CW00455975

Which? way to buy, sell

Consumers' Association, publishers of **Which?**
2 Marylebone Road, London NW1 4DX

edited by	Edith Rudinger
illustrations by	Peter Smith
cover illustrations by	Julie Tennent

Which? Books are commissioned and researched by The Association for Consumer Research and published by Consumers' Association, 2 Marylebone Road, London NW1 4DX and Hodder and Stoughton, 47 Bedford Square, London WC1B 3DP

ISBN 0 340 41623 8
and   0 85202 369 3

Photoset by Paston Press, Loddon, Norfolk
Printed and bound in Great Britain by
Richard Clay Ltd, Bungay, Suffolk

Which? way to buy, sell and move house

Contents

SCOTLAND

There are major differences between Scottish and English law in relation to the purchase and sale of houses and flats. Although most of the practical aspects of moving house are the same in Scotland as in England and Wales, the procedure of buying and selling, as well as the legal aspect, is very different in Scotland.

So, if you are moving house in Scotland, or if you are moving to Scotland from another part of the United Kingdom, look particularly at the chapters **Buying a house in Scotland** and **Selling in Scotland**.

Foreword

For anyone who has never bought a home before, or who has bought but not sold, or who needs to be reminded of what buying, selling and moving home entails, this book sets out what happens and what to do.

Moving to a new home means setting about finding somewhere to live, arranging to buy it, selling your present home, getting your goods and chattels out of the one and into the other, completing all the practical and administrative arrangements, and organising any work needed at the new home.

As for the first edition of this book, to help us know the problems most likely to arise during all the transactions, a questionnaire was sent in April 1987 to 1,000-plus *Which?* subscribers who had recorded a change of address during the preceding six months, asking them what had happened when they bought, sold, moved home. The questionnaire also asked what part of moving house people had found most difficult and what hints, warnings and advice they would give to someone about to move.

Much of the information in this book is drawn from the response to these questions. We are grateful to the *Which?* movers who gave so much care and thought and time to completing the questionnaire, for their good humour and good sense, and would like to thank them for their willingness to make moving easier for others by passing on what they had learnt the hard way through their own move.

We have used direct quotes (Q) from many of them to illuminate points and problems throughout the text.

One mover commented: "How can one summarise the infinite number of points that require careful consideration? They would make a volume."

Here is that volume.

Throughout this book

for 'he' read 'he or she'

Moving where?

A common reason why people move is a change of job or a transfer of place of work. Another common reason is that family circumstances bring a need for more accommodation – or for less.

A home may have become too big after the family has grown up and left, or after the loss of a husband or wife. Or it may have become too expensive to run because financial circumstances have changed.

Where the financial situation in a family has improved, a couple may decide to move into a better house or flat as a way not only of improving their standard of living but as an investment.

Retirement or the period just beforehand is often the time when people decide to move into accommodation suitable for older age – perhaps a flat or a bungalow – or have to move if they have been living in 'tied' accommodation.

Whatever the reason for the move, it may provide the opportunity to make an additional change – by switching from town to country living, or vice versa. Before making the choice, any cost of living differences between one part of the country and another – for example, the higher cost of living in the home counties – should be considered, and also any climatic differences, particularly moving from south to north.

The 'pro' points of country living are aspects that have already appealed to you and which may be why you are considering making the change. But the seaside village that looked so nice during the summer holiday may be like a bleak graveyard out of season. And there are other 'con' points which you may not have thought about and which you have to balance against the attractions relevant to you.

living in the country

PRO

environment
Natural beauty of the countryside; facilities for walking and other outdoor activities; fresher unpolluted air; no overcrowding; usually quieter than town living.

housing
Often more land with house; more garden space with safer play areas for children; chance to grow own produce; often more bungalow housing available; suitable for retired; insurance rates lower for burglary cover, also for motor insurance.

services
Could use coal or wood as alternative heating fuel (seldom smoke control restrictions), perhaps cheap wood supplies.

social life
Pace of living slower than town; more personal contact with neighbours; easy involvement in local activities.

CON

environment
Areas may be inhospitable in winter – fog, wind, cold; smells not always agreeable from nearby farms, can be unpleasant in hot weather; country not necessarily always quiet (aircraft flight paths?); in holiday area, influx of summer visitors.

housing
Not as wide a choice; free-standing houses in exposed position costly to heat; may have to buy more land than wanted; if in 'green belt' area, planning permission may be restricted.

services
May be no mains gas laid on (have to rely on electricity); may not be mains drainage but septic tank or cesspool (emptying required); in many places, no street lighting; public transport may be limited (or non-existent) for getting to work, shops, schools; difficulties in wintry conditions; might need second car for family; doctor, baby clinic, hospital, chemist may be some distance away, health visitors or district nurses fewer; schools may be limited in number and type, nursery schools few or non-existent; adult classes and library facilities may be limited or far away; choice for shopping limited, village shop(s) within walking distance may be expensive.

social life
Lack of choice (have to get on with neighbours, be prepared to join in local community activities); may take time to get accepted in village community; public entertainments and sports facilities limited; may be fewer neighbouring children for yours to play with; guests will need transport (yours or theirs) to visit you.

living in a town or city

PRO

housing
Usually more choice of neighbourhood and houses; more flats available; possibly some saving on heating costs (terraced or semi-detached houses and flats keep each other warm).

services
More public transport, health care and school facilities; shopping more convenient with more choice; may be more facilities for older people (sheltered housing, local welfare and social clubs), visiting easier.

social life
Closer proximity of neighbours can be useful in times of emergency; children may benefit from nearby children to play with; wider range of entertainments, sports and recreations.

CON

environment
Close proximity of neighbours; house or garden may be overlooked; pace of living likely to be faster; hustle and bustle, pressure of people always around; traffic or factory noise and smells; clothes and home likely to need more cleaning because of traffic or industrial pollution; parking difficulties and expense.

housing
Higher prices, may have to accept smaller house and small or no garden; may be no garage; restricted or non-existent playspace for children; insurance rates for burglary cover more expensive (or unobtainable), also higher rates for motor insurance.

services
Health and welfare services may be over-stretched, particularly in holiday or retirement resorts.

social life
Can feel isolated in large city; friends may not be immediate neighbours but have to be made through job or hobby.

Moving to what?

If you are considering living in a different kind of home, weigh carefully the new factors involved. You may have been living in a rented flat and are to become the owner of a house, perhaps with a garden, for the first time. Or the change may be from a large house with its responsibilities into a small flat with lesser ones.

To a flat

The Consumer Publication *Buying, owning and selling a flat* explains in simple terms the areas of law of particular concern to actual and potential flat owners.

Most flats in England and Wales are leasehold, which means that the ownership will revert to the lessor after a set period of time (usually 99 years but it can be 999 years). The resale value decreases towards the end of the leasehold period.

Nowadays, a building society, bank or other lender is not likely to look any less favourably on making a loan for buying a leasehold flat than a house. A couple whose family has grown up and who sell their family house could buy a flat for cash in the same area, with something left over for investment.

In most blocks of flats, there is a service charge to cover porterage, cleaning of communal areas, insurance and the maintenance of the building, drains, garden, driveway. You are committed to pay; the charge is bound to increase annually and you have little or no control over how much. In addition, you will have to pay your share of any major repair work to be done.

On top of that, the physical nature of a flat will mean that you have less independence and less direct say about what is going on. This will be reflected in the terms of the lease. One of its longest sections will consist of the 'lessee's covenants' (i.e. the rules for the flat owner), which will cover everything from repairs to rates, from windows to window boxes and from pets to pianos. The lease will also contain complicated provisions for dealing with the repair of the building and the supply of services to the flat owners.

Q

Further complications can occur if you are moving between different parts of the country where the local markets differ (e.g. from the North, where it may be a buyers' market, to the South, where it may be a sellers' market) or between different types of property (e.g. from a house which may not be in demand to a flat which may be much sought after).

There may not be any garaging facilities which you may previously have been used to. Having to park on the highway or outside will affect the car insurance premium, and you may have to pay for a resident's parking permit. Also, you lose the workshop or storage area a garage provides.

You will probably need less furniture, and there will be less storage space. You will have to decide what to take and what to dispose of and a ruthless, pre-move sort-out will be essential.

There may be restrictions on keeping pets.

The garden may be a communal one, or there may be none at all. This may be one of the advantages of flat living you are seeking; on the other hand, if you are a garden lover, think whether you can live without one.

You must be prepared for other people living above and around you, and you should consider other aspects of daily living in a flat which you may not have thought about:

living in a flat

CON

less privacy; your comings and goings (and those of your callers) are observed; windows may overlook or be overlooked

noises from adjoining flats and corridor, footsteps above, TV from next door, loud music and voices (including other people's quarrels); conversely, you have to watch your own noise levels

kitchen smells may pervade living rooms, bedrooms

may be no choice of fuel; communal heating can be inflexible and may not be individually adjustable; if heating or plumbing goes wrong in another flat, yours may be affected or cut off, too.

PRO

neighbours easily contacted; no need for elderly to go out-of-doors to find company; probably a porter or caretaker to take deliveries, let in meter readers, servicemen

less need for heating where adjoining flats help to keep each other warm; easier to keep clean; compact layout; no stairs.

In addition, there are disadvantages and advantages of living on the different floors in a block of flats which you should consider when looking at specific flats.

From flat to house

Moving to larger accommodation can mean additional expenditure for more furniture, carpets and curtains. Heating costs are likely to be higher. If there is a garden, there will be the expense of tools and plants, and the added cost and time required for its maintenance.

A householder changing from a flat to a house must be prepared to accept a greater degree of personal responsibility for the property and be prepared to devote a considerable amount of time to it: roof and gutters, fences and walls, plumbing and drains have to be kept in good repair. But you can choose when and how to get repairs done, and stagger the outlay.

In a flat, insurance for the building was probably not your personal responsibility; in your own house, it is up to you to take out the insurance for damage to or destruction of the building (as well as any insurance you may want for the contents).

Having a house may mean having a garage for the first time, which can be a big advantage – not only for housing the car, but space for storage, freezer, tools, workbench.

Although a housewife may find that, with more space, she has better facilities these will be on more than one floor and she may find this physically more demanding, particularly at first. Various household activities will have to be re-organised and housework re-planned to avoid unnecessary numbers of journeys up and down stairs. If there are small children, it may be less easy to keep an eye on them.

A house can give more privacy and, within reason, permit more noisy activities without worry of disturbing close neighbours. A piano or a highly amplifying sound system may be possible for the first time – and so may a Great Dane.

Q

Every property viewed had something missing. The house we finally settled on was just what we wanted – the only thing that had to be done was the kitchen. This was done by wife and myself before we moved in: it took us about two months working weekends but the end result was very gratifying.

Changing in size or type

When moving into a bigger house or flat, you should budget for more expenses. Perhaps more or new household furniture and appliances will be needed, more curtaining and floor coverings, followed by higher running costs in the future. If moving to a smaller place, there may be large items to get rid of and smaller (and perhaps more expensive) replacements to buy.

When considering a larger property, bear in mind that the insurance is likely to be higher. You have to insure for the cost of re-building and this is calculated by taking a figure based on building costs per square foot and multiplying this by the area of the building. For a thatched house, the insurance premium may be as much as four times more.

A bungalow is sensible for older people because there are no stairs to climb and it can be run easily and with less risk of accidents. But a bungalow has to be maintained, like a house with a greater roof area, and often has a garden. And a lifetime of 'going up to bed' can inhibit some people from sleeping easily on the ground floor.

If the reason for a possible move is to get more accommodation, then consider extending your present house. Moving is expensive and an extension may be less costly. If you are looking for less accommodation, think of converting your house into two flats – or even taking in lodgers.

Changing style

You should try to anticipate what changes the move to another house or flat may bring in the pattern of your daily life and outgoings, both immediately and in the long term.

Aspects that might be affected include

- mortgage
  monthly payments may be higher/lower
  (you may previously have been paying a weekly or monthly rent)
- life insurance premiums
  perhaps payable now on an endowment or protection life insurance policy for mortgage

- rates and water charges
  may be higher if a larger house or in a different authority's area
- household insurance
  premiums increase if moving to larger premises or to a more burglar-prone area
- fuel consumption and costs
  may be different (more on electricity, less on gas or vice versa; oil instead of solid fuel or vice versa, etcetera)
- telephone bill
  will be higher if fewer calls within local range
  (it is going to be a big one for the period of the move, anyway)
- daily travel
  change in method of getting to work/schools/social or cultural activities (more by car, less by public transport or vice versa)
- car
  second car (or none) may be needed; garage may be needed; insurance premium may be higher/lower
- daily timetable
  may get home earlier/later; have to get up earlier (dark in winter); more/less housework; opportunities expanded/restricted for part-time or voluntary work
- neighbours
  adjustment to new (more or fewer, different ages); difference in access to friends and/or family (more or fewer visitors)
- clothing
  different category of clothes and footwear required if moving from town to country or vice versa
- upkeep of property
  may be more maintenance and redecorating (higher ceilings, more wood-work, windows, doors to paint)
- garden (maybe for first time)
  may want to alter layout and/or contents; cost of restocking; upkeep of fence or hedge, walls or other boundaries; surfacing of paths or driveways; tree care.

None of these items need be a deterrent to moving to the place you want to go to. But you may have to adjust your priorities and purse.

Q

If moving to a new area, visit the local pub and chat to regulars – we did: very interesting!

Q

Above everything else, remember position is all important – a house can be changed beyond all recognition by extensions, alterations etc but it cannot be moved!

The money for buying

Before you start hunting for a new home, you have to work out how much money you will have available so that you know in what price range to look.

Add together

○ likely net proceeds from sale of your present home
○ other available capital or savings
○ maximum possible mortgage.

Deduct from the total of these the estimated expenses of moving including the various fees and stamp duty and allowing for essential repairs, possible redecoration or improvements. The result of this calculation will give you the approximate maximum price you can afford for your new home.

NET PROCEEDS FROM SALE OF THE PRESENT HOME

Estimate what price you think your home will fetch. If you have had an estate agent's valuation, you can use this as a guide – but you might get more, or less, depending on the state of the market. If houses in your area change hands frequently, you could ask neighbours and friends how much they bought or sold their house for. You then deduct from this the balance of any mortgage to be paid off on your present home and the estimated costs of selling it:

● estate agent's or other seller's fee
  This can vary from 1 to 2½ per cent of the sale price, plus VAT. Some agents and property centres charge a flat fee instead of a percentage. If you intend to sell privately, allow for the cost of advertising.
● legal fees connected with the sale
  For very rough budgeting purposes, allow 3 per cent of the sale price to cover these expenses.

ANY SAVINGS

Calculate how much you have available in

– building societies or bank deposit accounts
– other investments, such as in national savings accounts, certificates, bonds, shares, unit trusts, government stock (but your move may not coincide with the best time of selling)
– a life insurance policy (but current cash-in value may not yield enough to make it worth doing).

Q

Most people have a rough idea of what their house is worth, but become a little optimistic once they have thoughts of selling.

Remember that you should always keep some of your savings intact in case of any emergency quite unconnected with house purchase. And you may want to keep some of your savings aside to help pay for such items as new carpets and curtains, or for redecorating your new home.

money for the deposit

You will be asked for a deposit of up to 10 per cent of the purchase price to put down on the house or flat you are buying when you exchange contracts. Do not rely on being able to use any similar deposit which your solicitor or agent may be holding in respect of the property you are selling.

If you do not have the necessary deposit available in ready money, you can usually get a bridging loan from your bank (and should allow for the extra expense of this), repayable on completion of the sale of your present house. Alternatively, there is a deposit guarantee scheme, through solicitors, where the premium is generally less expensive than a bridging loan for the deposit.

for a first time buyer

There is a government home purchase assistance scheme called **Homeloan**, intended to help first time buyers who save with a recognised institution such as a building society, bank, trustee savings bank, friendly society, and who want to buy a home below a certain price. (This price varies according to geographical region.)

Anyone who has saved for at least 2 years after joining this scheme and has saved at least £300 may qualify for a tax-free cash bonus of up to £110, depending on how much has been saved, and, if this is at least £600, a loan of £600 interest-free for 5 years. Details of this **Homeloan** scheme are given in a leaflet obtainable from banks and building society offices.

Getting a mortgage

A report on mortgages was published in **Which?** April 1988.

Not many people can afford to buy their own home without having to borrow at least part of the cost. Loans made to home buyers are usually in the form of a long-term mortgage on which you pay interest at the lender's current rate, with your home as security. What this means is that the lender has the right to sell your home if you do not keep up your mortgage payments. Lenders can thus be reasonably certain that they will get their money back.

Before lending any money, the lender (*mortgagee*) will want to make sure that you (*mortgagor*) can keep up repayments and that the house you want to buy is worth enough to cover the loan if you default on your repayments.

How much you will be able to borrow will depend on:

○ your income – and therefore how much you can afford in mortgage repayments
○ the home you want to buy.

how much can you borrow?

Q

Beware of maximum mortgage: we took less than offered by building society and still have to be careful to make ends meet.

Most lenders work out the maximum they are prepared to lend by using a multiple of your annual income before tax. For instance, a single person might be allowed to borrow between $2\frac{1}{2}$ and 3 times the annual income. So, if you earn £10,000 a year, you would be allowed to borrow up to £25,000 or £30,000 depending on the multiple used.

A couple who are both earning would usually be able to borrow up to $2\frac{1}{2}$ or 3 times the higher income plus 1 to $1\frac{1}{2}$ times the lower income. (Lenders are not allowed to discriminate against women by applying the larger multiple to the husband's income when it is not the higher of the two.) Some lenders use a different formula by adding the two incomes together and multiplying by 2 or $2\frac{1}{2}$. This variation can mean that the same couple could be offered different loans by different lenders.

Some lenders may use different multiples for first-time borrowers.

Unmarried couples are in most cases treated in exactly the same way as a married couple – few lenders seem to worry about making loans to such couples. And other couples or groups of friends can apply for joint mortgages, too. But you may need to shop around quite a bit because lenders are likely to be rather more cautious and the maximum loan could be quite a bit smaller than the total of your incomes might suggest. If you are thinking of applying for a joint mortgage with friends, it is worth remembering that each of you is responsible for paying the whole mortgage. If one of you cannot afford to keep up payments or moves out, the other (or others) will have to take over the payments.

The multiples used by lenders vary depending on the lender and on the current rates of interest charged to borrowers. In general, the higher the interest rate, the lower the multiple.

The length (or term) of the loan can also affect the multiples used, with larger multiples being available for a 35-year term than for a 20-year term.

what counts as income?

Broadly, 'income' is your basic salary before tax or other deductions. Some lenders will include overtime payments or commission or bonuses but only if guaranteed: they will probably want confirmation from your employer that these payments are likely to continue. In exceptional circumstances, some lenders may take into account future increases in salary or promotion prospects.

Income from investments is not usually counted and neither (normally) is income from social security or other benefits.

Account may be taken of such ongoing financial commitments as hire purchase debts or payments made under a court order.

SELF-EMPLOYED

If you are self-employed, the amount you can borrow will usually be based on the average of your earnings over the last three years or so. Some lenders may base it on your last year's profits but will look at previous years to make sure it was not an exceptionally good year. The lender will not simply take your word as to what your annual income is but will want to see your annual accounts or/and your tax assessments.

If you are newly self-employed or have been in business for a relatively short time, you may well find it difficult to get a mortgage. And even if a lender is prepared to grant a mortgage, it may be for a relatively small amount.

but how much can you afford?

Q

They seemed willing to give me far more than I could have paid for!! And I had declared the exact amount of maintenance payments to my wife and daughter, which should have made it clear to them! So I determined the limit I could pay for.

Just because a lender is prepared to give you a mortgage of a certain size, do not be led into thinking that you can necessarily afford it. Lenders' formulae are based on averages, and your situation could be far from average. For instance, if you have exceptionally high travelling costs to get to work, you will have far less income available than someone who lives only one mile from the office.

Another thing you should consider is whether your income is likely to drop soon – for example, if you are planning to have children or if you might have to take on caring for an ill or elderly relative.

Having heavy financial commitments already could mean that you do not really have enough spare income each month to cope with the maximum loan a lender will make without problems. Also, bear in mind the costs of running a home (particularly if you are a first-time buyer): there are rates and water charges to pay, repairs and maintenance to be done and so on. So check your finances carefully.

What is the home you want to buy worth?

You are not usually able to borrow the whole of the asking price (or the price eventually agreed). Lenders have to make sure that they would get their money back if you do not keep up your mortgage payments and they have to get a court order to re-possess and sell your home.

This means that the lender is unlikely to lend to you the full price even if this is within the amount you can afford to repay. Instead, you will be allowed to borrow a percentage. Lenders have a normal maximum percentage that they will offer without qualification. This maximum varies periodically according to market conditions. At present (October 1988), most lenders' normal maximum is 75–85%; it may be lower for more expensive homes.

The percentage you can borrow is not a percentage of the purchase price but of what the lender's valuer reckons that the property is worth. So if the valuer reckons the house is worth less than the asking price, even a 100% mortgage might not be enough to enable you to buy. If the valuation is higher than the purchase price, however, the percentage you can borrow is likely to be based on the purchase price, not on the valuation.

In general, the higher the value of the house, the lower will be the normal percentage that the lender is prepared to lend.

MORTGAGE INDEMNITY POLICY

Q

This extra security is for the protection of the lender. If you default in your payments and the lender has to draw on the security, the insurance company paying out can make a claim against you for this money.

Many lenders are prepared to lend a higher than their normal percentage (up to 100%) if the borrower is able to provide extra security for the loan. While a lender may be prepared to accept anything as extra security which could be turned into enough cash if needed, such as a charge on a second property or share certificates, the usual way is through a mortgage indemnity policy. This is an insurance policy which guarantees to pay the lender the outstanding balance of loan, if the home has to be re-possessed and sold for less than the amount of the mortgage.

The lender arranges the policy with an insurance company. There is a single charge for this, usually around £3 per £100 you borrow above the lender's normal limit. You may have to pay this at the time you take out the mortgage or, more usually, it is added to the loan so that you repay it along with the mortgage.

What sort of home is it?

Finally, how much a lender is prepared to lend will also depend on the sort of home you are buying. If the house is unconventional or unusual in its construction and therefore likely to be difficult to sell, the loan could be based on a lower than usual percentage of the valuation, or the term allowed to repay the mortgage could be shorter than usual.

In England and Wales a lot of property (particularly flats) is bought leasehold: you are buying the right to live in the property for a certain number of years after which it reverts to the landlord. You should find no difficulty getting a mortgage on a leasehold property, although the lender will need to check the lease and be satisfied about two things in particular. First, there needs to be a clear and legally-binding agreement about who pays for the repair and maintenance of the building. Secondly, most lenders will lend only if there is a reasonable amount of the lease left after the end of the mortgage term. Many lenders want at least 20 years left at the end of the mortgage term; with others, it could be as much as 40 or 50 years. The result of this is that it could be difficult to get a mortgage on a property with less than 50 or 60 years, or even longer, to run on the lease.

It is very difficult to get mortgages on freehold flats or maisonettes, mainly because of the difficulties in enforcing agreements on who should maintain and repair the structure of the building. (In Scotland, there is a different system of land law which means that leasehold properties are very rare and there are not the same difficulties over getting mortgages for the equivalent of freehold flats as there are in the rest of the UK.)

Getting a mortgage on recently converted flats can sometimes cause problems: lenders will want to be satisfied that the job has been done well and not by cowboy builders.

Many lenders are quite happy to give a mortgage on a property that needs a lot of renovation and repair but may hold back (or retain) part of the loan until the work is done.

If the property you want to buy has a sitting tenant in part of it, you will have difficulty in getting a mortgage – quite apart from potential other difficulties. This is because it would be harder to sell a home with such a tenant and very difficult to get rid of the tenant, particularly if he or she has been there for some time.

You could also experience difficulty in arranging a loan if the property is used partly for business and partly for living – for example, if it is a case of living over the shop.

How long a loan?

In theory, a mortgage term by the end of which the loan has to be repaid can be anything from as little as five years. But the usual term is 20 or 25 years; longer term loans – 35 years or more – are available from some lenders. Lenders may insist that a mortgage finishes before you reach retiring age. But many are prepared to offer shorter term loans to people who are retired.

If you are buying a leasehold property, the building society may insist on a term which allows a certain number of years of lease left at the end of the mortgage.

For example, if they require 40 years left and the lease has 60 years to run, the maximum length of loan will be 20 years.

Tax relief

When you borrow to buy your own home, you do not have to pay tax on the amount of your income which goes towards paying interest on the loan. In other words, you get tax relief on the interest, and the loan therefore costs you less. (Tax relief used also to be given on loans taken out for home improvements. Since April 1988, home improvement loans do not qualify for tax relief.)

You cannot claim tax relief on more than £30,000 of loan and the relief is available only on money borrowed to buy your main home, not for a second home.

Under the scheme known as MIRAS (mortgage interest relief at source), you make payments to the lender less basic rate tax. In 1988/89, with basic rate tax at 25%, you pay only £7.50 on each £10 of interest owed: £2.50 tax relief is deducted from the gross payment. You would benefit from this even if you did not have enough income to pay tax. If you pay income tax at higher than basic rate, you get the extra tax relief either through your PAYE code or by getting a reduced tax assessment. If you borrow more than £30,000, you will get tax relief via MIRAS on the £30,000 and pay the interest on the rest in full.

Up to 1 August 1988, where two or more people not married to each other bought a home together with a mortgage, each could claim tax relief on up to £30,000 of loan. This multiple tax relief will continue for the life of a mortgage taken out before 1 August 1988 but is not available for any further or future mortgage.

Types of mortgage

With a mortgage, you have to pay back the money you have borrowed (the capital) and pay the cost of borrowing the money (the interest). There are two main ways of doing this:

○ with a **repayment mortgage** you repay the loan in instalments along with the interest, so that at the end of the term of the loan you have paid off the capital
○ with an **endowment mortgage** you do not pay back any of the capital until the end of the term. You pay interest on the whole amount of the loan throughout the term and you also have to pay premiums to an investment-type life insurance policy. At the end of the term, the loan is repaid from the proceeds of the insurance policy.

There are two other types to consider:

○ **pension mortgage**
○ **unit-linked mortgage**.

'Alternative' types of mortgage currently on offer were explained in **Which?** June 1988.

Repayment mortgages

The payments you have to make every month are the same throughout the term (unless there is a change in interest rate).

How much you pay each month depends on how much you have borrowed, the interest rate charged and the length of the loan. The longer the period of the loan, the longer there is to pay off the capital so the smaller the monthly repayments. But over the course of the whole loan, your total payments will be much higher because you are paying interest for longer. (There would, however, be nothing to stop you increasing your monthly payments as the years go by, thereby paying off the loan more quickly.)

Q

Different lenders operate different charging policies, but usually a lump sum to a building society is best made shortly before 1 January.

In the early years of a repayment mortgage, most of each payment you make goes to pay the interest on the money you have borrowed and only a very small part goes towards paying off the capital. But as the years go by, the capital you owe reduces and so the proportion of each payment which is interest goes down and the proportion that is paying off the capital goes up – until in the last few years only a very small part of each payment is interest. The table overleaf shows an example of this.

how capital is paid off

Amount borrowed: £20,000 over 25 years at 12.75% interest
monthly repayments after tax relief: £177.48 (£2,129.76 a year)

year	capital repaid in year £	interest paid in year £	capital owing at end of year £
1	217.26	1,912.50	19,782.74
2	238.04	1,891.72	19,544.70
3	260.80	1,868.96	19,283.91
4	285.74	1,844.02	18,998.17
5	313.06	1,816.70	18,685.10
10	494.24	1,635.52	16,609.25
15	780.27	1,349.49	13,332.00
20	1,231.85	897.91	8,158.10
25	1,944.76	185.00	—

Since tax relief is given only on the interest part of the loan and the interest portion of each payment gets less throughout the length of the mortgage, you might expect that the amount you have to pay each month would rise. But most lenders prefer to keep mortgage repayments the same by averaging out the tax relief over the whole length of the loan. This means that the borrower knows exactly how much has to be paid each month. This type of mortgage is known as a **level repayment mortgage** (or **constant net mortgage**) and is the sort of repayment mortgage you are most likely to be offered.

With an **increasing repayment** (or **gross profile**) mortgage, the tax relief is not averaged out, so that repayments start off lower than with a level repayment mortgage. But as the amount of interest drops, so does the tax relief and the result is gradually increasing payments. The adjustment is made once a year, not every month. The advantage of an increasing repayment mortgage is that in the early years of a loan you get more tax relief because the interest element is higher, so that your payments are less in the early years than they would be with a level repayment mortgage. In later years, the payments are higher but by that time your mortgage payments are likely to be a much smaller proportion of your income.

Some lenders are prepared to offer formal **low-start** mortgages whereby you make lower-than-normal payments for the first few years and pay interest only (on which you get tax relief). This could help if you are very hard pressed financially. It means that you do not start making repayments of capital for a few years and have to make larger payments in later years.

mortgage protection insurance

If you have people who are financially dependent on you, or if you are buying a house as a couple, you should consider getting insurance which would pay off the loan if you (or your partner if you have a joint mortgage) were to die. A **mortgage protection policy** is a relatively cheap form of life insurance because the amount the policy would have to pay out goes down as you pay off your mortgage. If you have a joint mortgage, it may be better to take out two separate policies, one for each borrower.

Information on mortgage protection policies was included in the report on mortgages in **Which?** April 1988.

WHAT HAPPENS IF YOU MOVE?

With a repayment mortgage, you pay off the loan when you sell your house with the money you get for selling it. If you are buying a new home, you then get a new mortgage for that.

WHAT HAPPENS IF YOU CANNOT AFFORD TO CONTINUE THE PAYMENTS?

The lender may agree to extending the term of a mortgage – for example, from twenty to thirty years. This will not necessarily reduce the monthly payments by very much (especially in the early years of the mortgage when interest forms the largest part of each payment). Or the lender may agree to your paying interest-only for a short period, particularly if your problems are likely to be short-lived.

If interest rates rise, you may be able to extend the term of the mortgage rather than have to increase your monthly payments.

Endowment mortgages

With an endowment mortgage, there are two separate payments to make.

You pay interest to the building society or bank on the full amount of capital you have borrowed for the whole length of the loan. As the amount you owe does not change, your monthly payments to the lender are constant no matter how long the term of the loan. (The size of your payments will change if the interest rate or the basic rate of income tax alters. If interest rates rise, you have to increase your monthly payments.)

The mortgage is linked to an endowment life insurance policy for which you have to pay regular (usually monthly) premiums to the insurance company for the whole term of the loan. The policy is taken out for a period to coincide with the term of the mortgage so that, at the end of the term of the loan, the endowment policy 'matures' and the proceeds are used to pay off the capital. Life insurance is automatically included so that, if you die, your mortgage can be repaid by the insurance policy, however short a time the insurance had been in operation. How much an endowment policy costs will depend largely on your age and health: the older you are, and the poorer your health, the higher the premiums. The longer the loan, the lower the endowment insurance premium should be because your 'fund' has longer to build up the amount required to repay the loan.

A simple **non-profit endowment** policy guarantees to pay out just enough to pay off the capital borrowed and no more. A full **with-profits endowment** policy also guarantees to pay enough to cover the capital borrowed but in addition you will share in the profits made by the company as a result of their investing your premiums. How much you get at the end depends on how well the insurance company's investment fund does over and above the guaranteed amount to repay the mortgage loan.

Q

. . . low-cost endowment policies – ask them about the commission they earn. Insist on seeing full *specimen documentation. (Why can't this documentation be available, with all the small print, at the building society? why were we treated so rudely when we requested specimen policies?)*

A **low-cost endowment** policy is a with-profits policy but costs much less. You are guaranteed only that it will pay off about half of the mortgage which is why it is cheaper than a policy which guarantees to cover the whole loan from the day you take out the policy. The insurance company hopes that the rest of the loan will be covered by the profits made by their investment fund during the period of the loan. If their profits were to be not as much as expected, you would have to fund the balance needed to repay the mortgage. Although this sounds risky, in practice it does not need a very high rate of return for profits to build up over a 25-year period and if you should die before the end of the mortgage term, the whole loan will be repaid by the insurance policy. Lenders will accept low-cost endowment policies only from insurance companies they are sure are sound.

Some lenders may offer **low-start, low-cost** endowment mortgages, allowing you to defer paying all or some of the interest in the early years. In later years, you will then have to pay more: the amount you owe will have increased by the amount of underpaid interest.

WHAT HAPPENS IF YOU MOVE?

You will have to pay off the loan from the proceeds of selling the house and arrange a new loan for your new home. The endowment policy you had for your old home remains in force and can be used to cover the new loan (if the lender agrees). If it is not large enough for the new loan, a second endowment policy can be taken out to make up the difference. Or, if the original policy allows, its value and length can be increased to cover the whole of the new loan. (But you should be aware that with an endowment policy on which tax relief is being given – that is one taken out before 14 March 1984 – a change of this sort will mean that you lose the tax relief.)

If you do not want another endowment mortgage, you have to choose what to do with the policy:

○ cashing-in the policy (especially in the early years) is likely to give a very low return, so is not something that should be done hastily
○ making the policy paid-up means that you need pay no more premiums and will get a lump sum at the end of the policy but this will be a much smaller sum than if you had carried on paying the premiums
○ or you can go on paying the premiums, treating the policy as an investment (although not one with a very good return).

WHAT HAPPENS IF YOU CANNOT AFFORD TO CONTINUE THE PAYMENTS?

Extending the term of the mortgage would not make any difference to the payments you have to make because the amount of interest you owe would still be the same. And, again unlike a repayment mortgage, there is not the option of reducing payments by paying interest-only because that is what you have been doing all along. Moreover, you have to keep paying the endowment insurance premiums as otherwise the loan is not covered and the lender may foreclose on the mortgage or force you to sell your home. The only option is to consider changing to a repayment mortgage and cashing in your endowment policy. If you are several years into your mortgage, the proceeds of the endowment policy could be used to reduce the amount of capital you owe.

Pension mortgages

A pension mortgage is similar in some ways to an endowment mortgage. You have to pay interest on the whole amount borrowed throughout the term of the loan. In addition, you pay regular premiums to a pension plan. When you start drawing your pension, part of it can be taken as a lump sum and used to pay off the mortgage and the remainder provides a regular pension.

The main advantage of pension mortgages is that as well as getting tax relief on the interest on the mortgage loan, you also get tax relief (at your highest rate of tax) on the contributions you make to the pension plan. This makes a pension mortgage extremely tax-efficient, particularly for higher-rate taxpayers.

But there are disadvantages. The most important one is that you are using part of your pension fund to repay your mortgage loan, so that a smaller sum is available to provide your pension. And you may be tying yourself to taking your pension at a fixed date in the future, even though this may not be convenient. Very young borrowers who intend to retire and start their pension 35 or 40 years ahead will find it difficult to find a lender willing to grant a loan over such a long term.

Pension mortgages are available mainly to people who are self-employed or who are employed but have a personal pension plan. Some employer's pension schemes also offer pension mortgage facilities. There are limits to the percentage of earnings that can be paid in pension contributions to qualify for tax relief.

Not all pension mortgage plans include life insurance and lenders are likely to insist that borrowers take out enough cover to repay the mortgage loan. Anyone who qualifies for a personal pension plan can include life insurance as part of the personal pension plan and get some tax relief on the premiums.

WHAT HAPPENS IF YOU MOVE?

If you move before your pension plan has paid out, the loan will have to be repaid from the proceeds of selling your old home. You can then link the mortgage for your new home to the pension plan. If the new mortgage is larger than the old one and the lender does not think that the pension plan will pay out enough to repay the loan, you might have to take out another pension plan to cover the extra (subject to the maximum percentage of income allowed for tax relief on premiums) or take out another type of mortgage in addition.

WHAT HAPPENS IF YOU CANNOT AFFORD TO CONTINUE THE PAYMENTS?

As with an endowment mortgage, you do not have the option of reducing your payments to the lender by extending the term of the loan or making interest-only payments. And if you stop making the pension plan payments, the lender has no guarantee that the loan will be repaid so could ask you to pay off the mortgage, forcing you to sell your home. Unlike an endowment policy, a pension plan cannot be cashed in early so there is no chance of being able to get a lump sum to repay part of the capital and then transferring the rest to a different sort of mortgage.

Unit-linked mortgages

As with an endowment or pension mortgage, interest has to be paid to the lender on the full amount of capital throughout the whole mortgage term. You also have to make regular monthly payments which are used to buy units in an insurance company fund which invests in shares, property and so on.

At the end of the mortgage term, the units are cashed in and the proceeds are used to pay off the loan. But unlike an endowment policy or pension plan, the value of the units can go down as well as up and the moment when you need the money may be one when the market is low. Because of this uncertainty, not all lenders run unit-linked mortgage schemes. And those that do may only accept unit-linked policies which guarantee enough to pay off the mortgage.

Interest-only mortgages

These are generally available only to older borrowers – some lenders offer them to people over 50, others restrict them to those over pension age. The borrower pays interest only, and the loan is not repaid until the house is sold or the borrower dies. In general, the percentage of the home's value that can be borrowed is rather less than with an ordinary mortgage.

Interest rates

Most mortgages have a variable interest rate which means that the lender can increase or decrease the percentage charged (and usually such changes happen with all building societies at more or less the same time). However, many lenders allow borrowers the choice of having their mortgage payments fixed for a year at a time, no matter what happens to interest rates. This helps borrowers cope with increases but means they do not benefit immediately from cuts in rates. From time to time some lenders offer fixed rate loans where it is guaranteed that the interest rate will not change for a stated number of years (say, 3 years), usually for large loans.

Interest rates do not vary greatly between the major building societies at any given time but there may be a difference of up to 2% with some others. A few charge a higher interest rate for loans over a specified amount (which may be as low as £15,000 or as high as £60,000).

All lenders issue brochures, or mortgage packs with a lot of information. It is not easy to compare like with like, but they all have to show the APR (annual percentage rate) in their printed information.

The APR is generally higher than the quoted rate of interest: it includes one-off charges such as arrangement fees, valuation and legal fees and takes into account the way interest is calculated on a repayment mortgage. Most building societies calculate the interest you owe only once a year and divide that into equal monthly amounts: this ignores that each payment reduces the capital you owe – but the APR takes account of this. Where a lender recalculates the interest part of a payment on a monthly basis (as some banks do), the APR is lower.

If you want to compare current interest rates and conditions for mortgages from various sources, look at a copy of *What mortgage* (£1.20 every month on bookstalls) which publishes regularly updated comparison tables of the major lenders, including for top-up or second mortgages. (The magazine also has useful articles on other aspects of house buying and finances.)

Where to get a mortgage

The first rule these days is to shop around: there are well over 200 institutions in the mortgage market.

Make sure you know what sort of loan you are being offered; check what costs are involved; find out whether life insurance is included or not or is compulsory; do not take on too big a loan just because the lender offers you that much.

Get and study the literature of potential lenders: different building societies, banks, insurance companies, and other financial institutions.

BUILDING SOCIETIES

Until relatively recently, almost all mortgages for home buyers came from building societies who funded the loans from people's investments with them.

Each society has its own guidelines about to whom it is prepared to lend, how much to lend and on what type of home. Branch managers may have some discretion to vary the conditions and it is worth discussing your particular case with the manager even if it looks as though the guidelines seem to rule out a loan to you.

The Building Societies Association has produced a booklet *Starting point – a building society guide to house purchase*, with accompanying leaflets on taxation, on assistance with mortgage repayments, on questions most frequently asked; available free (send 39p s.a.e. 10in × 7in) from the BSA, 3 Savile Row, London W1X 1AF.

When a building society has more potential borrowers than money to lend, it may impose a form of rationing. This could take the form of giving priority to people who invest with that society or who already have a mortgage with the society. So, if you are planning to buy your first home, it may be a good idea to open an account with one or more building societies, just in case. Before doing so, check the society's lending policies to make sure that it would be prepared to lend to you when the time comes.

BANKS

Over the last few years, banks have become an important part of the mortgage market, particularly for large loans. All the High Street banks now offer mortgages and less well-known foreign banks are also in the market. But a bank (unlike a building society) can decide at any time not to offer any further new mortgages.

There is often little to choose between a bank and a building society as mortgagee. If you are after a big loan, check what the banks, particularly the foreign banks, have to offer.

OTHER LENDERS

Insurance companies who offer life insurance may also be in the mortgage market. The chances are that you will be able to get only an endowment mortgage linked to their own policy – few allow a free choice of endowment . policy or offer repayment mortgages.

Local authorities have to give mortgages to council tenants who want to exercise their 'right to buy' option. A few authorities may offer mortgages to people prepared to buy and renovate derelict housing.

Employers, particularly banks and other financial institutions, often offer mortgages to their staff, usually at low interest rates as a fringe benefit. But before you take one, check what would happen if you were to leave and change jobs: would you be allowed to keep on the loan and if so, at what interest rate or would you have to repay it?

Finance houses and credit companies may be prepared to lend you more than other lenders, but at a higher interest rate. They are unlikely to offer repayment mortgages. There may be a high redemption charge if you want to pay off the mortgage in the first few years (in order to move to a cheaper lender perhaps).

Builders or the developer of a new site may offer to arrange mortgages for prospective buyers, perhaps offering to get 100% mortgages or lower-than-normal interest rates for the first year as part of a package to induce you to buy.

Private mortgages are not common but are a possibility. If a relative or friend offers to lend you money to help buy a home, at a low interest rate, or none, it would be a cheap source of finance. But make sure a proper business-like arrangement is made between you, with a mortgage deed. You can claim tax relief on any interest you pay on a loan under £30,000, but the lender will have to declare the interest received as income for tax purposes.

You should be careful if the person from whom you are buying a house offers you a loan. It may be just because the seller is desperate for a quick sale but it could be because he knows that getting a mortgage will be difficult due to structural or other problems. You should get your solicitor to check the terms carefully before agreeing.

Q

Our buyer obtained mortgage through employer (an insurance company) – this proved very slow, surprisingly.

Q

Don't rush into arranging your mortgage through a broker. Most of the time, building society and bank mortgages are easy to come by – and they do not charge a brokerage fee (though some banks do charge a 'setting up fee').

Under the Financial Services Act 1986, a broker (or any other professional adviser) giving financial or insurance advice must be authorised by a recognised professional body, such as FIMBRA (Financial Intermediaries, Managers and Brokers Regulatory Association).

USING A MORTGAGE BROKER

Mortgage brokers do not themselves lend money but make arrangements for you to borrow from someone else. If mortgages are not in short supply and you want to buy a fairly ordinary house with an average sort of mortgage, there is little point in using a broker. But if you are hoping to buy an unusual house, or one which most lenders are not too keen on (for instance, one with a sitting tenant or a home combined with a shop), or if you want a very large loan, or mortgages are in short supply, a broker could be useful or even essential.

If a broker offers you a repayment mortgage, you will usually have to pay an arrangement fee of 1 or 2 per cent of the loan. But you are more likely to be offered some sort of endowment mortgage, or a pension mortgage, in which case you should not have to pay a fee as the broker will get commission from the insurance company who provides the endowment policy or personal pension plan. If the broker asks you to pay a deposit, it must be repaid to you (all but £3) if you have not taken up any loan arranged by the broker within six months.

A good broker should give you a choice of mortgages to suit your circumstances. Get written quotations setting out all the payments involved (including any arrangement fee) and study the figures carefully. If you are in any doubt about anything, ask for an explanation and get your solicitor to look over anything you have to sign. And there is nothing to stop you going to a second broker to see what that one has to offer you.

Anyone called an 'insurance broker' has to be registered with the Insurance Brokers' Registration Council. But anyone can call himself a 'mortgage broker' or 'insurance consultant'. Many mortgage and insurance brokers belong to bodies which have codes of conduct for their members to follow and which will investigate customers' complaints. You could write to one or both of the following bodies for lists of members in your area:

British Insurance and Investment Brokers' Association (BIIBA)
BIIBA House
14 Bevis Marks
London EC3A 7NT

Corporation of Insurance and Financial Advisors (CIFA)
6-7 Leapale Road
Guildford
Surrey GU1 4JX

FINDING OUT FROM A LENDER

As soon as you start looking for a house or flat to buy, it is worth going to visit several potential lenders to discuss a loan.

What you should find out from booklets or a personal visit includes

- the interest rate:
  for different amounts lent (rate may be higher for larger loan)
  for different types of mortgage (repayment/endowment/unit linked/pension-linked)
  for first-time buyers
- what payments you will have to make per £1,000 borrowed
- when and how payments have to be made:
  in the first month
  in the rest of that financial year
  thereafter
- what will happen when the interest rate changes
- what percentage of valuation is the normal maximum loan
- how much more you can borrow with extra security (and what security is acceptable)
- whether there will be a redemption charge if you pay off the mortgage within so-many (how many?) years.

Under the Financial Services Act, firms that sell endowment or pension mortgages have to be authorised to carry out their business and have to abide by a set of detailed rules. One important feature of these rules is that firms have to make it clear whether they are giving completely independent advice to their customers on what their best choice is, or are tied to selling one company's products.

Applying for a mortgage

You may be asked at an early stage to fill in a form giving some details of your income and commitments. Many lenders offer a **mortgage certificate** to potential borrowers. This states how much they would be prepared to lend you (subject to the value of the property you will want to buy). Such a certificate constitutes an offer to lend but is usually valid for a limited period – six weeks perhaps, or three months.

A mortgage certificate could be useful if you need to persuade a seller that you are a serious buyer who will have the finance to proceed.

The application form asks for full details of your (and any joint borrower's) financial commitments and income. You will have to give details of your employment, your bank, any previous mortgage or your landlord. The lender will probably contact all of these to check that you are a credit-worthy and reliable person to lend to.

A self-employed person may have to submit audited accounts. If you are freelance or working on an irregular basis, you may find it difficult to get a loan unless you can produce a large part of the purchase price yourself. With what is known as a 'non-status' mortgage, the amount borrowed is not related to earnings, but some evidence of financial stability will be required, such as an accountant's or bank's reference, and the interest rate may be higher.

Q

If you are not sure about your own status (i.e. ability to repay) you can always ask the lender to conduct the status enquiries first, thus saving a wasted valuation fee if it is you, rather than the property, that is unacceptable.

when you have found the house

Once you have made an offer for a house or flat, you will have to apply formally for the loan.

You have to give details of the house you are wanting to buy, including the price. You also have to say how much you want to borrow and may be asked where the rest of the purchase price is coming from.

Once you have filled in the application form, you will have to pay for the lender to value the property. This is a valuation only, not a full structural survey. The fee is based on the purchase price (or the valuation, if that is higher). If the lender decides not to give you a loan as a result of the valuation, you will not get the fee back. Neither can it be refunded if you decide not to go ahead with the purchase, whatever the reason.

When the valuation has been done, the lenders will let you know whether they
are prepared to lend, how much and on what terms.

mortgage conditions

Conditions will be laid down by a lender which the borrower has to undertake
to observe. These may include

○ undertaking to carry out certain repairs or improvements within a specified
  period
○ keeping the home in good repair
○ not letting all or part of the home without the lender's permission (this means
  you would need to ask before you have tenants in the basement, for example,
  or take in lodgers or paying guests)
○ not altering the property without the lender's permission
○ informing the lender of any local authority proposals which would affect the
  property
○ keeping the property insured.

INSURANCE
Insurance for fire and other risks to the building is always a condition of
granting a mortgage. Most building societies and banks offer to arrange the
insurance with a selected insurance company. Normally, a borrower is entitled
to choose from a number of insurance companies named by the lender. If he
wants to use another company (perhaps his current insurers), he would have to
get the lender's approval (and may be charged a fee for this).

The loan

If the amount you are offered is enough to allow you to go ahead, you should
have no problems. But you could either be turned down or not be allowed a
large enough loan to enable you to complete the purchase.

TURNED DOWN FOR A LOAN?

If your application is rejected, you must ask the reason. It could be
– because of your circumstances (your income, age or occupation), or
– because of problems with the property such as its condition or type, or
– because the lender does not have the money available to lend.

If the problem is you or the house, a different lender may well use different lending criteria.

If the problem is a shortage of funds, the lenders may be prepared to commit themselves to granting your mortgage in the near future, perhaps within the next month or two. But there would be no harm in seeing whether a different lender does have funds available.

For older properties, particularly if in need of repair, the loan may be a lower percentage of the price than normal. Most lenders stipulate that the loan is conditional on repairs being carried out within a specified period, and may hold back some of the loan until these are completed and the lender's inspector has approved the work.

need a larger loan?

If the loan you are offered is limited because the lenders will not lend more than a certain percentage of the valuation, they may be prepared to lend more with a mortgage indemnity policy.

If the reason for the offer being low is your income, do think carefully whether you really can commit yourself to the loan you were requesting. Perhaps if you looked at a cheaper home, you would have no problems in getting the (smaller) loan you need.

TOP-UP LOAN

You should think hard about whether you are being realistic in thinking you can cope with the amount of loan you applied for. If you know you can cope, you may be able to get a second mortgage or top-up loan from an insurance company or bank. The first lender will normally have to give permission (not all lenders allow borrowers to have a top-up loan) and to approve the insurance company or other provider of the second loan.

You are likely to have to pay a higher interest rate on the top-up loan than on the main mortgage and may have to take out an insurance policy to cover it. The conditions of the top-up loan may be stringent: for example, you could be asked to pay three months' interest as a charge for early repayment.

Cost of obtaining a mortgage

The costs which have to be paid by you, the borrower, are

○ the lender's valuation fee
○ the lender's solicitor's fee for handling the mortgage application
○ your own solicitor's fee (if you use one) for handling the mortgage.

The lender's solicitor's job is to check the legal ownership of the property, and to draw up the mortgage deed laying down the conditions of the loan.

Your own solicitor may also charge you a fee for providing the lender with the documents about the ownership, and for checking the mortgage deed.

If you are getting a building society mortgage and the same solicitor is acting for both you and the building society, the Building Societies Association and the Law Society have published a list of basic charges, as a guideline to their members, for the work done on the lender's behalf.

There are also guidelines suggested by the Building Societies Association for solicitors' charges when acting for only the building society.

These charges are based on the size of the mortgage loan and whether the mortgage is a repayment one or is linked to an endowment policy.

Possible additional costs connected with the mortgage

If you have

● *a mortgage from a bank,* you may have to pay an arrangement fee when you take it out
● *a second mortgage or top-up loan,* there may be a charge for obtaining this and the bank or insurance company solicitor's fee for handling it; your own solicitor may also make an extra charge, especially if he is not acting for the second lender
● *an endowment mortgage,* the lender's legal fees will usually be higher than for a repayment mortgage
● *a mortgage indemnity policy or guarantee bond* (required if your loan is for more than a certain percentage of the value of the property), this would entail a single premium, payable as a lump sum or added to the mortgage loan

Q

In practice, most solicitors will charge less than the scale if they are acting for you and the lender at the same time when you are buying a house. Some make no extra charge at all.

- *repairs stipulated by a lender* (for example, eradication of dry rot or wood-worm) and the lender retains a sum out of the mortgage loan until the work has been done to its satisfaction; there may be a fee for inspection
- *a bridging loan* from the bank to make up the purchase price; the bank makes a charge for arranging such a loan
- *a mortgage other than an endowment,* premiums for a mortgage protection policy to provide cover for the sum being borrowed may have to be paid throughout the period
- *a newly-built house which is still being constructed,* and the lender is releasing the mortgage loan in stages, you have to pay a fee for the lender's surveyor's inspection and certificate at the various stages and will have to pay the interest on the earlier parts of the loan from the time you first receive any money.

insuring in case of hard times

Some lenders offer insurance policies which pay your mortgage payments if you are unable to earn because of illness or unemployment. These policies are not cheap, perhaps adding £10 to £15 to the monthly payments on a £30,000 loan.

Read the small print carefully before agreeing to have one of these policies.

- The wider the circumstances in which you can claim, the better. Some policies pay out only if you are unable to work because you are ill or have had an accident. Others include redundancy – though not always if you volunteer for redundancy. A few policies cover a wider definition of unemployment e.g. if you are sacked or lose your job but are unable to claim redundancy payment, perhaps because you have not worked for the firm for long enough.
- Make sure that your work is covered by the policy. Some do not pay out if you normally work part-time, even if you earn good money in that time and have been doing so for several years. Most policies cover self-employed people only for periods of illness, not for unemployment.
- Some policies do not pay out on redundancy or unemployment if you have been with your employer for less than a certain time.
- Most policies will only pay out for mortgage payments for one year, some for two years; you are unlikely to find policies paying out for longer than this.

Buy first or sell first?

Q

The decision to buy first or sell first must depend on circumstances: we've done it both ways and it worked out all right either way.

Probably the most difficult question to resolve is the timing of the whole operation.

If you are selling and buying at the same time, you will want to make sure that you do not risk getting into the position of being the owner of two houses at the same time – or even none.

Although bridging finance is available if you want to conclude your purchase before your sale, it is not to be recommended if you are bearing the cost yourself. It is hardly ever advisable to take on what is known as an 'open-ended' bridging loan when you commit yourself to your new home without having exchanged contracts on the old.

Once you have a pretty clear idea of how much you can afford to spend on your next house, start looking around. If you decide to put the house on the market at that stage, make it clear to the agents that you will not sell until you have found a house to buy. When you find a house you want, then you should try to run the two transactions together.

Q

Your sale gives you first hand experience of 'state of the market' – especially if you intend to buy in the same area.

All things being equal, it is probably sensible to put your house on the market as soon as you think you have found the house you want. Should you lose the house you are buying, you could then withdraw the one you are selling. If all goes well with the offer, the survey and the mortgage for your new one, you will then not have lost time before starting to find a buyer for your present home. When you get an offer for it, you should try – as far as is practicable – to arrange with your buyer for the final completion date to link as closely as possible with the one for your new home.

The matter can become complicated where there are further links in the chain: a prospective buyer for your house has in turn to find one for his, and so on. Difficulties can arise either if one of the houses in the chain proves slow to sell or if one of the purchasers finds that he cannot get a mortgage. For one reason or another, a prospective buyer may have to back down from a purchase after having made an offer, leaving the owner to find another buyer, or even abandon his own purchase.

Q

To buy a house you have to have sold yours and to sell your house you have to have somewhere to go: Catch 22 – you have to muddle through somehow.

So, before you decide to go ahead with a purchase, you should be fairly certain that you will be able to sell your present home reasonably quickly. And you should check with your bank manager that you would be granted a bridging loan if you should need one.

The pros and cons of selling first

PRO

o you will know how much money you have for buying
o no bridging loan necessary
o as a buyer with ready cash, you will be more attractive to sellers (and estate agents)
o no worry about having to sell quickly when you find the house you want

CON

o you could be forced to move out
  – before you have found a new home
  – before you get possession of the house you are buying
  – before the building of a new house is finished and incur costs of storing furniture, two removals, renting accommodation (plus worry and inconvenience)
o house prices could rise sharply between sale and purchase
o you are put under pressure at the buying end which may adversely influence your judgement about what to buy
o being unable to offer a completion date, you could lose a potential buyer

The pros and cons of buying first

PRO

o you have somewhere to go
o there may be time for preparing the new house before moving in.

CON

o a bridging loan may be necessary
o you may have to pay outgoings (e.g. rates, insurance) on two houses.

A break in the chain of seller-buyer-seller may make your preference irrelevant because the situation will no longer be in your control.

Expenses of moving

Q

Get quotes for all professional services (our combined sale/purchase solicitors' quotes ranged from £400 to £800).

REGISTERED TITLE
title or ownership of freehold or leasehold property which has been registered at the Land Registry, so that ownership is guaranteed by the state.

selling

solicitor's fee	no scale fee: allow for up to 1 per cent of the price (+VAT); or flat fee
estate agent's fee or own advertising	allow 1 to 2½ per cent of the price (+VAT) up to you
mortgage redemption charge	if repaying within short period (say, under 5 years) may be up to 3 months' interest, or administration/legal fees in the region of £15

buying

solicitor's/conveyancer's fee	no scale fee: allow for around 1 per cent of the purchase price (+VAT); or flat fee

Statutory fees applicable to the majority of sales:

Land Registry fee on the transfer of property with registered title on a scale related to the purchase price

IF HOUSE COSTS £	FEE £	IF HOUSE COSTS £	FEE £
0– 20,000	25	90,001– 100,000	160
20,001– 25,000	30	100,001– 150,000	180
25,001– 30,000	35	150,001– 200,000	200
30,001– 35,000	40	200,001– 300,000	225
35,001– 40,000	50	300,001– 400,000	250
40,001– 45,000	60	400,001– 500,000	275
45,001– 50,000	70	500,001– 600,000	300
50,001– 60,000	80	600,001– 700,000	325
60,001– 70,000	100	700,001– 800,000	350
70,001– 80,000	120	800,001– 900,000	375
80,001– 90,000	140	900,001–1,000,000	400

STAMP DUTY
a duty payable to the government on some deeds and documents, including conveyance or assignment of property above a certain price.

SEARCH
an enquiry for, or an inspection of, information recorded by some official authority, such as the Land Registry, Land Charges Department, local authority.

Q

Realise exactly how much cash you will need to have available to pay for solicitors, removals, searches, surveys etc + of course the deposit before moving into new home.

---

stamp duty

tax payable on the purchase price of houses costing above a certain figure (at present, 1% if price over £30,000)
for example:
house at £29,500 – stamp duty nil
house at £32,500 – stamp duty £325

local authority searches

set fees payable to local authority for information about planning in area and suchlike (allow about £22); nominal fee in Scotland

---

mortgage

lender's legal fee

fee of solicitor acting for mortgagee (bank, building society, insurance company)
for building society mortgage, guideline scale for fee (+VAT)
for example:

loan of	acting for b.s. only	acting for both
£15,000	£ 93.75	£62.50
£20,000	£101.25	£67.50
£25,000	£108.75	£72.50
£30,000	£112.50	£75.00

(fees are higher with an endowment mortgage)

own solicitor's fee

for dealing with borrower's side of mortgage; no guideline scale fee

valuation fee
allow for more than one valuation fee during house-hunting

for lender's surveyor's valuation, fee based on price of house (+VAT); varies according to lender's arrangement with valuers. For instance, allow around £70 for £40,000 house, £90 for £80,000 house

top-up loan (if needed)	valuation and legal fees
mortgage guarantee bond or indemnity policy (if required)	for loan above normal percentage: single premium of about 3% of amount of extra loan
bridging loan (if required)	interest at 3 to 4% above current bank base rate; bank's charge for arranging loan (say, £120 or 1% of loan)

structural survey

surveyor's fee *allow for more than one survey during house-hunting*	for full survey allow £250 to £400 + VAT (could be a reduction if combined with building society valuation); if old property, budget for possible extra charges if tests by specialist firms needed (eg. drains, electrical, central heating) for a surveyor's intermediate report, fee linked to price of house: allow, say, £150 for £45,000 house

house-hunting expenses

travel and subsistence	allow for meals out, telephone calls, fares/petrol for several visits, overnight accommodation if some distance involved
time off work	?

insurance

buildings insurance	first premium payable in advance (budget for £1.90 per £1,000 of sum insured)

Q

Expenses: several days of eating out at both ends while cleaning/packing up and unpacking and not being able to get at things to cook; not being familiar with where the best/cheapest food shops are initially in new area.

removal expenses

by professional firm *get estimates from three*	for example: contents of 3-bedroomed house moved 20 miles, allow at least £180 (+ VAT and insurance); contents of 3-bedroomed house moved 100 miles, allow at least £420 (+ VAT and insurance); allow for tips
by doing-it-yourself	packing materials; cost of hire of self-drive van (+ VAT and insurance) plus petrol for several journeys, including for the return of the van; fare for own return; food and refreshments for helpers
insurance	allow for minimum premium of £25

services

gas	disconnection and reconnection charges
electricity	perhaps costs of having inspection and tests; perhaps installing additional circuits e.g. for cooker at new house
telephone	installation of new telephone at new home (up to £105) or for taking over existing telephone (£16) plus VAT
mail	redirection of letters: £2.75 (1 month), £6.25 (3 months), £15 (1 year)
plumber	perhaps for disconnecting and reconnecting automatic washing machine and/or dishwasher

Q

Make sure you can afford to move – don't forget you get gas, electricity, phone bills soon after moving from your old property, plus, depending when you move, your mortgage due up to the end of the month.

incidentals

notifying change of address   cost of cards and postage

rubbish disposal

new locks and/or security devices
in new house

kennelling

thank-you presents for helpers: child keepers
                                       animal keepers
                                       strong friends who heaved furniture and cases
                                       gentle friends who provided meals and
                                             comfort.

As well as the expenses of actually moving, also take into account the cost of any immediate repairs (for example, rewiring), improvements or redecoration which might be required in the old and/or new house.

contingency fund

You must allow for the costs of purchases (or sales) which fall through, and for once-only expenses that could occur.

The contingency fund should allow for paying for immediate repairs to put right faults in items you have taken over from the previous owners and for buying replacements for fittings you expected to inherit (or believed were included in the price) which the previous owner has taken.

If you buy a 'secondhand' house, the purchase price will include the fixtures. But if the house you are planning to buy is newly-built, you will have an initial outlay on many items, which, although inexpensive in themselves, mount up.

It is not possible to do more than set an arbitrary figure for contingencies – say, 3 per cent of the total of the purchase price plus all other expenses.

If you are going into a smaller place, you could find yourself with additional money through selling any surplus furniture – in which case, your contingency fund can be marginally reduced.

Q

Allow sufficient money to cover all costs – they really do mount up. Better to have an extra £1,000 on mortgage to allow for home improvements than no money at all.

Q

Make sure before you start that you know how much the move will cost:
    estate agents fees
    solicitors fees/stamp etc
    survey fees
    removal costs etc
and add 20%!

BASIC CHECK LIST OF EXPENSES	ESTIMATED	ACTUAL
	£	£
Maximum possible price to pay for house		
Solicitor's/conveyancer's fee		
Estate agent's fee (if used for selling house)		
Advertisements		
Land Registry fee		
Stamp duty		
Fees for local searches		
Mortgage		
– lender's solicitor's fee		
– own solicitor's fees		
– lender's valuer's fee		
– top-up loan: charges		
– mortgage indemnity policy		
Structural survey		
– surveyor's fee		
– fees for specialist tests		
Insurance		
– buildings insurance premium		
– removals insurance premium		
Bridging loan		
– bank's fee		
– interest		
House-hunting expenses		
– transport		
– accommodation		
– time off		
– other		
Removal expenses		
– firm		
– hire		
– other		

TOTAL CARRIED OVER

BASIC CHECK LIST OF EXPENSES	ESTIMATED	ACTUAL
	£	£
TOTAL BROUGHT FORWARD		

Services
– disconnection
– reconnection
– installation of new equipment
– carpet laying
– mail redirection
Incidentals
– change of address
– boarding animals
– meals out
– rewarding helpers
– telephone calls
– tips
– other

	ESTIMATED	ACTUAL
Contingency fund (percentage of total)	£	£
FINAL TOTAL	£	£

Q

As this was a company move, everything had to be done 'by the book' – rules and regulations caused a headache!

Q

Being a serviceman, a move for us follows a well regulated pattern, unlike our civilian counterparts.

Q

The peace of mind offered by company scheme is very often undermined by the hassle of having to deal with yet another body of people in addition to the normal group of bank/building society/solicitor etc.

Q

We selected our area very quickly and found house which was later withdrawn leaving us to start again: without bridging from my company, the whole process would be much too problematical to tackle (move was 250 miles).

Help with expenses of moving

If you are offered a new job which will necessitate a move, you may be able to make it a condition of accepting that you will get help with removal expenses.

For some employees, such as civil servants, doctors, and members of the armed forces, the moving allowances are laid down. *Civil Servants on the move* is a guide for staff on transfer, available from personnel offices. Doctors who are members of the British Medical Association can get a guidance note on removal and associated expenses from their local BMA office.

Some private employers undertake to bear the costs of moving when they transfer any of their staff from one branch to another, or if the firm itself moves its premises from one area to another.

Be sure to find out beforehand what the employer means by 'costs of moving' and whether this will include

- ○ all solicitors' fees
- ○ other fees, such as Land Registry fee, stamp duty, search fees
- ○ any surveyors' fees
- ○ estate agent's fee (for selling)
- ○ removal firm's charges
- ○ temporary storage of furniture
- ○ temporary rented accommodation while you house-hunt or wait to get in
- ○ fares
- ○ overnight hotel expenses for a two-day move.

If you find you need a bridging loan because of the timing of your buying and selling, it is worth approaching your employer to see if he will advance you this, perhaps interest-free or at a low rate of interest. If the move is at his request, the onus is on him to help you with it.

If it is your employer (or the state) who will be paying, get and keep receipts for everything. If it is not, make this clear to the removal firm (who may assume if you are 'Dr' or 'Sgt' or 'Capt' or 'Rev' that your expenses are being paid for).

Buying a newly-built house

Many buyers prefer a new house to an old one. This could be a house designed and built to your specification on your land. For most people, however, buying a newly-built house is one being built or just completed by a developer, often on a new estate.

A house may be advertised before it has been built. The developer or estate agent can show you the site but only the plans of the house, with perhaps a glossy brochure, or there may be a show house for you to look at before you choose a site.

If you need a mortgage for buying a newly-built house, you will find that lenders such as building societies normally only lend on new houses built under the supervision of an architect or surveyor employed solely by the buyer, or which are built by an NHBC-registered builder.

National House-Building Council

National House-Building Council
Chiltern Avenue
Amersham, Bucks HP6 5AP

in Scotland:
5 Manor Place
Edinburgh EH3 7DH

in Northern Ireland:
Bedford House
Bedford Street
Belfast BT2 7FD

The National House-Building Council is a non-profit-making body with a register of some 25,000 builders and developers who undertake to build houses to a set of standards drawn up by the Council.

Each house built by a registered member is covered by the NHBC's 10-year **Buildmark** warranty and protection scheme, introduced in April 1988 to supersede the previous NHBC protection scheme. A promotional booklet *What the Buildmark means to you* is available free from the NHBC.

The scheme is not a full 10-year guarantee for putting right all faults that may occur in that period. It is an undertaking to repair faulty work within the first two years, followed by an 8-year insurance cover if major structural faults develop. The Buildmark scheme applies to flats and maisonettes as well as houses and bungalows.

- If the builder goes bankrupt before the house is completed, the NHBC will either reimburse the buyer's lost deposit or pay the cost of completion (up to a maximum of £10,000).
- During the first 2 years (the initial warranty period) after the house has been completed, any defect resulting from a failure to comply with NHBC technical requirements must be put right by the builder at no cost to the buyer.
- During the following 8 years (the structural warranty period), insurance

cover is provided for any major damage due to structural defects caused by a failure to comply with NHBC requirements. This includes, for example, major settlement or subsidence, collapse or serious distortion of joists or roof structure, dry (but not wet) rot.

The most that the NHBC will pay for putting right any defects is whichever is the lower of: the cost of the remedial work at the date of payment of the claim, or the amount a reasonable person would spend of his or her own money for the work. To discourage trivial claims under the structural warranty cover, there is a £75 investigation fee, refunded if the claim proves to be valid.

The builder registers the house just before he starts to build. The buyer is given an 'offer of cover' form by the builder, together with a Buildmark booklet giving full details of the scheme. He completes the acceptance form and sends it to the NHBC. NHBC inspectors carry out spot checks on registered buildings under construction and when the inspector is satisfied that a house has been built substantially in accordance with NHBC's requirements, a 'Ten Year Notice' is issued to the builder. The NHBC sends a copy of the notice to the buyer's solicitor or licensed conveyancer and to the buyer (to be kept with the booklet and handed on to the new owner if the house is sold within the 10-year period), and another copy goes to the buyer's lender.

The Buildmark booklet incorporates a *Home Owner's Guide*, giving advice on running in and taking care of the new home, and also explaining further what can and cannot be claimed from the Buildmark scheme, what the payment limits are, and how to appeal to the NHBC's conciliation and arbitration procedures should a dispute arise over rectifying defects.

the advantages of a newly-built house

- major repairs and redecorations should be unnecessary for the first few years
- if, as is probable, it is built to NHBC standards, it will come with their 10-year warranty and protection scheme
- if the house is not yet built or not yet completed, you may be able to get some features changed to suit your requirements – the position of a door, sockets, kitchen work surfaces, cupboards, for instance. But you will have to pay extra for this (and the builder may not agree to undertake any variations until after contracts are exchanged)

Q

A new house has the advantage of not having to clear up other people's mess, but there are still a lot of DIY jobs to add your own fittings etc.

- deposit required may be small
- it may be easier to get a mortgage on a new house than an old one. Many builders arrange mortgage facilities for a whole estate in advance. There is often a link between the property developer and a particular building society which makes it possible for a loan of a high percentage of the purchase price (sometimes as much as 100 per cent) to be given.

the disadvantages of a newly-built house

- the house may not be finished for some time
- there may be no more than the site and a plan to show to solicitor and building society or other mortgagee
- most building societies or other lenders will not release the final loan until all the work is completed – down to the last coat of paint
- you generally have to put in fittings, such as cupboards, which previous owners would already have installed in an inhabited house
- there are often teething troubles – plaster drying out producing cracks, for example
- the roads on an estate may not have been finished (this may cause problems with a building society's loan – and muddy floors in the house)
- the garden may have to be laid and planted and there may be restrictions on what you can do to the front garden (front gardens on an estate are often landscaped by the developers)
- you may not get your money back if you have to sell within one or two years (particularly if the newly-built price was a package including 'free' extras, fixtures and fittings which depreciate; general inflation takes care of longer periods)

A crucial disadvantage is that the date you are first given for the house to be ready is unlikely to be met. This could lead to delay and difficulties over the sale of your present house and extra expense with your removal arrangements – and wear and tear on you. If possible, you should try to get the builder to agree a 'long stop' completion date, so that if he does not finish the work by that date, he will be in breach of contract and liable to pay you compensation. Ask your solicitor to advise on this.

The builder could go bankrupt and so be unable to complete the building or not be available to carry out any work to remedy defects.

Q

I would advise buyers of new houses to

– beware of minor costs of installing amenities which are taken for granted in an old house (e.g. mirrors, toilet roll holders, towel holders, door bell)
– remember you've got to lay the lawn.

Q

Don't underestimate the cost of a new house – fitting carpets, curtains etc and then coping with the new garden – patio, lawn, shrubs – is huge – much more than you get for any fittings or mature garden you leave behind, however dreadful.

Q

They were still partitioning internally on the day we moved in.

Looking for a newly-built house

When touring an area, look out for signs of building works, either single houses or estates. Advertising boards may have been put up by

○ a national firm which has its own sales organisation (the address to contact will be on the board)
○ a large building firm working in the district
○ an estate agent working in conjunction with a building firm
○ a local builder.

It is worth asking local builders, or a national firm, whether they have any future plans for putting up houses in the area. Ask local estate agents not only for details of houses being built or just completed but also about any plans for future estates. They may recently have sold land to a builder or developer for this purpose.

A builder who is not on the NHBC register may be an excellent builder with a good local reputation but he may be just a good jobbing builder with no experience of house building – or he may be one who may have been expelled from the NHBC scheme. In either case, you will have difficulty getting a mortgage; you may have difficulty also when you come to sell if your prospective buyer cannot get a mortgage.

Advertisements

There are some monthly magazines which, between them, contain much useful information on new estates being built, all of which have regular articles on different areas of the country, with a lot of information about new developments, a round-up of mortgage prospects, and frequent supplements on specific aspects of new-house building and buying. The main ones are *Home Finder, House Buyer*, *New Homes News* and *What house*. From these specialist magazines, you can get the names of large developers and the areas in which they operate, so that you can apply to them for details in the area of your choice and in your price range.

The local paper may carry notices with details of property developments, and advertisements of recently-granted planning permissions may appear with the names of builders and developers. The local authority planning officer and the building control officer know about ongoing and projected developments, and may be prepared to give you information.

TIMBER FRAME HOUSE

If you want to buy a timber-&-brick house (constructed with prefabricated timber panels as against a house of conventional masonry construction) the **Timber & Brick Homes Information Council** (Kingsgate House, 536 King's Road, London SW10 0TE, telephone 01-835 1222) can be asked for the names of registered timber frame builders and for a copy of its twice-yearly list of newly completed timber-&-brick houses in each county. *The Timber & Brick Homes Handbook* (£1.95), which may be provided by the builder/developer, contains information about what is involved in buying and owning a house of timber frame construction.

PROMOTING NEW HOMES

The **New Homes Marketing Board** is an offshoot of The House-Builders Federation (82 New Cavendish Street, London W1M 8AD), established to promote the selling of new homes. The NHMB has produced a free booklet *Open up a brand new home*, describing all the advantages of a newly-built house and explaining how to set about buying one.

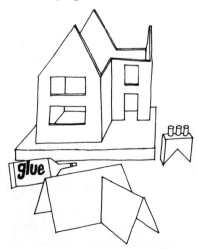

Finding out about the house and the estate

Find out as much as you can about the reputation of individual builders or developers. If possible, talk to people who live in their houses; if an estate is still being built, talk to anyone who has already moved in. Ask:

– have there been many problems with the houses?
– has the builder put them right quickly?
– does he keep his promises?

Ask if there is a show house on the estate. Some developers complete one house and furnish it as a demonstration model. (But remember that the show house may have a number of optional extras fitted as if they were standard.) A small builder may have put up a similar house in the district which he could arrange for you to look at.

Where you have a drawing rather than a finished house to consider, check at the actual site or compare the drawing with the ordnance survey map in the local authority planning office. A site plan may be accurate as to what it does show, but fail to show the proximity of railway lines, sewage works, quarries, factory estates and other unsuspected horrors.

For the inside of the house, get confirmation of actual dimensions of room and stairways.

Some builders fully equip a house and then sell it on its merits. Others provide a basic shell and offer a long list of options – types of doors, floor finishes, kitchen equipment, bathroom suites – to suit the taste and pocket of prospective buyers.

There are all sorts of permutations. The brochure may appear enticing, but it is the detailed specification which it is vital to study if the house is not already finished and available to be seen. The developer's or agent's particulars are sometimes not as detailed as they might be perhaps because the builder is wary of naming specific materials or fittings, in case at a later date these become unobtainable. The quality of fittings tends to vary, so try to get what you want written into the specification as part of the contract for your house. Be sure to confirm all variations in writing and obtain a written acknowledgement (builders' memories are notoriously bad).

Q

Nearly got caught out with lack of rear access but fortunately spotted it before paying a reservation fee.

Q

Make sure what you get for your money i.e. showhouses are full of 'extras' (what was standard in the showhouse was extra).

Q

Builders need continual surveillance when the house is under construction if individual specifications are to be met.

Take special care to check exactly what you are paying for. Is the garage an optional extra, for instance (or obligatory even if you do not want one)? Find out what type of heating is to be installed and be sure not only that you like the type but can afford the fuel. Some estates are all-electric with no gas laid on – you may feel strongly about cooking or heating with one fuel rather than the other.

ROADS

On a new estate, the cost of building the roads and laying the drains is usually included in the purchase price of the house. The water authority becomes responsible for the drains, the local authority for the roads, cleansing and lighting.

Most local authorities insist on the base of the road and kerbs being laid before building work starts. Later, when the top surfacing has been completed to their standard, the roads are adopted and maintained by the authority. There can be delays since the final making up of the roads is done at the end of all the construction work (and a building society may withhold some of the mortgage money until the roads are completed).

The roads will not be adopted by the local authority unless they are satisfactorily completed. Even then, it may be some time before the local authority passes the necessary resolution to adopt and there may be no street cleansing until formal adoption is finalised.

WHILE THE HOUSE IS BEING BUILT

A prospective buyer who has a specific house allotted to him should, if possible, make regular visits to see what is going on and check regularly whether the target date is likely to be met and that the construction is being carried out in accordance with the plans and specifications. Builders can, and often do, make changes in methods and materials. These may not affect the value, but they may not be precisely what you contracted for. If mistakes are found (a yellow suite where blue was ordered, for instance), the earlier the builder is warned, the better.

A survey towards the end of the work might be advisable – to check, for example, that the agreed boundaries have not been altered.

Q

There needs to be tightening up over the location and size of plots – ours 'shifted' several yards to one side from plan to completion – there is nothing that can be done about this afterwards.

Q

Make regular visits (at least weekly) during building and discuss things with builder.

The price

A builder may quote for a house that has yet to be built a price which he undertakes to hold for a specified period. Once contracts are exchanged, he will have to keep to that price unless the contract specifically provides for price fluctuations. You may be asked to pay a small deposit for the offer to be kept open.

The price of a newly-built house is seldom negotiable, especially if it is part of an estate. National firms fix their asking prices and are not likely to reduce them. A smaller firm who finds one or more houses on a particular site remaining unsold may (particularly if interest rates are high or money is tight at the time) make some reduction in order to complete the scheme and so release funds to finance the next development.

INCENTIVES TO BUY

Depending on the state of the market, builders may offer financial incentives to persuade you to buy. Amongst them is reduction in price if you exchange contracts within a specified number of weeks. The catch is that if you do not meet the date, you lose the house at that price and the deposit.

The builder may offer to buy your present house in part-exchange for the new one. This avoids the risk of a chain but you may find that the builder's trade-in price is lower than the open market price for your house. Or the builder will pay the estate agent's and solicitor's fees.

Some builders have their own 'pet' solicitors whom they will encourage you to use. But you are free to use the solicitor or conveyancer of your choice.

Another incentive is for the builder to arrange a 100 per cent mortgage and/or to offer a mortgage subsidy for a year in the form of a reduction in mortgage rate or a refund.

paying

Some builders insist on being paid by instalments and they will put the price up if you do not want to pay for the home in full until it is finished.

Q

The builder operated a scheme in which he offered me 95% of the value (one independent valuation) of my old house provided the price differential between the two houses was at least £10,000 – also no stamp duty or estate agent fees payable.

Q

Discounts are available on new houses if you go at the right time i.e. when first house built on site and when houses are built and not sold – we saved £4,750 which was 10% discount.

Q

Check new property with 'fine toothcomb' and don't complete until fully satisfied. Force builders to carry out work properly.

Q

It is certainly a costly business having to install all fixtures etc. Also there were annoying teething problems – plumbing leaks, oil tank drain-plug not tightened properly, air-locks in central heating system. Most were willingly and quickly rectified by the people concerned. However, I would think twice before buying another new house.

If you are obtaining a mortgage and want to have stage payments as the work progresses, at the various stages the lender's surveyor will have to inspect (and be paid a fee).

It is important to tell your building society when you apply for a mortgage that you will be needing instalment payments. Building societies are generally quite happy to release a mortgage advance by instalments, so long as the value of the work done at any stage covers the amount they have advanced, and so long as the stages in construction tie in with their own requirements.

The society will issue an offer which spells out the stages at which money will be released. Generally, these are as follows:
1. roof plate level
2. roofed in
3. plastered out
4. final completion.

You should make sure that the payment stages in the builder's contract are the same as in the mortgage offer. If there is a discrepancy, you may find it easier to get the builder to change than the building society. Get your solicitor to send a copy of the mortgage offer to the builder with a request that the building society payments are accepted instead.

Even though the lender's surveyor will inspect the house at the end of the construction work before paying out, you yourself should check on doors and window finishes and decorations, whether all the services are connected and working and whether any extras you ordered have all been provided. Unless everything is in order, you would be wise not to complete. If the date of moving out of your previous home is irrevocable, you may need to move to rented accommodation.

It is unlikely that the builder will let you in before he is paid, so if the building society will not advance the money until the house is completed to the surveyor's satisfaction, there may be a critical and frustrating period when the house is to all intents and purposes finished but cannot be occupied. If the date of moving in is vital, you may have to get a bridging loan from the bank.

House-hunting

It is sensible to use all methods of looking for a new home: estate agents, advertisements, searching the area, and word of mouth.

Let it be known to as many people as possible that you are looking – friends, relations, neighbours, colleagues, solicitor, shopkeepers, bank manager, postman, landlord of the pub.

Look out for 'House/Flat for Sale' signs. These may have been put up by the owners themselves but more commonly they are notices erected by estate agents on behalf of a seller. Unless the board says that viewing is 'by appointment only' or 'no callers at the house', there is no reason why you should not approach the owner direct. The board may even say 'apply within'.

If the owner is selling direct and you are interested in viewing, you can either call and ask if it is convenient to look around immediately or make an appointment to see it later. But if it is in the hands of an estate agent, you will usually have to see him first. Although the board may be that of one agent, the house may be on the list of other estate agents as well.

At times when there is a sellers' market (that is, few houses or flats for sale in relation to the number of buyers), property may be bought up so quickly that the agents do not need or have time to get their boards put up. In which case, there is little point in searching a district for boards: go straight to the agents' offices and put your name and requirements down with them to be given details of any likely properties.

A directory of members is available from the National Association of Solicitors' Property Centres, 30 Station Road, Cuffley, Herts EN6 4HE.

In London and many areas of the country, there are 'property shops' where details of houses and flats, including a photograph, are displayed. You can get particulars there of any property you think looks suitable and make arrangements directly with the vendor to go and see it. Some property shops or centres, in particular those set up by solicitors, offer a package deal including the conveyancing. Some firms of solicitors have established a specialist estate agency department within the firm and are more directly involved in the practical and financial aspects of buying and selling property as well as handling the legal side.

Estate agents

Q

A truthful estate agent is like gold dust – not a lot of it around!

To find the names and addresses of local estate agents, start by looking for the names of firms advertising property in the local paper. Also look in the Yellow Pages or other business directory.

Most of the estate agents in England and Wales have principals or senior partners who are members of professional associations and are bound by their codes of professional conduct.

The National Association of Estate Agents (NAEA)
 Arbon House, 21 Jury Street, Warwick CV34 4EH

The Faculty of Architects & Surveyors (FAS)
 15 St Mary Street, Chippenham, Wiltshire SN15 3JN

The Incorporated Association of Architects & Surveyors (IAAS)
 Jubilee House, Billing Brook Road, Weston Favell, Northampton NN3 4NW

The Incorporated Society of Valuers and Auctioneers (ISVA)
 3 Cadogan Gate, London SW1X 0AS

The Royal Institution of Chartered Surveyors (RICS)
 12 Great George Street, London SW1P 3AD

A country-wide list of members is available from the head offices, and professional estate agents will normally have a list of their fellow members.

When you have located the offices of estate agents, study any advertisements outside. Most agents have window fronts in which they display particulars of property they sell, sometimes accompanied by a photograph. These can give you a rough guide to prices and types of property in the area handled by that agent. Agents do not advertise only in order to sell a particular property, but advertise also to establish their identity in the market: "I have this type of property for sale, I operate in this area. Entrust me with the sale of your house and I'll handle it like this" – are what estate agents are trying to put over.

Call on agents who seem to advertise the kind of property you are looking for. If you are restricted to weekend viewing, check which agents are shut on saturdays and/or sundays.

Buying the right house is so important that you should certainly not restrict yourself to what is on offer from just one agent. Enquire of all the agents in a locality. The least flamboyant agent may have just the house you are looking for.

The agents you visit will want to know fairly exactly what kind of accommodation you are looking for. So, decide beforehand what is important to you: how many living rooms, bedrooms and bathrooms are the minimum you need, whether with or without a garage or garden and, most importantly, how much you are prepared to pay. Unless you feel very strongly about alternatives such as detached versus semi-detached, house versus bungalow, keep an open mind and let the agent know you are doing so.

The agent will ask for your name, address, home and work telephone numbers so that he can put you on his register and mailing list.

You, as buyer, are not charged by the estate agent and you are under no obligation to him. Estate agents are in business to arrange the sale of a house or flat on behalf of their client – the seller. They act as negotiator between seller and buyer but since they make their living out of the commission they charge the seller, their duty is to him and not to you, the buyer.

To get an indication of the kind of buyer you would make, the agent may ask you whether you will be a cash buyer or need a mortgage. He will do all he can to make it easy for you to buy (it is in his interest, too) and will be as helpful and cooperative as he can – offering advice about mortgage, survey, solicitor.

Q

Be pro-active in looking. Do not just wait for the estate agents' blurb to hit your letterbox. Telephone a selected group of agents regularly every week, obtain details of properties entering the market before the leaflet is printed.

Q

We disliked having estate agents rub their hands at the thought of us buying from them – put us off and we never went back to them.

Q

View as soon as possible and be able to make a fast decision. I first heard about the property we bought at 6.15pm. I made an appointment to view it at 8.00pm. Got there at 7.45pm having driven 75 miles, and made an offer subject to contract that evening. It is worth making the effort to get what you want!

Q

Looking for a property involved weekend trips to the area; once there, the estate agents' descriptions of properties were continually disappointing. How on earth they manage to get such good photographs of some properties is a puzzle.

The better contact you have with an agent, the more likely he is to think of you and get in touch with you specifically when a suitable house is put in his hands. Be prepared to spend time initially calling in or ringing up regularly in order to establish a good relationship with the agents.

in a new area

It is not easy to house-hunt at a distance. You are unlikely to know the area well enough to be able to assess advertisements or agents' descriptions: sometimes two streets, although adjacent, can be quite different in style and standard, as can opposite sides of the same street.

Estate agents in the locality may send you details of houses but many of these will be no longer available by the time the information reaches you: someone on the spot has beaten you to it.

If you are not able to go to the area, you can call on an agent in your home town and ask if he has any contacts with fellow agents in the other area. He may have the professional journal *Estates Gazette*, which publishes a monthly regional directory of agents.

A **National Homelink Service** is operated by members of the National Association of Estate Agents to provide a referral service for anyone moving from one area to another. The Homelink member in your present locality will contact another Homelink member in the area to which you are moving, giving details of your requirements, and the agents 'on the spot' will send you details of likely properties. The names and addresses of Homelink agents in any area can be obtained from the NAEA.

Some agents are linked to a regional or national multi-list computer system. For instance, the **Team** group of estate agents have combined to offer their clients a computerised multi-listing service in southern England. You register your requirements with one Team agent, and will receive details of properties that match your specifications currently on the books of all the others.

If the area to which you will be moving is some distance away, the cost of travelling to look at houses can be quite considerable. A good estate agent can be helpful in preventing you making unnecessary journeys. He should know each property thoroughly and a telephone call to him for more details or an

Q

If moving to a new area, then apart from usual searches etc, buy an up to date Ordnance Survey map – it gives details such as sewage works!

opinion may help you decide whether a potentially interesting house is worth a journey. He can also arrange appointments for seeing several houses during one visit.

It can be profitable to take time off to go and stay for a few days in the prospective new area so that you can see and assess the place for yourself and make a few personal contacts.

Arm yourself with a large-scale map or street guide so as to make looking easier and quicker. (Many estate agents provide a free map or guide.) Start touring round the area to get the feel of different streets or districts and mark on your map the ones you like.

RELOCATION AGENTS

There is an increasing number of agencies offering a 'relocation' service throughout the country. They act solely on behalf of buyers and set out to help them find and get the type of property they want in the area they want. Originally, such agencies were used mostly by firms for the relocation of staff being moved because of their job. Nowadays many more agencies deal with individuals moving who do not have the time, opportunity or inclination to undertake the tracking down of potentially acceptable properties, particularly in an unfamiliar area of the country.

Relocation agencies vary from the individual consultant to fairly large organisations offering a full range of relocation-related services in the UK and abroad. They advertise in the national press, and many agencies are members of the **Association of Relocation Agents,** 1 Castle Street, Edinburgh EH2 3AH.

The ARA can be asked to send a list of their members in any area of the country, with a brochure setting out the rules of conduct that an ARA member will abide by.

An agent's knowledge of the local property market should enable him or her to offer advice on suitability of property and location according to a client's requirements. The agent should advise on a particular property's value and condition, on planning consideration and resale possibilities. An advantage of using a relocation agent is that he or she is working for you, the buyer, and will get details of properties, view on your behalf, sift and select property within

your specifications, so that you do not waste time and risk disappointment seeing hopeless candidates. An agent will negotiate terms for a client, if required, and can also be asked to oversee the sale of the present home.

Relocation services can include whatever the individual client requests, including introductions to legal and financial advisers, making all the removal arrangements, organising storage of possessions, the cleaning and preparing of both the new and the old home, providing information about the new area and facilities.

It is usual to be asked to pay a 'retainer' or registration fee (anything from £25 to over £200) for the initial work of researching and selecting suitable property; when a purchase goes through, a further fee (perhaps 1% of the price) is payable on exchange of contracts. Any additional or further work the relocation agent is asked to do will be charged on a negotiated basis.

Estate agents' particulars

Whether you call in person, telephone or write, the agent will give you what are known as 'particulars' – details of available properties which he thinks may be of interest. The information may be in the form of a list or even a glossy brochure or individual sheets for each property. He may send particulars to you at frequent intervals until you tell him to stop, or until he gets tired of you if you do not follow up any of them.

Q

When houses are offered for sale by multiple estate agents, then sometimes the price varies, and all too often each estate agent quotes different room sizes in the house.

"None of the statements contained in these particulars as to this property are to be relied on as statements or representations of fact."

"Any intending purchaser must satisfy himself by inspection or otherwise as to correctness of each of the statements contained in these particulars."

One of the hazards of the house-hunting game is that by the time a list has reached you, you may find that the house which you particularly like the sound of has already been snapped up and is 'under offer'. This is a good reason to make good contact with agents and ask that they telephone rather than write to you.

Agent's particulars are part of his service of marketing the house for the seller, who would not thank him if a description were so worded as to deter potential buyers. It is intended to act as an inducement for the buyer to inspect: the assumption is that no one buys a house on the strength of particulars only. However, the facts given in the description of a property must be accurate – about, for instance, the number of floors or size of rooms. But you may find that because a room is on an upper floor, it is counted and described as a bedroom when it may not really be big enough to hold a bed. So, check the room measurements if they are given, and beware if none are quoted. Measurements are usually given straightforwardly: reception room 16'6" × 20'. 'Maximum' dimensions may mean that the room is not square: it may be L-shaped or have an alcove.

You have to learn to notice what is not said and extract the details from the traditional estate agents' descriptive style, which uses such terms as 'exceptional' or 'beautifully proportioned'. Beware of 'immaculate decor' or 'tastefully decorated' which has to be a matter of opinion – usually only the owner's and possibly only the agent's.

euphemisms

suitable for conversion	in need of a lot of repair and redecoration
bijou	can't swing even a cat
cottage	anything old and small
townhouse	front entrance through the garage
easy to manage	pokey
spacious	too big for most people to decorate or heat
exceptionally spacious	cold and draughty
full central heating	four storage heaters
conservatory	porch 18in × 3ft
full double glazing	constant traffic noise

Q

*Reference was made [in particulars] to
"magnificent views to open countryside"
and "superb views from the property over
to Wychwood Forest in the distance".
comment: at the rear of the property from
where the views are to be beheld is a
school playing field. At the time of the
production of the particulars, the County
Council had already resolved to sell a strip
round two edges of the playing field with
outline 'medium density' planning
permission for 23 houses. These will
effectively cut off the view except so far as
it is visible through the gaps in the new
housing.*

interesting	only if you're selling it (can't think what it's for)
individual decor	paper peeling off walls
convenient motorway/railway	runs at back of garden
convenient buses	bus tickets fall into your front garden
convenient school	children fall into your front garden
quiet cul-de-sac	children's playground early sunday mornings and school holidays
secluded	the shops are a long way away
rural views	views of allotments, cabbage fields, pig sties, or all three
open views	faces league football ground
reasonably priced	overpriced
reduced for quick sale	still overpriced
potential garage space	if only there were access
potential anything	if only money/time were available (we would have but are moving instead)
full of character	full of woodworm, dry rot, damp
exposed beams	on which to hit exposed heads
light and airy	expensive to curtain
deceptively spacious	too many small rooms
potential for extension	cramped
garage space and driveway	no parking
neat garden	minute yard
garden laid to lawn	grass patch
mature garden	overgrown wilderness
sea view	standing on seat in wc
merits further improvement	can only get better
suitable for keen d-i-y	present owners did nothing
ideal for modernising	quick before it falls down

The particulars may also give the rateable value, whether it is freehold or, if it is leasehold, the length of the lease and the amount of the ground rent and sometimes any maintenance charge, and, finally, the asking price. The letters "o.n.o." (or near offer) after the price are an indication that the price is set high and the seller might be prepared to come down.

Q

The road on which the house stands is a bit busier than we had expected and the shortness of the front garden does little to distance the sound of passing cars from our front rooms.

An estate agent must, by law, inform you if he has a personal interest in a property (perhaps a house is owned by one of his staff). Such a 'personal interest' statement may appear on the particulars.

Photographs of houses serve as a rough guide to the kind of property involved but can be misleading – for instance, they may have been trimmed of their less attractive surroundings, or may even be of similar property in the same road – and should be regarded with caution. Remember the agent is being paid to sell the house; to do this, he has got to present it in the most favourable light, without deliberately misleading or blatantly misrepresenting it or its size or position.

advertisements

Estate agents often advertise in the local and national press the properties they handle. Although these may well have been sold by the time the advertisement is published, it is worth studying advertisements to get an idea of prices and of agents and because they are a useful pointer to the current state of the market.

Owners who wish to sell privately often advertise in the 'Property For Sale' columns of newspapers and magazines. Do not be put off buying a house which is advertised privately rather than through an agent. (An agent gives no guarantee of the quality of the house he is selling – and remember, he is acting for the seller and not the buyer.)

For an area you are unfamiliar with, ask at the local reference library what papers cover the district. It is important to find out on which day property advertisements appear, and get your copy immediately.

Advertisements in the national dailies and sunday papers and glossy magazines are likely to be for houses at the upper end of the market; local morning and evening papers and weeklies will give a wider choice. Weekly magazines worth consulting include: *Exchange & Mart, London Weekly Advertiser, Daltons Weekly, The Lady*. Top-of-the-market property is advertised in such magazines as *Tatler, The Field* and *Country Life*; often these are houses which are to be sold by auction.

HOUSE-HUNTER'S ADVERTISEMENT

You can yourself put an advertisement in the 'Wanted' column of a local or national newspaper. Specify what you want:

> flat/house/bungalow
> location/position
> size/number of rooms
> (garden?)
> (garage?)
> price (approximate)
> and why you would be a good buyer, such as 'no chain' or 'mortgage arranged' or 'bank employee'.

Local newspapers are likely to be more useful and less expensive. Most newspapers offer reductions for repeated inserts; take their advice on which days to place the advertisement. If you are lucky enough to find a house in this way, you can ask the seller if he will reduce his price since he will not be paying an agent's commission.

Buying an old house to do up

If you want to buy an old house and modernise and improve it, you must be prepared for it all to take a long time. Applying to the local authority for and receiving planning permission and an improvement grant could take anything from 2 to 12 months or longer, plus a further 6 months or more for the building work to be carried out. In some cases, it may not be practicable to live in the house while the work is being done.

Before you buy the house, you ought to find out more about planning permission for the work you would like to do and the possibility of getting a grant. Go to the planning department and the environmental health department of the appropriate local authority and ask what the position is likely to be in your case. The more accurate and realistic the details you are able to provide, the better.

Conservation officers working for district or county councils can sometimes help with general advice.

house improvement grants

Local authorities administer and give grants (towards which the government contributes the greater part) for improving or renovating property, provided that the house is freehold or has a lease with at least five years to run, and is not a 'second home'. You have to declare that you intend the property to be used in the same way for at least five years. A house may be more difficult to sell while the grant conditions are in force. If you as an owner-occupier sell to someone who will be using the house for letting, this could result in the grant (or part of it) having to be repaid with interest.

A Department of the Environment housing booklet (no. 14) *A guide to home improvement grants* is available free from local authority offices. Many local authorities produce their own notes of guidance for prospective applicants. In Northern Ireland, the Housing Executive issues a leaflet *Renovation grants*. The Scottish Development Department's booklet *Improve your home with a grant*, available free from local district council offices, is a guide to house improvement and repair grants, and gives full details of the conditions for getting a grant.

The grant you can get is a percentage of an amount called the eligible expense of the cost of the improvement plus some repair work.

An **intermediate grant** is for putting into a house for the first time certain basic standard amenities: basin, hot and cold water supply, bath or shower, flush lavatory – coupled with essential repairs or replacements. You may have to provide all these facilities to get the grant, but not all at the same time.

Intermediate and improvement grants are available only for property built or converted before October 1961.

There is also an **improvement grant** to help owner-occupiers improve older houses to a good standard. Unlike an intermediate grant to which one has a right, an improvement grant is paid at the local authority's discretion, and only for property with an existing rateable value below a specified limit (at present, £400 in Greater London, £225 elsewhere). Many local authorities impose strict eligibility criteria for discretionary grants. You may not get one.

A local authority can make it a condition of a grant that you carry out certain repairs – for which you may not get a grant. Thus you might finish up getting only 25% of your total expenditure, even though a 50% grant was promised.

For pre-1919 houses, there is a discretionary **repairs grant**.

For any grant, it must be approved by the local authority before any work is started. Local authorities do not have discretion to approve grants retrospectively for any work which has already been started.

planning permission

You do not need to be the owner of the property to apply for planning permission (but you must inform the owner).

The Department of the Environment booklet *Planning permission* is a guide for householders; available at local authority planning departments and housing advice centres.

Planning permission is required for many alterations and extensions to a building, particularly if it affects the external aspects and appearance, and for changing the use of a building. The permission has to be obtained from the local planning authority. The fee for applying for permission to alter or extend a property is £33.

Permission is not required for what is specified as permitted development – for example, extending the house within certain limits. But the rules are very complicated and you would be well advised to contact the planning department of your local authority for informal advice from a planning officer. Sometimes the permitted development provisions do not apply to certain areas, such as conservation areas.

Whether planning permission is needed or not, building regulations will apply to the materials and method of building. The local authority's building control officer should be consulted about getting building regulations approval (in Scotland, building control consent).

listed buildings and conservation areas

Under the town and country planning legislation, the Department of the Environment compiles lists of buildings of special architectural or historic interest. A listed building must not be altered or extended in any way which would affect its character without authorisation from the local planning authority. This is a separate issue from planning permission, but getting listed buildings consent can be dealt with at the same time. The listing extends to the whole of the building inside and out, and the site, even though only a part may be 'of interest'.

Also, local authorities have designated conservation areas – perhaps a whole town or village, or a square, a street or even part of a street.

Any property in either of these categories must not be demolished without consent and all trees within a conservation area are automatically subject to preservation orders.

You can check whether a house is in a conservation area or is a listed building by going to the local authority offices to inspect the list. Do this before buying a house if you have ideas of making alterations or extensions to it at any time. Not only very old houses are listed – a building may be listed that is only 30 years or so old, if it is of outstanding quality or design.

Certain grants may be available from the local authority in respect of essential structural repairs to a listed building, and to repair or retain aspects of architectural interest; ask about this possibility at the local planning authority. Grants may also be made by English Heritage (the Historic Buildings and Monuments Commission for England) for buildings of outstanding interest where the cost of eligible items of repair is over £10,000. Notes for guidance and an application form are available from **English Heritage**, Fortress House, 23 Savile Row, London W1X 2HE.

Ancient or unusual properties

If you are prepared to buy a decayed or historic building, the **Society for the Protection of Ancient Buildings** (37 Spital Square, London E1 6DY) compiles for its members a quarterly list of historic buildings for sale which are in need of sympathetic owners to repair and maintain them.

Some people prefer the challenge of finding a building not originally designed as a home, and converting it themselves. If you would like to know whether there are any redundant properties available in your chosen area or happen to see a disused or unoccupied one, the organisations to get in touch with are

for redundant church, rectory or other church building	apply to diocesan office or registry (address in local telephone directory) or ask the vicar
for disused railway property	ask the British Rail Property Board (Great Northern House, 79–81 Euston Road, London NW1 2RT) for the names of regional estate surveyors and managers to apply to in Birmingham, Bristol, Glasgow, London, Manchester, York
for buildings in the forest	the Forestry Commission sells some of its property by auction or by tender through regional offices; free mailing list for area/price required from the head office at 231 Corstorphine Road, Edinburgh EH12 7AT

for unoccupied warehouse or other derelict property	trace ownership by contacting local authority for name and address of whoever is responsible for the rates on the property
for redundant schoolhouse	ask the local education authority
for redundant pub	ask the estate manager of the brewers

How to view

When you have spotted a house or flat or been sent details of one you wish to look at, you should make an appointment 'to view' immediately. If you are the first person to view, you stand a better chance of getting the house should you decide it is the one you want.

The estate agent will make the appointment on your behalf; it is one of the services he offers. Sometimes he will accompany you; this can save time. If the owner is out, or the property is vacant but still furnished, and the agent has the key, he will want to go with you since responsibility for the house or flat is his. If it is empty, you may be allowed to borrow the key to look round on your own.

If you have an appointment but cannot keep it, you should let the owner or agent know. If, when you get to the outside of the house, you decide without even going in that it is not what you want, it is common courtesy to cancel your appointment there and then by knocking on the door and saying "sorry, but no".

Always take pen, paper or notebook and a measuring rule with you, and the agent's particulars, so that you can check dimensions, particularly where measurements are quoted as 'max' or 'overall' or 'approx.'. Ideally, husband and wife should view together but if one or other cannot do so, it will help in later discussions if there are notes or plans to refer to.

It is no bad thing to make up a short check list. Write down on the left-hand side, line by line, all the factors you can think of – rooms, situation, all the merits you want and any demerits you do not want – with a few spare lines for points occurring as you go along. Draw vertical columns to the right of these headings, put the address of the house (and succeeding houses) at the top of the columns and then tick off 'yes' or 'no', '3', say, opposite 'bedrooms' or 'good' or 'bad', and so on, so that you have a ready reminder of the comparative merits of possible houses/flats.

first look

It can be distracting to assess a house or flat when it is decorated or furnished to another's taste or in need of decoration. Try not to be influenced by 'wrong' colours and furniture – or none at all – but concentrate on absorbing a general impression and imagine yourself and your family in it. You are equally likely to

Q

Try to view properties without estate agent – this alleviates being 'rushed around' and being placed in awkward situation on likes and dislikes of property: the vendors themselves know more about the property than the estate agent likes to think he does!

Q

Have a check list and/or pointing system to grade and catalogue each property viewed. Invaluable when the memory starts flagging at the 25th viewing.

Q

When choosing house, put position first. You can alter a house extensively but not move it nearer shops, school or commuter route.

be misled by a beautifully furnished and newly decorated home – you can fall for it as it looks, forgetting to think: "How will it look with my paltry possessions in it?"

A strange house on several floors can be confusing at first sight: it may help to make a floor by floor plan as you go. But do not waste too much time on this. It is better to go back and do a second tour. Do not let yourself be rushed or pressurised by the estate agent who accompanies you or embarrassed by the presence of the owner.

As you go over the house, concentrate on the layout of each floor and each room. Do not forget to look at the windows. An empty house without curtains gives an impression of light rooms, but can turn out dark and dismal when curtained and furnished.

The height of the rooms is something to note from the point of view of heating and redecorating and how your furniture will fit.

An open-plan house where the dining and sitting area and the kitchen lead into each other, without dividing walls or doors, means the need for a powerful heating system and good insulation. There are advantages for a mother working in the kitchen being able to keep an eye on a small child playing in the adjacent living area, but there can be problems about privacy, and difficulties when children reach school age and need a quiet place to study or play on their own or as teenagers to entertain their friends.

If the house or flat seems to provide what you need in the way of basic accommodation – sufficient bedrooms, living rooms and so on – and if your first impression of it as a possible home is a favourable one, you should consider it in more detail.

Looking in more detail

No one house will provide all you want. It is up to you to decide what points are most important or relevant, and which – because others are so satisfactorily provided – you are prepared to forgo.

Think also how permanent you expect your stay to be in the new home. If you are likely to resell shortly, consider whether any aspect of the property may affect your chances of finding a buyer when it is your turn to sell.

Q

I always asked in casual conversation style where they were moving to. If locally: "How can you leave this lovely house?" caught on the hop, surprising answers sometimes emerged. At least you should be able to detect confusion and subterfuge.

Here are points to consider carefully. If the answers to the majority are not positive, the house is probably not suitable for you. The answer to some of the questions may be 'no, but could be arranged'. But take into account that alterations or improvements will put up the cost – quite apart from the time factor.

POINTS TO BE CONSIDERED INCLUDE

○ is the accommodation what you want?
○ is the layout suitable?
○ is the situation and location of the house right?
○ what are the facts about the heating, lighting and other services?
○ what is the state of the structure?
○ what is the state of the decorations – inside and out?
○ what about the garden?
○ what about any garage, drive and roadway?
○ when will the house/flat be available?
○ what is included in the price?

accommodation and layout

entrance (hall)   – is there an outer porch? (as protection against weather, for delivery of parcels)
– is there space for parking a pram, pushchair, bicycle, shopping trolley?
– is there anywhere to hang coats, store wellington boots, gardening shoes, umbrellas?
– is it well lit?
– which direction does the front door face?

living room(s)   – are they adequate in size? (in any irregular-shaped room or one with a bay window, take the exact measurements)
– is the dining room or dining area convenient to the kitchen? are there steps up or down from the kitchen? (making a trolley impracticable, carrying trays hazardous)
– is there space for the children to play?
– is there space for the piano? (preferably not against a neighbour's adjoining wall)

– are the windows in convenient places?
– where are the electric sockets and are there enough of
  them?
– where are the lights and switches?

kitchen
– is it large enough, particularly if you want to be able to eat
  in it, work in it?
– does it lead off hall/living room/dining room? how
  convenient is it for carrying food, shopping to, garbage
  from?
– is there an outside door, into garden, for access to garage
  or dustbin?
– is there a back porch?
– what does the window look on to? which way does it face?
  (if south or west may get too hot) could you keep an eye
  on a child in the garden?
– is the window easy to open? is there an air extractor
  system?
– does the layout of worktop and sink area suit your way of
  working?
– is it well lit?
– what storage is there for food: is there a larder? is there
  space for your refrigerator? for your freezer?
– will your existing equipment fit?
– is there enough cupboard space, drawers, shelves? tall
  cupboard for vacuum cleaner, brooms?
– is the floor covering in good condition? comfortable to
  stand on? likely to be easy to clean?
– is gas laid on? (check particularly if the present owner has
  an electric cooker)
– where and how many electric sockets are there? is there
  one for a cooker?

utility room
– is there one? or what facilities are there for washing and
  drying clothes?
  indoors: space for a washing machine/tumble dryer?
  ironing area?

outdoors: space for hanging clothes to dry? are there any restrictions on hanging washing outside?

staircase
- is it easy to climb? (for small children or the elderly) are the treads wide enough? risers not too steep? are there awkward curves or bends? are there handrails? is it well lit? (top and bottom)

bedrooms
- how many?
- are they large enough? for double bed/twin beds/four poster/bunk beds?
- will other furniture (chest of drawers, wardrobe, for instance) fit in? (measure, do not guess)
- is there built-in furniture?
- is there a washbasin? (if so, fill it up and let it drain, and do the same with any others – they can be noisy and react to the plumbing elsewhere in the house)
- are the rooms convertible to nursery/playroom/study/ bedrooms? (consider future needs as well as current ones)
- do they face a noisy road or a bright street light?
- how soundproof are the walls between?

bathroom(s)
- how many?
- is there a separate wc?
- plumbing: can another bathroom/extra basin/shower/wc be installed easily? (check where the water supply and waste piping runs in the building)
- does everything work?
- is there an airing cupboard/linen cupboard or space to make one?

other
- is there an extra room which you could use as spare bedroom/study/sewing room/boxroom for storage/playroom/workshop?
- is there a loft? could it be used for storage or converted into a room?
- cupboards: are there any built in? or space to put some in?

Q

I find people don't know north from south etc. I got in the habit of saying "Where is the sun at midday?"

situation and location

You probably already know or, if you do not, you should decide now, how important to you it is to have a sunny living room, kitchen or bedroom. A kitchen or living room which never gets any sun can be especially dark and gloomy in winter – and these are the rooms in which a housewife spends most of the daylight hours. So, check which rooms are north facing (cold and dark), which east facing (morning sun, best for waking up/breakfasting), which south or west facing (warm and sunny for most of the day). This is especially important if you are viewing on a dull day or a winter evening. If you cannot work it out for yourself, ask the owner or agent and mark the direction of the rooms on your plan. Similar houses on opposite sides of a road may be quite different inside from the light and warmth aspect – and may be different in price, too, on this account.

Work out whether the garden gets the sun all day or only part of the day, or is always shaded. Consider how important this is to you – as a sun lover or as a gardener.

Look to see whether any trees, foliage or adjacent buildings take away light from any room. If you are viewing in winter, be especially observant and allow for trees in leaf during the summer. Do any houses nearby look into the windows or garden? If you are viewing in summer, study whether the trees obscure some overlooking building. Also, trees in leaf are a good barrier to traffic noise, so it may be much noisier in winter.

Think about any possible winter hazards: if the district is hilly or the approach to the house is steep, icy conditions might make access difficult or impossible. Draughts coming through front or back doors and along passages may be fierce in winter – but absent on the gentle summer's day when you are viewing.

Is there a river or any streams close by which could cause flooding? (this may affect insurance cover).

The exterior of a house in an exposed position, on high ground, or by the seaside may need more attention in the way of upkeep and insulation. If there is industry nearby, note whether the prevailing wind would send any dirt, smoke or smell towards the house rather than away from it.

Q

Make one view in the wettest, most horrible weather possible.

If you are at all interested in the house, it is essential to go back again to see it at a different time of the day, on a different day of the week, and in different weather conditions, if possible.

What about the siting of the house – the immediately adjacent vicinity (neighbours), the general location and the effect on your journeys to work?

Check on:

distance from
- railway station (are there parking facilities there?)
- bus stop and bus routes (and London underground)
- post office, bank, library, shops, launderette, health centre (will it be uphill carrying home heavy shopping or pushing a pram?)
- schools (how safe is the route?) or college
- church or chapel

access to
- countryside/sea
- park or recreation ground
- cultural and leisure activities

neighbours
- how secluded is the house?
- are neighbours likely to be a nuisance (children or pets) or vice versa?
- in a terraced or semi-detached house, which rooms have the party walls?
- what is the division between gardens?
- is the next-door garage near your boundary? (late/early car starting)
- are nearby buildings likely to cause a nuisance? (restaurant, pub, club, fish-and-chip shop or take-away, could cause parking problems and noise at night; cooking smells, piles of rubbish; a factory can produce smoke, noise or smells; a farm may bring in smells or flies or straying animals)
- on a new estate, could further building work or future buildings obscure a pleasant view?

Q

Burglar alarms of nearby shops – tendency to go off frequently – very disturbing, especially when it goes on all night.

Other factors that you could find either a nuisance or an advantage if next-door

Q

Walk round the neighbourhood in the evening and at weekends.

Q

Apart from checking proximity of amenities required, also check for path of sun around home (we prefer rear of house to face south, approx); watch for nearby traffic problems; possible re-development in the area e.g. large house being demolished and number of flats built.

Q

If vendor asks you to call back in ½ hour or so, although viewing at appointed time, ask yourself why? in my case, the reason was to give heating system time to quieten down.

or nearby might be a school, a police station, fire station, hospital, church, garage or repairer, kennels, swimming pool, sports ground.

If the next-door property is uninhabited (particularly if it is derelict) find out who owns it and what is likely to be happening.

If you are viewing on a weekday, try to find out whether things change at weekends. Or if you are there at a weekend, consider the other days of the week. For a market town, make at least one visit on market day.

Watch and listen for traffic noise and inconvenience:

– are there heavy lorries going by on weekdays? (none at weekends)
– are there traffic lights/junction/hill/bend close by? (constant stopping/starting/gear noises)
– is it a favourite route for L-drivers?
– do commuters or shoppers pass or park on weekdays?
– do tourists pass or park at weekends or in summer?
– do nearby sports grounds cause parking problems and noise at weekends/evenings?
– do trains pass within hearing distance?
– is there a motorway or by-pass near enough to be noisy? or are there plans to build one?
– is there an airport or airfield near and is the house under the flight path?
– are there any nasty but short-lived noises such as milk depot loading crates at 4am for two hours every day?

If you can find out about the ownership of the adjacent land or buildings, try to discover if there are plans for further developments. Knowledge of the district if you live there already will obviously be a help. Local papers and local gossip are other sources of information. It is unlikely that the seller will tell you that he is putting his house on the market because a new battery chicken 'farm' is to be set up in the field opposite.

heating and other services

How is the house heated? Is all or only part of it centrally heated? (Look for radiators in all rooms; a note on a plan can help later when working out arrangement of furniture.) When was the system installed?

Is electricity the only laid-on fuel? Or is there a gas supply, even if not currently in use? (when was it last used?)

Is there an alternative to fall back on if the electricity is cut off or the central heating supply fails, such as an open fire or a stove? Are there working fireplaces and what can you burn (is it a smoke control area)?

If you view during cold weather, you should be able to tell straightaway whether the heating system works effectively. If you view in summer, ask for the system to be switched on, if practicable. You should get it properly tested later as part of the survey.

Ask the owners what the past year's fuel consumption and heating costs (including maintenance) have been – if they are able to tell you. When assessing any figures, remember to allow for differences in your ways of life – whether out all day, with or without children or of different ages, elderly people in the household.

Q

If we had known how inefficient the solid fuel central heating proved to be, might have offered lower and set about changing it sooner.

if oil-fired	where is the storage tank (and its vent pipe)? is it unobtrusively sited and what is its capacity? where is the boiler?
if solid fuel	do you mind having to stoke a boiler? carry fuel? clean out ashes? what type of fuel has to be used? where is the fuel stored – is it convenient for the house/for delivery?
if gas-fired	where is the boiler? how old is it?
if off-peak electricity	electric storage heaters – how many and where, what size, capacity, how old and run on what tariff? underfloor or ceiling heating – in which rooms? warm air ducting – where are the vents/grilles?
loft insulation	is there any, and of what type and thickness?
water supply	is it on direct mains water? if not, what water supply is there?

Q

The loft insulation had only been fitted near the trap door so the brief view I had didn't show that the sub-contractor had 'economised'.

what are the water charges per year? is there a meter?
how is the water heated?
is the cylinder likely to be large enough for your needs?
where do the pipes run?

electricity	ask how old the wiring is and has it ever been re-wired (professionally or d-i-y?) are there plenty of sockets? if you want to cook by electricity, is there a separate circuit (30 amp, at least) for the cooker?

gas — if there are gas fires, how old are they? (older types may not be efficient)

drainage — is the house connected to a main drainage system? or is there a septic tank or cesspool? (if so, what are the costs of maintenance and arrangements for emptying?)
Note where any manholes or access points are: if on your premises, you are independent in case of trouble; if on someone else's land, there may be delay in getting a stoppage cleared. (On the other hand, if the communal manholes are on your site, you may be inconvenienced by calls to get obstructions cleared.)

TV aerial — is there one? if you see a lot of fancy aerials on nearby houses, it is likely that reception is poor; if the house is under a cliff or hillside, it may be inaccessible to radio signals.

Q

Check EVERYTHING works – if the central heating is not in operation, insist on the system being run to check operation (replacement boilers cost approx £850!) check all waterworks and plumbing e.g. for noisy pipes, poor water pressure, poor flushing toilet.

Q

Make several visits to the house you are buying, try all taps, lights, central heating . . . don't feel as if you are imposing on the seller's privacy: have a long slow look around.

the structure

Even if you will be having a professional survey of the house or flat done by a qualified surveyor, during a preliminary visit try to get as good an impression as you can of the structural condition of the building. If it looks to you to have a lot of faults, you could save yourself the cost of a survey by deciding then and there that the cost of repairs would not justify the cost of the house – or that the repairs would not be possible on your budget. Ask the owner what structural work has been carried out recently, when and why.

Q

... that the hot water took a very long time to reach the kitchen sink and was low pressure – but, fair do's, we didn't tell our buyers that their kitchen would be infested by ants every spring!

An owner is under no obligation to tell you of any faults: it is up to you or your surveyor to discover them. On the other hand, he is under an obligation to give honest answers to direct questions: for example, whether he has ever had any problems with dry rot or an insurance claim for flooding. If he does not answer truthfully and you can show that you relied on his answers, you can sue him.

INSIDE

From a structural point of view, the main things to look at inside are the walls and ceilings.

ceilings	– are there stained patches? (tell-tale sign of leaks)
	– are ceilings sagging or cracked? (Cracked plaster ceilings in an older house may just be a matter of papering over the cracks, but if cracks look to you alarmingly wide or run into corners or over window lintels, there may be a problem.)
walls	– are there stains on walls around the skirting, and crumbling plaster? (signs of rising damp)
	– are there any long, diagonal cracks in walls which look as if they have been repaired but have re-cracked? (this may be a sign of settlement)
	– is the existing paper or paint shabby, dirty or damaged? (note to what extent redecorating would be immediately necessary and include this in your budget)
	– if the house is newly painted inside, ask yourself why? are they just houseproud – or covering up?
woodwork and floors	– is woodwork showing cracks or shrinkage (going crinkly), especially skirtings? (a possible sign of woodworm or rot)
	– if floors are springy, they or the joists underneath may be rotten (on the ground floor) or wormy (anywhere)
	– ask what the floor surface is under a fitted carpet, vinyl or lino covering
	– are any floor tiles cracked or wood blocks loose or bulging?
	– are any floor coverings worn in places that take a lot of traffic? would any need replacement?

Q

Have a thorough look around the property you are buying: don't listen too much to vendors as they can distract you from faults in the house.

OUTSIDE

Go outside and study the building from top to bottom. A pair of binoculars can be useful for scanning roofs and chimney stacks. If things look bad from below, they probably are worse up there, and inside too.

If any major re-roofing or repairs have been carried out, find out what, when, and whether any guarantees were attached. For a flat roof, find out how long ago it was laid (felt roofs last about 10 years, asphalt up to 30).

Points to look for or ask about are:

roof
— look for any loose or broken slates or tiles, particularly near chimneys and roof valleys. Walk down the garden or to the other side of the road and have a look at any roof valleys that may be visible (if they are cluttered with slipped slates or tiles, the whole roof may be likely to need rehanging)
— do chimney stacks look in good condition or is brickwork in need of repointing?

main walls
— any bulges or cracks? (may be caused by settlement of the foundations or by tree roots – own or neighbour's)
— what is the state of the pointing between the bricks? (it should look smooth and full: gaps or cracks allow damp to penetrate)
— is there a damp proof course? (not all old houses have one) are there signs of damp at ground level?
— guttering and down pipes: are there signs of rust or leaking, stained or green walls (damp could penetrate brickwork, or cause wet rot)
— when were the walls last painted? with what material? will they need doing immediately? and how often thereafter?
— is the paint peeling very badly? (there may be a damp problem)
— are walls covered with a cement rendering? what condition is it in? (it will be an expensive maintenance item)

doors and windows – do they fit well? do all windows open and close easily?
- does woodwork look in good condition? is there any rust on metal frames?
- what is the condition of the paintwork?
- when were they last painted (or varnished)? (on average, every three years is a recommended interval, more frequently in south facing walls or if the house is at the seaside)

If you decide to go ahead to the stage of having a professional survey done, tell the surveyor of anything you have noticed that you think may be sinister. If he confirms your suspicions, you can ask him to give you an idea of how much it would cost to be put right.

There is more likelihood of there being heavier maintenance and repair costs with an older house, so it is even more important to have an old house surveyed and get an idea of how well it has been looked after over the years.

Some prefabricated reinforced concrete house-types have been designated as defective. Before buying a PRC home, a prospective buyer should check with the local authority whether the dwelling is one of these. If so, find out whether it has been repaired in compliance with the Housing Defects Act 1984 and carries a warranty issued by the National House-Building Council.

THE GARDEN

How important is a garden to you for general recreation (sunbathing, barbecues), for the children and as a gardener?

- is it the right size/too big/not big enough?
- how sheltered is it?
- how much sun does it get?
- is it suitable for a child to play in? are there any hazards? (trees, pond, stream, unsafe access to road)
- is it easily accessible for a pram?
- is it overseeable from the house?
- is it on a steep slope? easy to maintain?
- what state is it in? (if not yet laid out, this could be expensive: purchasing topsoil, laying a lawn)

– is there much grass to cut/hedges to be kept trimmed? (would this present a problem?)
– is there somewhere to store garden tools?
– if outhouses or a greenhouse are included in the sale, what condition are they in?
– is there a standpipe or tap for watering? (may involve additional water charge)
– is it possible to reach the garden at the back of the house without having to go through the house? (also relevant for dustbin emptying)

Trees can be a hazard if they have grown too big or been planted too close to a building or walls (including the neighbour's). Roots spread underground, growing outwards generally in proportion to the canopy of the tree and can affect the foundations of a building and damage drains. Poplars, elms and willows are especially greedy (willows can signify a very damp environment or underground stream).

In some areas, trees in private gardens have tree preservation orders placed on them, prohibiting the owner from lopping or cutting them down without first getting permission from the local authority. Ask the owner if this applies to any tree on his property.

The boundaries of the property may be marked by walls, fences or hedges, for some of which the owner may be responsible. If the piers of a brick wall or the posts of a fence are on your side, it is more likely than not that the wall will be yours and your responsibility. In any case, it is sensible to inspect the state of any brick walls, wooden fencing or gates.

GARAGING THE CAR

– is there a garage?
– how far is it from the house?
– will your car fit in? (size of garage is not usually stated in estate agent's particulars; be sure to know the measurements of your own car, including its width with the door open and the height if a hatchback)
– are the garage doors easy to open, keep open, shut and lock?
– is there light and a power point inside?
– what is the approach to the garage made of? what sort of upkeep will be necessary?

Q

Make sure that you have evaluated the proposed house for all important aspects e.g. must it be south facing, are there any potential nuisances such as young children next door or large dogs or large trees obscuring light. In short, look at the outside and the location of the house as well as the inside. (Resale value of the house may also be affected by the area and within small bounds i.e. in some roads the value of the property rises much faster than the average).

– what is the access from the driveway/garage to the road like? (if the road is narrow, will a car parked on the opposite side stop you getting yours out?)

and if there is no garage:

– is there a car port (a roofed-over area at the side of the house) or where can your car be parked? in the garden, yard or on the road? (this affects the insurance premium)
– is there plenty of parking and turning space?
– are there parking restrictions outside? or a residents' parking scheme? (involving an annual charge)
– is there space and access to road for you to put up a garage? (needs planning permission)
– where can visitors park?

Viewing a flat

Flats are usually on one floor level but sometimes include some internal stairs to a half-landing level. Units on two or more floors are usually termed maisonettes.

Bear in mind the advantages and disadvantages to you of a ground floor or basement or upper floor flat, since you will probably be looking at a number of all three kinds.

GROUND FLOOR FLAT

ADVANTAGES	DISADVANTAGES
no stairs, no dependence on the lift; easy access with baby and pram, small child or pet, also for elderly, invalid or handicapped person; direct access to garden, road, car: easier and nearer for carrying in heavy shopping or child	you may prefer to sleep upstairs; not as good views and less light from windows than from higher floors; generally less secure; may be overlooking dustbins, parking space, garages; more noise – from traffic, neighbours en route to other flats, main door banging shut, people outside

UPPER OR TOP FLOOR FLAT

ADVANTAGES

often good view and light;
less problem of sound from traffic, neighbours or outside
noise; no overhead noise on top floor

DISADVANTAGES

stairs, may be no lift (a disadvantage when selling, even
if not for you);
lift may be slow or insufficient, subject to breakdowns;
any leak from roof or tank likely to affect top floor first;
poorly insulated roof could make heating more
expensive than in lower floor flat (or too hot in summer);
in high-rise flats, exposed to wind;
in case of fire, less easy escape than flats nearer the
ground

BASEMENT FLAT

ADVANTAGES

not many stairs or steps;
may have own front door direct to outside;
possibly cheaper to buy than flat on other floors;
may lead to garden or have own patio or area;
easier for small child, animals

DISADVANTAGES

any stairs may be steep;
may be dark if windows below street level;
view restricted to people's feet passing by;
can be liable to damp problems, leaks and overflows
from flats above; blocked drains or gulleys can cause
unpleasantness;
may be looked down into by passers-by;
security problems

There are specific points to consider when looking at a flat rather than a house
or bungalow.

accommodation and layout

In a house converted into flats, the designer may have been compelled to make
the best he could out of the existing layout, and some things may be less than
ideal.

Q

Next time would ask people upstairs to move around so that we can hear if there is noise (if possible).

It is important when viewing to imagine yourself living in the flat and to look out for potential inconveniences or drawbacks as well as the advantages:

– do rooms lead off each other, or all off a corridor or central area?
– does the kitchen lead off the hall, living room or dining room? are kitchen smells likely to pervade the living areas?
– how far is the kitchen from the front door of the flat? (imagine carrying rubbish or shopping through)
– is there space in the entrance hall for a pram, bicycle? if not, is there anywhere in the building for these?
– is there another door out of the flat: for example, on to a balcony or landing?
– is there a fire escape? where does it lead to?
– is there a balcony on which you could put plants, a baby's pram, a chair? does this get the sun?
– are there features of layout, staircases, balconies that would make the flat easy to burgle?
– what arrangement is there for disposal of rubbish (an important consideration for a flat-dweller): dustbins or rubbish chute? where are they located? is there a sink waste disposal unit? (if there is not, may not be allowed to install one)
– how is the bathroom/wc/kitchen ventilated? if there is no window, check on the method of ventilation (if by electric fan, it should start with the light being switched on and remain on for several minutes after the light is switched off)
– where are the bedrooms in relation to the living room? would there be a sound problem with small children sleeping next door to the room where grown-ups watch TV or entertain?
– are there sufficient storage facilities in the flat? are there any additional ones available in the block?
– is the front door of the building kept permanently locked? if so, is there an entryphone in the flat which operates it, or have callers to be received personally at the front entrance (perhaps two or three flights of stairs down)?

In some purpose-built blocks, the flats are on either side of a central corridor so that the windows in any one flat all face one direction. So, if you want a sunny living room, you have to have a kitchen which may get too hot. South-facing flats normally are higher priced – if one flat is cheaper than a similar one in the block, check which way each is facing.

Q

Keep eyes skinned when viewing – will your furniture get through the narrow corridors of a converted flat?

The higher the floor in the block, the less traffic noise there will be (and the more expensive the flat may be). A flat near the lift or rubbish chute may be noisy, both mechanically and because people congregate.

What the soundproofing is like beween adjacent flats and the ones above and below is one of the most important aspects of flat life, and is a difficult one to check when viewing. Make a point of listening for extraneous noises in each room with the windows shut, and if you can hear the TV or the barking of a dog in an adjacent flat, or plumbing noises, be warned.

Try to view the flat again at a different time of day and on a different day of the week.

GARDEN

If the block or building has its own garden, you will need to know whether it is a communal one. If so, is it big enough for everyone? Look to see if it is well-kept, ask who is responsible for its maintenance, and check about access to the garden.

Where a large house has been converted into a number of flats, it is quite common for either the ground floor or the basement flat to have sole rights to the use of the garden and responsibility for its upkeep and perhaps also for maintaining the garden walls or fencing.

GARAGE/PARKING

Most custom-built blocks have garages, sometimes underground, for use by tenants. Older blocks or houses converted to flats may have only forecourts or driveways, often quite inadequate for parking all the cars of residents (let alone their visitors). Some have no provision at all. Points to check:

– can you park conveniently near to the flat for unloading?
– has the flat its own lock-up garage? is there an extra charge?
– what are the rates payable on the garage?
– if parking is on the forecourt or in communal underground car park, is it a free-for-all or are there allocated spaces? any charge?
– is there somewhere for visitors to park?
– does the flat overlook garage/parking area? (likely disturbance by cars coming or going early or late)

HEATING AND OTHER SERVICES

If there is a communal heating and hot water system, have the flats any individual control over their heating? With a central system, a lot of the bother and worry is taken off your hands, but you have less control of temperature and timing and costs. And if it needs servicing or if it breaks down, it may take longer to repair than a smaller system.

Can mail, newspapers and milk be delivered to the flat door? Who cleans the communal parts of the building? maintains lighting, lifts?

Is there a porter? is he resident? available at night? what are his duties? A good porter can be a considerable advantage as far as security is concerned, also for looking after deliveries, organising parking, giving access to workmen such as window cleaner or plumber, doing or organising small maintenance jobs for tenants.

outgoings

There are various set-ups for maintenance and administration of the building.

For some aspects, it is either essential or convenient for the property to be managed as one unit, because it would be impossible or absurd for each owner to act independently. For example:

– insurance of the property for fire, flooding, subsidence, and other such risks
– the maintenance, repair and renewal of lifts, entrance hall, staircases
– the repair of the roof, foundations and the exterior of the building and redecoration
– the maintenance of gardens and forecourts
– porterage
– central heating and hot water (where these are provided communally).

These matters may be dealt with by the landlord of the whole building who divides the cost amongst the flat owners each year by way of a service charge and/or a maintenance charge.

MAINTENANCE AND SERVICE CHARGES

You should find out what the service or maintenance charges cover and what they are based on. Are they variable according to the flat or shared equally?

The type of structure (and the services provided) governs the amount of the maintenance or service charges. For instance, a two or three storey modern block, built of brick with a tiled roof, with aluminium windows, basic staircases and landings and set in a simple grassed area will have much lower charges than, say, a high rise block with lifts and a resident caretaker or an old conversion with painted stucco elevations, wooden sash windows, high parapets and inaccessible roofs and chimneys.

There are different ways in which tenants have to pay for the cost of repairs to the whole building. When you get a surveyor's report, it should cover not only the flat itself but, as far as can be done, the rest of the building. There may be defects – in the roof or foundations, for example – which do not directly affect the flat in question, but a share of the cost of repairs to these will almost certainly be the legal responsibility of every flat owner in the building (even if the cause had arisen during the previous owner's occupation).

Managing agents often display a small notice near the entrance of blocks of flats, giving their name, address and telephone number. Ask them when the next account is expected to be sent out. This could be a nasty shock if it arrives just after you have moved in. If asked, they will also be able to advise if they are contemplating any substantial expenditure in the near future.

Find out what the arrangement is for paying for communal redecoration when this falls due.

You will be expected to redecorate the flat internally every so many years and will be fully responsible for the repair of the inside. Like a house owner, the owner of a flat is also personally and directly responsible to the public authorities for the payment of rates and water charges; buildings divided into flats are almost invariably assessed as separate units for rating purposes.

Unlike a freehold property, there is an annual ground rent to pay for a leasehold. This is generally a fixed sum, and usually quite modest. Some ground rents rise at intervals of, say, 20 years or 33 years. But watch out for any terms in a lease which provide for the figure to be 'reviewed'.

Q

If buying leasehold and vendor says that he does not know of any outstanding bills or work to be carried out, get it in writing.

The landlord may be a property company which delegates the administration of the building to a firm of managing agents (whose fee, a percentage of the annual charge, is included in the charge paid by the leaseholders). The alternative may be a cooperative organisation to which all flat owners belong, running the building on more or less democratic lines. Be sure to ask the seller or his estate agent what the set-up is, both formally as specified in the lease and in practice.

the lease

Most flats and maisonettes in England and Wales are leasehold. This means that the landlord (the lessor) grants a tenancy for a relatively long period (99 years or even 999 years) to the tenant (the lessee). To buy the lease involves paying a price (called a premium) to the vendor, who may be the developer or the previous lessee. If you buy from the developer, you will get the full term of the lease (for example, 99 years) but if you buy from the previous lessee, you will get only the part of the lease remaining. The previous lessee has no power to grant you a new lease.

Whereas the purchase price for a flat or maisonette is just as negotiable as for a freehold house, the provisions of the lease are not so. They are drawn up to ensure that each flat owner complies with the necessary obligations for maintaining the standard and condition of the building.

The length of the term of a lease is important as it can affect the value of the property. Where the term exceeds 75 years, the variations in value are minimal, but below 75 years the value can progressively and increasingly fall as the term diminishes. Building societies usually require 30 years left on a lease after repayment of the mortgage, so if you are looking for a 25-year mortgage term, the lease of the property at the outset must have at least 55 unexpired years. It follows that properties with only 30 years left on the lease would not be considered suitable security for mortgage purposes. It may be less difficult to get a mortgage loan from a bank or insurance company for a flat with a relatively short lease.

A guide for flat buyers *Buying a flat? don't buy a lifetime of problems as well*, produced by the Law Society and the Royal Institution of Chartered Surveyors (available from them and/or from their members), includes a check list of questions to ask your solicitor and surveyor when considering purchasing a flat.

Before making an offer

If you like what you have seen, look to some formal aspects before you make an offer.

Find out approximately when the seller is able and willing to move out. He may be waiting to sell before he starts to look for a house or may be waiting for a mortgage or be part of a lengthy chain. If timing is important to you, this will affect your decision about the house.

The legal and financial set-up will have to be gone into in great detail when it comes to the stage of conveyancing. At this preliminary stage, however, there are some relevant points to check.

FREEHOLD OR LEASEHOLD

If it is a leasehold property, you should ask about any annual or other financial commitments such as

– ground rent payable (how much? fixed or subject to review?)
– maintenance charges for repairs or redecoration (is any payment imminent? has the seller been informed of any future expenditure, and what payments have been made over the last three years or so?)

If it is freehold, there may nevertheless be annual charges for maintenance – for example, roads on a private estate.

COVENANTS AND RIGHTS

Are there any restrictions on the use of the house – for example, on putting up a brass plate or even on hanging out the washing? Restrictive covenants are obligations imposed by covenant on the owner of a property, preventing him from doing certain things on the property, such as running a business or putting buildings on parts of it. (You may in any case need planning permission if you want to carry on a professional business from your home address.)

Do other people have rights such as to walk across part of the property? This should come to light when your solicitor receives the draft contract or details of the lease at a later stage. But if there are any indications of this sort of thing, tell your solicitor so that he can make more enquiries.

PLANNING PERMISSION

Has planning permission for any alterations to the property ever been applied for? If granted, what work was carried out and by how much did this increase the size of the house? (this could affect your need for planning permission for any future alterations). If permission was refused, why? Has an enforcement notice been issued?

If you think you would like to make alterations – for example, add a large extension or put in new windows – try to discover before you get too involved what the local planning authority's attitude is to such alterations.

Also you can find out by going to the local authority planning department whether there are any plans (or projects) for local buildings, new roads, motorways or industrial development. Every local authority keeps a register of planning applications and the register is open to inspection (as is the register of enforcement proceedings).

RATEABLE VALUE

The rateable value, or perhaps the rates payable, may have been quoted in any particulars you have been provided with by agent or seller. If not, ask for this information. If only the rateable value has been given, you can find out from the finance department of the local authority what the rates per £ are for the area. Water and sewerage charges are levied separately by the local water authority in England and Wales, based on the rateable value of a property.

VACANT POSSESSION AND SITTING TENANTS

Normally, a house is sold with vacant possession: when it becomes yours, the seller leaves and it will be empty ready for you to occupy. But if there are already 'sitting' tenants in the house – that is, the owner has let part of it to other people – you may assume that you cannot get immediate possession of those parts of the property. (Some sitting tenants even have the right to transmit the tenancy to the widow[er] or another generation.) You would also probably have considerable difficulty in raising their rent above its present level, should you want to. The subject of sitting tenants is complex and you should get legal advice before you take any steps towards acquiring such a house.

What does the price include?

The estate agent's particulars may mention specific items which the owner would like to sell with the house or flat. When the agent or owner is showing the house, he or she may point out in each room any items being included in the sale, or being offered separately. These would be additional to what are usually termed 'fixtures and fittings', which are accepted as being part of the house.

fixtures and fittings

An area of the buyer and seller relationship liable to cause friction is the question of what are regarded as fixtures and fittings. It is vital from the point of view of any buyer – and equally any seller – to establish clearly which items are, and which are not, included in the sale.

The basic concept is that anything that is part of the fabric of the house is included. Over the years, various removable items, known in law as 'chattels' ('moveables' in Scotland), get fixed to the house and lose their original nature of chattels by becoming part of the structure. One test is the extent to which the items are actually attached and cannot be removed without causing irremediable damage; the other is to consider what might have been the intention of the owner in installing them. But the distinction between a removable and a not-removable item remains difficult to establish.

For example, a case was brought to court which concerned some garden seats and sculptured statues which were free-standing on their own weight and not fixed to the ground. These were judged to be essentially part of the architectural design of the garden and so were not removable. In another court case, valuable tapestries had been firmly fixed to the walls of a house in such a way that they could not be removed without causing substantial damage. These were, nevertheless, held to be removable because the aim in attaching them was to enjoy them as tapestries and not that they should form part of the house. So it is not easy for seller or buyer to know exactly what the law would say in a case of dispute.

Many sellers and buyers are ignorant about what they can take or can expect to have bought, so you should be particularly careful on this point. It may not always be practical or desirable to go through all the items on a first viewing, but at a point before you negotiate a price, you should establish exactly what you are buying and be sure that the seller – as well as yourself – has this clear. Bathroom fittings, light fittings, curtain rails and tracks and TV aerials are commonly disputed items. What has to be done in each case is to clarify what are

items not removable	because they form part of the structure	included in price
uncertain items	which buyer and seller may regard differently	whether to be included in price should be agreed at the time of making an offer
items removable	since they do not form part of the structure	price to be agreed if sold to buyer

Q

A gas fire in the property when I viewed had been replaced by an older one when I moved in; likewise with a light fitting.

EXAMPLES OF ITEMS NOT REMOVABLE

plumbing and heating installations integrated into the structure
gas or electric instantaneous water heater
electric sockets, wall switches and wiring (including lamp socket holders but not light bulbs)
garden sheds and greenhouses built on foundations and not free-standing
trees and shrubs in the garden

EXAMPLES OF ITEMS REMOVABLE BY THE SELLER

free-standing gas or electric cooker
refrigerator, freezer
dishwasher, washing machine and any similar detachable equipment
heaters connected to mains supply only by plugs or detachable means of connection
electrical fittings beyond the point of contact with mains supply
lamp shades, light bulbs
carpets, underlay and felt, curtains
free-standing garden furniture and sheds

UNCERTAIN ITEMS

Curtain rails and tracks including brass and wood rods and pelmets
fitted bookshelves and other shelves
built-in kitchen units/appliances
built-in cupboards and wardrobes/bedroom furniture
} *the test being the extent to which they are fixed to the structure*
electric storage heaters, water softener, wall lights
decorative door furniture and door chimes
bathroom fittings, lavatory paper holders
roof TV aerial
plants in garden
free-standing garden ornaments (depends on their purpose).

When you reach the point where you have decided to go ahead with an offer, ask the owner to go through the house or flat with you, agreeing and listing room by room

○ any fixtures and fittings, whether referred to in any particulars or separately agreed between you, which are included in the sale price
○ any items he is willing to leave but for which you would have to make a separate offer.

It could be helpful to make a list such as the one on page 103 to go through with the seller.

You should in due course draw up an itemised list together with the seller, with copies for your solicitors, so that there will be no confusion later. (You should check when the time comes that the actual item(s) get left for you and not inferior substitutes.)

You should assume that anything not on the list of items the seller is to leave behind will be moved by him – indeed, he must do so in order to give you vacant possession.

what you buy

There is no reason why you should not vary any of the 'rules' as to what is or is not removable, provided it is agreed and written into the contract.

Whatever you intend to buy from the seller, inspect it very carefully to make sure that it works or is in good condition (any carpets, for instance, where rugs

Q

Garden – advertised as 'well stocked' but everything had been removed!

may have been covering up worn areas, any garden tools or lawn mower which may not have been well maintained) and is not going to cause you additional expense.

The prices for any separate items have to be agreed on the basis of their original cost, the wear and tear the items have had and their condition now, and what a replacement would cost at today's prices. The actual figures are generally wide open to negotiation. But whatever is agreed should be confirmed in writing (tell your solicitor, too).

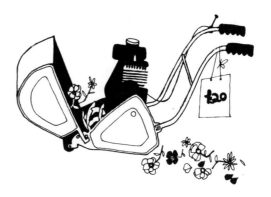

The owner may try to get you to buy some items which you do not want. If they duplicate what you already have, you are in a better position politely to refuse them. If you do not want them for some other reason – they are not to your taste, perhaps – you will have to judge whether buying them from him or not would affect your chances of concluding the whole deal.

The seller will probably be pleased if you agree to buy from him any residual coal or heating oil; the value of these will have to be worked out later, but the principle can be agreed now.

LIST OF ITEMS INCLUDED AND EXCLUDED

Tick either "INCLUDED" *or* "EXCLUDED" *where applicable*

INCLUDED   EXCLUDED

WINDOWS
curtain rails and rings
curtain tracks and fittings
pelmets
blinds

ELECTRICAL
immersion heater
switches, points
wall and ceiling fittings
night storage heaters
fitted electric fire
TV aerial

BATHROOM
bathroom cabinet
bathroom heater
towel rail
toilet roll holder
heated towel rail
mirror

KITCHEN
kitchen cupboards
wall utensils

GARDEN
greenhouse
garden shed
garden trees, shrubs, plants
flowers and garden produce
garden ornaments
garden furniture

GENERAL
fitted carpets
fitted mirrors
door bell
door chimes
heating oil
solid fuel
fitted gas fire
fitted shelves

ANY OTHERS (*list them below*)

Making an offer

When you decide that you want to buy a particular house or flat, you should make an offer for it without delay. If the seller was offering the property through an estate agent, put the offer to the agent (he can then tell other potential buyers that the property is under offer). Do this even before you have had a survey done – the offer does not commit you provided it is made 'subject to contract and to survey'.

You must make it clear that your offer is subject to contract – whether it is an oral offer or in writing – so that you are covered if

○ you are unable to raise the necessary mortgage or loan
○ a survey decides you against continuing with the purchase
○ subsequent enquiries disclose some insuperable drawback: for example, road widening or compulsory purchase by the local authority
○ you change your mind for some other reason.

If there is any objection to the deal being on a subject-to-contract basis, do not proceed. And do not sign any kind of contract at this stage without taking legal advice.

the price

Most sellers fix a price which they believe to be the maximum they dare ask, and most will be prepared to come down unless several would-be buyers are competing.

To decide whether you are willing to pay the asking price or to make an alternative offer, you must take into consideration:

○ how much you can afford to pay
○ the state of the property market (the more potential buyers there may be after the house, the less scope there will be for bargaining)
○ how the price compares with that of similar properties in the area
○ how much you want the house and are prepared to pay over the odds to get it.

Having made your offer, you may have to sit back and wait: the seller may have other prospective buyers about to make offers, or he may still want to show the house to other viewers. You can try to persuade him by the figure you propose not to continue with other possibilities but provisionally to accept your offer.

Q

Buying and selling is not for the faint-hearted or for people who can't afford to be let down.

A strong bargaining factor is whether you can act quickly because

○ you have a mortgage certificate guaranteeing the offer of a loan
○ the sale of your own house is practically completed
○ you have ready money.

If the sale of your own house is likely to be delayed, it may be worth getting the promise of a bridging loan from your bank (or other source) to put you in an advantageous negotiating position. Also, being willing to buy all the extras the seller wants to leave behind – fittings, furniture, equipment – may improve your chances.

STAMP DUTY

Whether the buyer has to pay stamp duty on the transfer of a property depends on the price of the house he is buying. The duty is one per cent on the whole price when this is over £30,000; at or below £30,000 no stamp duty is payable.

If the price, including fittings such as carpets and curtains, that you are asked to pay is just above £30,000, ask the seller to separate the price of the house and that of the fittings if deducting their value reduces the house price below the stamp duty threshold.

PRELIMINARY DEPOSIT

At the point when you make a firm offer, an estate agent will ask you the name and address of your solicitor or conveyancer (if you are using one) and may ask you to pay a small deposit (say £100 or £250) as a token of your intent. Such an initial deposit has no legal standing and cannot, by itself, bind either party to the transaction. If you do pay such a deposit, you should get a receipt stating that the deposit was paid 'subject to contract and to survey'. You will not at this stage have had the house surveyed. If a survey should reveal any defects requiring attention but not serious enough to deter you or your source of finance, you may want to reduce your offer.

If, for any reason, the sale should fall through before contracts are exchanged, a sum paid by way of initial deposit has to be returned in full. Estate agents are required to have a separate 'clients' account' with the bank, into which clients' monies are paid.

Q

It is highly unlikely that an agent will insist that you pay a deposit if you are unwilling to do so. The deposit benefits the agent far more than it does you or the seller!

Valuation for mortgage

A buyer who is applying for a mortgage should notify the building society or other mortgagee that he has made an offer for a property, and ask that the lender's valuation should be carried out as soon as possible. You will have to pay the required fee for the valuation which is based on the price of the house. (If you lose the house before the valuer has been to it, tell the lender to cancel the visit and to return the fee or keep it ready for your next attempt.)

The valuation is carried out on behalf of the lender to assess whether the condition and value of the house is adequate security for the loan the lender has been asked to make.

A RICS/ISVA leaflet on mortgage valuations explains that the valuer takes into account:

○ age, type, accommodation, fixtures and features of the property
○ construction and general state of repair
○ siting and the amenities of the locality
○ tenure, tenancies, if any, annual payments or other liabilities
○ planning potential will normally be disregarded.

Valuation for mortgage purposes is the amount at which a qualified valuer believes the property would sell in the open market at the date of the inspection. It is not a structural survey, and in no way guarantees that the house is structurally sound and without defects, nor that it is worth the purchase price being asked. If, in the building society's valuer's opinion, the house is worth less than the purchase price, the proportion that will be lent may be calculated on his figure – and the amount of loan offered to you may therefore seem a strange percentage of the purchase price.

low valuation

The offer of a loan may be withdrawn after the valuation survey. You would then have to start again, with a different property – or a different lender. But most mortgage applications ask if you have already applied for a mortgage on the same property, so it is unlikely that you will get an unconditional mortgage from another building society for that house.

Q

We were able to fight successfully the inaccuracies in building society valuation by having our own house buyer's report from an independent source . . . in our case, the extra cost incurred was only £10.

The valuer can include a recommendation to the lender not to make a loan unless specified work is carried out, such as putting in a damp proof course or treating all timbers against rot. He may advise the lender to withhold an amount (say, £5,000 retention money or even £10,000) which will be paid out only when the work has been carried out satisfactorily. This can be a problem if you do not have spare cash available – the seller will want all his price on the nail. This is where a bridging loan may be needed.

If the lender does lay down such conditions and substantial expenditure is involved, it may be worth getting a second opinion from another surveyor, or there may be an opportunity to re-negotiate the price with the seller. If an agreement cannot be reached, it might be better to pull out of the transaction.

Your own survey

Although most building societies let the borrower see a copy of their valuation report, this should not be regarded as a substitute for your own structural survey.

Most building societies allow or even encourage an arrangement whereby the surveyor who does their valuation carries out a survey for the buyer at the same visit. The fee for your survey would be slightly less than it would otherwise be, in view of the fact that he is already going to visit the property for the building society.

There are standard forms of 'house buyers' valuation and survey report used by surveyors who are members of the Royal Institution of Chartered Surveyors (RICS) or of the Incorporated Society of Valuers and Auctioneers (ISVA). If you want to have your own survey done earlier (so as to avoid delay if there are many other potential buyers) and the RICS/ISVA report is acceptable to the lender, no further valuation report is needed (nor further fee payable).

The standard house buyer's report completed by a building society surveyor when doing the mortgage valuation is not a structural survey. But it provides comments on the condition of parts of the property that are readily accessible or visible and gives an opinion of the market value. There are extensive exclusion clauses in these reports and you are not getting a full investigation and report on possible defects. It may include recommendations for further tests or

Q

Do have at least a house buyers report: it will save you more than it cost to have if there is something wrong with the property and possibily stop you buying a house which has major faults which are not obvious to the untrained eye.

Q

The survey on the house we bought specified problems with rising damp but did not specify penetrating damp upstairs. We queried this afterwards and the surveyor agreed to pay us the £472 we estimated repairs would cost (but he denied liability).

Q

Essential to get proper survey if house elderly: I was mercifully put off what I thought a beautiful old cottage after a full survey revealed dry and wet rot etc etc; renovation would have been astronomic.

investigations that seem to be called for. The fee is about halfway between that for a straight mortgage valuation and that for a full survey.

A house buyer's report is unsuitable for many older properties and buildings of unusual construction – pre-1900 buildings, buildings over 200 square metres floor area and buildings over three storeys in height.

structural survey

A structural survey should be carried out by a qualified person who specialises in this kind of work, such as a building surveyor or architect. A qualified surveyor may be a member of the Royal Institution of Chartered Surveyors (with the letters FRICS or ARICS after his name) or of the Incorporated Association of Architects and Surveyors (FIAS or MIAS after his name) or of the Faculty of Architects and Surveyors (FFS or AFS after his name). These professional associations are responsible for maintaining standards within the profession. They can be asked for the names of any of their members in a given area who are qualified building surveyors.

Your solicitor may be able to advise on the choice of an appropriate surveyor if you are buying locally, or a friend may recommend one he has used. It is preferable to engage a surveyor local to the property being inspected since he may know of any relevant conditions in the area which might affect it. The estate agent/surveyor acting for the seller is not allowed to carry out a survey on the house (because of a conflict of interests) but may recommend a surveyor.

Ask the surveyor how soon he can do the survey and discuss with him how comprehensive a survey to carry out. You should obtain written confirmation from the surveyor setting out the extent of his inspection: this may avoid misunderstandings at a later date. The extent of the survey will depend on the age and condition of the property – and on how much you can afford. It is not only for old property that it is desirable to have a survey done: a recently-built house can have serious defects too, through bad design, bad workmanship or neglect.

The extent of a full structural survey is described in *Structural Surveys of Residential Property*, a guidance note prepared by the Building Surveyors Division of RICS. If you want a full structural survey, refer to this booklet.

Q

We recommend obtaining an independent structural survey – the cost of this is easily outweighed by the potential savings that can be made by revising your offer in the light of its findings.

Q

... be prepared for considerable expense if transactions fall through; be patient and calm – worry doesn't make things happen sooner.

Q

Only renovate if you're rich or can do structural work yourself, or if you don't mind living in turmoil!

THE COST

Fees are usually by negotiation and related to the time taken to inspect the property and write up the report. Generally speaking, the larger the property and the worse the condition of the building, the longer the professional survey will take.

The written report accounts for a large part of the cost, so if you are content to have oral comments, or a less detailed survey taking note only of any major structural defects, you would pay less. However, beware of relying on oral comments only. If defects show up later, you may have difficulty in establishing just what the surveyor actually said.

Be prepared to have to pay for a survey more than once during your house-hunting, not only because a survey may show that a property is not worth buying but because a deal may fall through for reasons beyond your control (gazumping, mortgage delay, seller withdrawing) – so that you have to start all over again.

THE REPORT

Give the surveyor as much relevant information about the property as you can, particularly details of any doubtful points you noticed when you viewed it (such as damp patches, odd smells, cracks, obviously-recent repairs, state of party walls) and on the siting of the house regarding potential flooding or subsidence.

If you plan to make any alterations or improvements, inform him before he does the survey in case there are any snags which he might spot. If, for example, you plan to demolish an inside wall to enlarge a room, this may turn out to be a load-bearing wall which it would be inadvisable, or very costly, to remove. And if you are planning complete redecoration, or a rewire or replumb, tell the surveyor. You will save his time and your money.

what a survey includes

You are likely to get a general description of the construction and materials used, and comments on the condition of

roof – timberwork, cladding, tiles, slates, chimney stacks, flashing, rainwater gutters, insulation

Q

If a qualified surveyor detects damp, his report should state the source or likely cause. Some degree of surface damp is likely in some localities (kitchen, bathroom) and does not necessarily indicate a need to initiate specialist inspection and treatment. True 'rising damp', however, would be a more serious matter.

walls – plasterwork, brickwork, pointing, insulation, decoration, any cracks, damp, bulges

foundations – soundness, damp proof course and external soil level, any subsidence, settlement

windows – state of frames

floors and joinery – soundness of timber, ventilation, any evidence of wet rot, dry rot, woodworm

plumbing – bathroom and wc, fittings, waste pipes, tanks and cylinders

drains – soil and rainwater

electrical installation – age of wiring

chimneys and flues

garden – state of paths, fences, outbuildings.

The report which the surveyor gives you should summarise the condition of these items in as much detail as you have agreed, together with any faults and their importance.

If the house is furnished at the time, it may not be practicable to make a very detailed inspection – which would involve lifting carpets and floor boards, for example. Much depends on how thorough an inspection the vendor permits.

The survey of the electrical installation may be confined to a 'visual examination'. Much of the wiring is hidden behind skirting boards and under floor boards, and it is possible that the surveyor will draw his conclusions only from what he can see. He will say so in his report, but you should be aware of the limitation.

Do not hesitate to discuss the report with the surveyor. He will be able to put the defects into perspective. Ask him to explain any technical terms that you do not understand.

You should ask the surveyor to tell you the approximate cost of putting right any faults he has found. Ask the surveyor to give you an estimate of how much you would need to spend to put the house into good structural order and try offering the seller a price reduced by that amount. Tell him why, and be prepared to negotiate. If the seller will not budge, you have to decide how badly you want the house. Your offer being subject to contract and subject to survey, if you decide that you do not want to buy the house, you are not obliged to go ahead: simply tell the estate agent or the seller direct that you are no longer interested.

specialist tests

There is a distinction between 'an inspection' and 'a test' of such services as the drains, the heating system, the wiring, timber. In particular, you should discuss with the surveyor whether any central heating system should be inspected or tested.

Where a house is old or appears to be in poor state of repair, the surveyor may recommend specialist tests. He will offer to call in specialists (and you have to pay for them). The fact that he recommends tests may be sufficient reason for you to incur this extra expense – he will usually have diagnosed a potential problem.

GUARANTEED TREATMENT

If your surveyor's report shows that specialist treatment is recommended (and you are still likely to buy the house), you can get free estimates of the cost from specialist firms. Lists of their members are available from the **British Wood Preserving Association** (6 The Office Village, 4 Romford Road, London E15 4EA) and the **British Chemical Dampcourse Association** (16a Whitchurch Road, Pangbourne, Berks RG8 7BP). It is worth getting more than one such estimate. You may want to offer less for the house to allow for the cost of treatment and other work needed.

If the firm is a member of the **Guarantee Protection Trust**, you can register the guarantee with the Trust (POB 77, 27 London Road, High Wycombe, Bucks HP11 1BW) so that if the specialist treatment turns out not to have been successful and the firm who carried it out has gone out of business and cannot honour its guarantee, the Trust undertakes to have guaranteed remedial work done again. The registration fee for £10,000 cover is £10 each for woodworm and for chemical dampcourse treatments, giving 20 years' cover.

Q

I even spent one hour under the floor with a young lady from the timber treatment specialist looking for dry rot which the structural surveyor was supposed to have seen!

NHBC

If the house is less than 10 years old, check whether it is covered by a National House-Building Council Buildmark scheme. (This in itself is no reason for not having a survey.) Find out how many years there are left on the NHBC scheme. The balance is transferred to a new owner, but only for defects which appear after he has bought the house. Defects which are (or could have been) apparent before he buys will not be remedied by the NHBC unless the previous owner has already claimed. If your surveyor notices anything that may come under the NHBC scheme, it is the seller who must make the claim.

EXISTING GUARANTEES

Advice about guarantees for home improvement work and treatments was given in **Which?** in February and May 1988.

The previous owner may have employed specialist firms to carry out remedial work for which a guarantee has been given – for instance, treatment for woodworm, for dry or wet rot or rising damp, or the use of special protective coatings for roofs or external walls. Such a guarantee can normally be transferred from one owner to the next. You should get the relevant document eventually – but ask if the surveyor can see it before he does his inspection. Make sure you get hold not only of the guarantee but also of the original report and estimate on which the guarantee is based. This will detail what work was (or should have been) done and any qualifications to the guarantee.

Guarantees for damp treatment are often conditional on other works being carried out (such as replastering in a special way or lowering the ground levels outside). These tasks are not usually carried out by the treatment company. If any problem arises, it is easy for the treatment company to put the blame on someone else.

Survey for a flat

A survey for a flat or maisonette, particularly if it is in a converted house, should cover not only the flat itself but an inspection of the whole building. This should include the roof, foundations, drains, gutters and so on; also any communal services such as electricity, water or gas supplies to the extent that you could be liable under the terms of the lease.

Tell your surveyor whatever you have found out about the repairing liabilities, maintenance and service charges, and give him a copy of the lease if this has already been made available to you or your solicitor. He can then relate his comments to your responsibilities for repairing and decorating the flat, and for contributing towards the cost of maintaining communal parts of the building.

A surveyor who is a member of the Royal Institution of Chartered Surveyors or of the Incorporated Society of Valuers and Auctioneers may offer a standard flat buyers' report and valuation. This will indicate the condition of the flat and of shared access areas and services such as central heating, and also advise on management arrangements. It is, however, not a full investigation and there are exclusion clauses in such a report.

step 1	see house you like go home and think/talk it over
step 2	go to view it again (preferably at different time of day and day of week)

if still OK:

step 3	make an offer at a price you can afford (or a little less if you dare) via estate agent or direct to seller. Decide who is to do the conveyancing; ask what solicitor's or conveyancer's fees will be; tell chosen solicitor/conveyancer of your offer and give him seller's name and address and his solicitor's

if offer accepted:

step 4	contact building society (or other mortgagee), complete application for mortgage; ask when valuation can be done (and name of surveyor if you want him to do report for you at the same time)
step 5	confirm offer in writing 'subject to contract and to survey' to seller direct or estate agent; copy to own solicitor or conveyancer
step 6	return mortgage application form with fee for valuation
step 7	let your solicitor or conveyancer have relevant details of any potential problems; find out when seller can move out; warn bank manager (if bridging loan likely to be needed)
step 8	get on with selling of own house (where appropriate)
step 9	if own survey required, contact surveyor, discuss extent of survey, draw attention to any aspects of the building you are uneasy about and/or want him to check particularly; decide how detailed a report you require (written/oral; specialist tests); confirm instructions in writing; ask what his fee/expenses will be
step 10	await the outcome.

What happens at this point of the transaction depends on the house, the buyer and seller concerned, and the state of the market. The best would be that your offer gets accepted straightaway. The house is then 'under offer' and the seller should be asked to agree not to entertain any other buyers.

Ask the owner (or the agent you are dealing with, if he knows) whether the house is on the books of another estate agent as well as the one who has told you about it. If so, you may be pipped at the post from another quarter without you or the other agent being aware of the likelihood.

Newspaper advertisements cannot be cancelled immediately; also people who have viewed before you may make an offer subsequent to yours. So, expect some bargaining to go on after your first offer.

If you are told, or you sense, that your figure is being matched or surpassed by another, you must decide fairly swiftly whether to withdraw or to increase your offer, and by how much.

During the period between making an offer and exchanging contracts, neither buyer nor seller has entered into a legally binding contract. So long as the buyer's offer is still subject to contract, the estate agent handling the sale is under a duty to pass on to his client, the seller, all other offers made – right up to the day when a contract is exchanged. So it is possible for a new buyer, or a previously unsuccessful under-bidder, to enter the field offering an acceptable price which the agent has to notify to the seller.

CONTRACT RACE

If two or more people want to buy the same property, the seller will sometimes tell his solicitor or conveyancer to send out a second (or even a third and fourth) set of contracts to the would-be buyers' solicitors. The buyers then have to race each other, and the first to send a deposit and signed contract gets the house. Solicitors/conveyancers are required to tell the legal representatives of all the known would-be buyers when there is a contract race.

GAZUMPING

The unattractive practice of 'gazumping', as it has come to be called, is where a seller, tempted by a higher offer, goes back on his agreement with his potential

Q

Beware of vendors who are listed with a large number of estate agents, some of whom apparently do not recognise the 'under offer' notice of a rival firm or indeed the 'subject to contract'.

buyer and accepts a later, higher bid. This practice has tended to occur during a rising market with more buyers about than houses. As the law and practice of house purchase now stand, a buyer is not protected against gazumping until he has entered into a binding contract. You have to weigh up whether the consequences of binding yourself to a contract prematurely before you have made all proper enquiries will be more serious than the chances of being gazumped.

PRE-CONTRACT DEPOSIT AGREEMENT

The Conveyancing Standing Committee set up by the Law Commission has recommended a pre-contract deposit agreement which is designed to help deal with the problem of gazumping. The principle is that each side pays a preliminary deposit of $\frac{1}{2}$% of the purchase price to a stakeholder and signs an agreement that there will be a final exchange of contracts within 4 weeks. If one side withdraws without good enough reason (the form of agreement specifies the precise grounds), both deposits are released to the other. So a gazumped buyer will at least have some compensation for the expense he has incurred.

The Conveyancing Standing Committee's recommended form of pre-contract deposit agreement, with an explanatory leaflet and guidance notes which should be read before signing, is available free from **The Law Commission**, Conquest House, 37-38 John Street, Theobalds Road, London WC1N 2BQ.

The shortcoming of the scheme is that if the seller receives a substantially increased offer, it will still be worth his while to lose the deposit. Nevertheless, the agreement may be some inducement to seller and buyer to keep their word.

ANOTHER OPTION

There is a workable way of avoiding gazumping put into practice by some solicitors. The seller gives the buyer the exclusive right to buy the house in return for a fee and on condition that contracts are exchanged within a specified time.

If you are buying through one of the Abbey National's Cornerstone agencies, you get insurance to cover the risk of being gazumped: if the seller permanently withdraws from the transaction, you can claim up to £100 in wasted legal fees and up to £250 of survey and valuation fees.

It works like this:

> Mary wants to buy Rose Cottage from Peter. Peter is ready to sell but Mary cannot exchange contracts yet as she is waiting for her mortgage offer and she has not exchanged contracts on her own sale. She is sure that all these things will be dealt with in the next few weeks. How does she make sure that Peter sells to her and no one else and that he does not put the price up in the meantime?
>
> The solution is for Peter to agree with Mary that she can buy Rose Cottage at the agreed price so long as she exchanges contracts within x weeks. Peter must be compensated for freezing the price and taking the chance that Mary will at the last minute not go ahead with the deal. He will therefore charge quite a large sum for committing himself to the sale before Mary does – say, £1,000. Mary will lose that money if she does not exchange contracts but not if she goes ahead. Peter should agree to reduce the purchase price by the amount of the option price (the £1,000).

But note: such an agreement should not be attempted without a solicitor (the buyer has to be protected by the agreement being registered in the Land Registry or Land Charges Department).

all is not lost

After perhaps a series of negotiations, which can be nerve-racking for a would-be buyer who at this stage wants very much to succeed with a purchase, you may be disappointed and have to start all over again elsewhere.

But after a seller has accepted a bid and the losers have been informed, it is not uncommon that some weeks later the prospective buyer has to withdraw from the transaction for one reason or another. At this point, a disappointed under-bidder may find himself being contacted by the seller or his agent to ask if he is still interested and willing to re-start negotiations.

If you are bitterly disappointed at being outbid for a particular house (you had already mentally moved in), it is worth letting the owner or his agent know this so that should anything go wrong with his buyer, he will remember how keen you were. And do not just leave it to the agent – if the board stays up a while without 'Sold' being stuck over it, a reminding enquiry might, literally, ring the bell at the right moment. Both agent and seller will now want to settle the matter without further delay and you will be in a good position to succeed at a second attempt.

Q

If the chain seizes up, at least keep in contact with everyone. I rang the estate agent I was buying from immediately any hitch arose (they frequently did – I must have rung him 10 times) so he began to trust me. He then encouraged my seller that I was bona fide and would eventually buy his house – he [seller] was trying to put the house on the market again for weeks and weeks but the estate agent said 'Don't'.

A report on mortgages was published
in **Which?** April 1988.

Conveyancing

The legal and administrative work which is involved in transferring the ownership of a property from one party to another is known as conveyancing. The aim is to ensure that you acquire good title to the property and that there are no factors which would restrict your use or enjoyment of the property.

Even with an ordinary house on an established estate, there are plenty of traps and pitfalls for the unwary. These can range from undisclosed mortgages, the seller's bankruptcy, Granny refusing to move on completion day, to difficulties over rights of drainage, disputes over fences or ancient common rights. The conveyancing process is designed to unearth and resolve such problems, along with any others that come to light.

As soon as you start seriously hunting for a new home, you should decide who you want to do the conveyancing work for you. The choice you have in England and Wales is to

– appoint a solicitor
– appoint a licensed conveyancer
– do it yourself.

A big advantage of d-i-y conveyancing is that you can save on solicitor's or conveyancer's fees (and VAT). Also, you are largely in control of events. It does away with the frustration of chasing up your solicitor to get him to chase up the seller's solicitor. You can dictate the pace and possibly eliminate delays. You will need a book which describes the procedure step by step and explains how to prepare and complete the necessary documents.

You should hesitate to do it yourself where the property you are buying is

– not registered
– not in England or Wales
– not a house
– not wholly occupied by the seller
– being sold to you as new by a builder or developer.

If you are getting a mortgage, the saving may not be great: you will still have to pay the lender's solicitor's charge.

Usually, if you use a solicitor, he will do the building society work as well and charge an all-in fee. If you do your own conveyancing, you will be charged more for the building society's solicitor's work.

conveyancers

For many years there have been a number of individuals and non-solicitor firms doing only conveyancing work. It is now unlawful for unqualified conveyancers (those who are not solicitors or licensed conveyancers) to draft conveyancing documents or contracts for a fee.

A Council for Licensed Conveyancers has been established under the Administration of Justice Act 1985 for the licensing and supervision of non-solicitor conveyancers. The Council has prescribed the examination and training requirements, and in May 1987, England and Wales saw the first licensed conveyancers. The Council regulates the conduct of licence holders and has disciplinary machinery to deal with complaints against licensed conveyancers. It has set up a master policy to provide indemnity insurance and has established a compensation fund.

The **Council for Licensed Conveyancers** (Golden Cross House, Duncannon Street, London WC2N 4JF; telephone 01-210 4602) can give the name and address of any local licensed conveyancers in an area and, for a fee, can provide a list of all licensed conveyancers in England and Wales.

The **Society of Licensed Conveyancers** has been formed as the official body for licensed conveyancers, whether practising on their own or employed. The name and addresses of members can be obtained from the secretary of the Society at 32 Craignish Avenue, Norbury, London SW16 4RN, telephone 01-679 1619.

Q

Some of the newer lenders in the marketplace use only a very limited panel of solicitors. You may in such a case have to pay not only your own solicitor's or licensed conveyancer's fees but the fees charged by the solicitor acting for the bank etc providing the finance.

Q

When dealing with a licensed conveyancer, you should never be given the excuse that he is in court and cannot speak to you (if he is, you should ask why!)

using a solicitor or licensed conveyancer

The choice between a solicitor and licensed conveyancer may be very much a matter of personal preference. Both should be able to provide a full house-buying service and carry out the basic legal work for you. The best ones will also give you guidance and support and act as a forceful intermediary if things go wrong. Licensed conveyancers are expected to be cheaper than solicitors but that remains to be seen. They are required to operate the same safeguards to protect the public as solicitors, and there may be little to choose on price, particularly as solicitors' charges have come down considerably over the past few years.

Licensed conveyancers will be able to offer a highly specialised service while solicitors, particularly in small firms, tend to have a more varied workload. The best indication of choice will come from someone who has used a particular licensed conveyancer or solicitor and still thinks he or she is wonderful when it is all over.

If you have used a firm of solicitors for any legal business in the past, you could start by asking to be put in touch with a member of the firm who is experienced in conveyancing, or you could ask for a recommendation from a relative, friend, colleague at work, bank manager, building society manager, estate agent, or by consulting the Law Society's regional directory in your local reference library or citizens advice bureau, or simply look for an advertisement in the local paper or Yellow Pages directory.

If you found the house you want to buy through a multi-firm solicitors' property centre, one of the other firms (not the one involved with the seller of your property) can be used.

One solicitor can act for you in both transactions if you are buying and selling at the same time (and probably also deal with your mortgage). Except in very few cases, one solicitor cannot act for both buyer and seller. One solicitor can never act for the builder/developer and the buyer in a just-built house.

It is not necessary for the solicitor to be local to the property being bought, although it can help if he is, particularly if you are moving to another part of the country.

Q

Next time, I will be more careful in my choice of solicitor. I made the mistake of employing the one who gave the cheapest quote. Although he must have done everything he was meant to, he didn't tell me what was going on and resented me asking questions, accusing me of not trusting him (which I didn't!).

Q

I reckon a good solicitor is a godsend: mine was . . . very good, quick, efficient etc – but I've heard a few stories about unsatisfactory service by solicitors.

Advice on conveyancing costs was given in **Which?** in January and April 1988.

An article on competition in conveyancing, published in *Fiscal Studies* August 1987, using data from a questionnaire to *Which?* readers, indicated that "where the client requests an estimate, his bill is reduced by an average of £35 . . . It would appear that such clients succeed in giving the impression that they are shopping around, thereby inducing an appropriate response on the part of the solicitor."

Q

When visiting your solicitor, don't chat about the weather etc. Mine charged me for the actual time spent with him, irrespective of what was being discussed.

HOW MUCH WILL IT COST?

Ask how the fee will be calculated. Solicitors and licensed conveyancers are free to charge what they choose.

The Law Society recommends that solicitors' fees should be 'fair and reasonable' based on the value of the house; how complicated the transaction is; how much time is spent; how much skill is involved; the number and importance of documents involved; the place and circumstances of the conveyancing; whether the land is registered or unregistered; the importance of the matter to the client.

It will be well worth getting estimates from more than one solicitor/conveyancer before choosing one. Many charge a flat fee for all the work involved.

Do not expect him to be able to tell you how long he thinks his side of your transaction will take – but his reply may give you some impression of his tempo.

You can ask at an early stage how much the other fees will be, such as search fees and the Land Registry fee and stamp duty on the transfer. (These amounts depend on the price being paid for the property.)

If you are getting a mortgage from a building society, fees have been agreed between the Law Society and the Building Societies Association as a guideline for solicitors to charge when acting for both buyer and building society. But often a solicitor will make no separate charge for the mortgage work if he is also handling your purchase.

Consult your solicitor or conveyancer at as early a stage as possible, to have him (or her) at the ready when you decide to make an offer and to advise on any legal snags before you become too involved, such as

○ local restrictions (perhaps preventing or limiting extensions or alterations)
○ the possibility of undesirable development in the neighbourhood.

conveying a newly-built house

For buying a newly-built house, particularly if it is part of a housing estate, your solicitor or conveyancer must check

● that the contract provides that the house itself be properly built with appropriate works and services laid on

Q

Don't be afraid to make your solicitor work i.e. ensure he is giving you his best attention and advises you of basic points like fencing, covenants etc (I had to ask and I should have been told).

- that the boundaries of the property are as shown on the plan
- that the seller is providing any necessary rights, such as rights of way and drainage
- that the builder has entered into an agreement with the appropriate local authority to make up the roads and that, when they are built, the authority will take them over and maintain them
- what restrictions there may be: these are often connected with the appearance of the estate – for example, no parked caravans in front gardens, no cutting down of trees, no swimming pools; there may be rules about keeping animals
- whether the original planning permission for the estate contained conditions which restrict or remove the normal permitted development rights.

Some formalities

Q

. . . the solicitor tended to use technical language which was difficult to follow. We found the Which? 'The legal side of buying a house' a useful book to follow the legal side and to know what should be happening next . . . information from the solicitor was sketchy.

One of the main things that has to be done when you buy a house is to make sure that the seller really owns it and has the right to sell it. Every time property changes hands, the conveyancer has to check on all previous transactions which affect the title – that is, the ownership of the property – such as sales, mortgages, the granting of rights over the property, rights of way, drainage. This is done by investigating a summary (prepared by the seller or his solicitor) of the title deeds covering at least the previous 15 years.

REGISTERED OR UNREGISTERED

Where the property is 'registered', instead of looking at all the previous documents, the buyer can get the information about ownership of the property (and other matters, such as other people's rights over it) from the Land Registry, where the details of registered titles are kept. This makes the transfer of registered property easier than of unregistered – many people do it themselves without a solicitor or other conveyancer.

Not all the land in England and Wales is yet registered, but in areas where registration is compulsory, a property there either has a registered title or, when the house is next sold, the title has to be registered by the new owner. (In Scotland, registration started during 1980.)

If the house you are buying is in an area of compulsory registration but does not yet have a registered title, your solicitor/conveyancer will deal with it as a purchase of unregistered property and, when you become the new proprietor, will register the title at the Land Registry. This should be initiated promptly, but the Registry may take longer than you would wish – or expect – to record the change. A fee is charged by the Land Registry for first registration, based on the price paid for the house but on a lower scale than the fee for transferring a registered property to a new owner. These Land Registry fees are always payable by the buyer.

JOINT OWNERSHIP

Where two or more people are concerned in the purchase – for example, husband and wife, or brother and sister – they should inform their solicitor or conveyancer as early as possible which of two kinds of joint ownership they want.

JOINT TENANCY
(the word 'tenancy' has nothing to do with its usual meaning)
Under this arrangement, neither can sell without the other's agreement. When one dies, the survivor will automatically inherit the other's share. This may be a suitable arrangement for husband and wife, but may often not suit other kinds of shared ownership.

TENANCY IN COMMON
Here, each joint owner is able to dispose of his or her share as he or she thinks fit, whether by will or during his or her lifetime. This form of joint ownership is generally chosen by co-owners who are not married, who prefer to retain this independence.

It is easy for a joint tenancy to be converted into a tenancy in common at any time – simply by one co-owner giving written notice to the other – but the reverse is more complicated and would need a lawyer.

The relevance of inheritance tax in the event of the death of either or both of the co-owners is a factor in deciding whether a joint tenancy or a tenancy in common is preferable.

In the event of a marriage breakdown, it is less complicated to preserve the rights of each spouse if the home is in the joint names. A divorce court, however, has discretion to decide what is to happen to the home.

Q

Try to ensure that if there are joint vendors, they are of a similar mind about selling.

Consumer publication: *Wills and probate*

Consumer publication: *Divorce: legal procedures and financial facts*

The draft contract

As soon as an offer has been accepted, a buyer and seller should exchange the names and addresses of their respective solicitors or conveyancers, giving the name of the actual person dealing with the matter. (The estate agent may do this for either or both.) Each should also send his own conveyancer/solicitor the details concerning the house, the agreed price and any other agreements reached. This initiates the sequence leading to exchange of contracts when you will both be legally bound to buy/sell on the agreed terms.

It is the seller's conveyancer who draws up a draft contract while your (the buyer's) conveyancer's job is to make whatever enquiries may be necessary to ensure that there are no points which might affect your decision to buy.

Your conveyancer will probably not see the house itself: all he will have to work from will be the draft contract, the agent's particulars and some information from the title deeds or the Land Registry. So, if you know of or can guess at any peculiarities about the property or if you have any proposals for using or changing the property in any particular way, tell him, in case they could create some legal problem.

The sort of items to be alert about include:

Q

Garage in house details but did not appear on land plans. Turned out to be owned (land) by council, garage put up by vendor, land rent to be paid. Solicitor unconcerned, we were alarmed, delayed buying until assured garage would be in our title deed.

- the boundaries of a property or the extent of a flat: sometimes an earlier mistake in the plan on the deeds has been carried forward, unnoticed, for some years. You should ask to see the plans and check them, or get your surveyor to do so. If they have to be corrected, it is better done at the vendor's expense than yours
- any shared rights of access: for example, drive shared with another property and whether there is any obligation to contribute towards the upkeep
- a separate access to the back garden: you may need a right of way to it
- other 'easements': for example, a short-cut through your property or the way a neighbour's drains join yours
- any structural additions or alterations carried out by previous owners, such as an extension or a garage: these might have required planning permission or building regulation consent which may never have been obtained
- any remedial treatments for damp or woodworm or any re-roofing or double glazing for which guarantees still operate

Q

Anxious situations: when seller has not much incentive to move (for instance, someone on the threshold of retirement looking for the ideal seaside bungalow); when seller is in process of divorce.

Q

solicitors: if you get regular updates from them, it seems to keep things moving; also pass on other information that you learn direct from purchaser/vendor as this can speed things up, or alert the solicitor to a problem.

- any declared reason for the sale which may give rise to problems over possession – for example, matrimonial difficulties. If the seller's house is not jointly owned by husband and wife, it may be desirable to get written consent for the house to be sold from the spouse who is not the owner in case of matrimonial dispute before completion; the conveyancer can check whether that spouse has registered a claim
- whether any part of the property is let or occupied.

Points like these will normally be dealt with in the contract, or cleared between the two parties before signing, but this can only be done if the points come to light. Do not assume that your conveyancer is a clairvoyant. Bring to his attention at this stage any features about the house, the neighbourhood or the sellers. It is much better to get things right now, rather than have to try to sort them out later.

The contract, which is produced by the seller's conveyancer, is at this stage only a draft because your conveyancer, to whom it is sent, has to be given the opportunity to check, change or add anything which he feels necessary as a result of the enquiries and searches he makes, plus anything you may have told him.

There are standard forms of questions (called local searches) which he will send off to the local authority, the answers to which may show, for example, whether there are any plans to build a trunk road nearby, or whether there are any serious defects which the local authority would require to be put right.

There is also a set of standard questions, known as 'preliminary enquiries' or enquiries before contract, concerning the property itself, boundaries, restrictions and so on. These are sent to the seller's conveyancer with such additional questions as your conveyancer thinks appropriate for the particular transaction, so as to get as much information about the property as possible before exchanging contracts.

The Conveyancing Standing Committee of the Law Commission has issued a practice recommendation on preliminary enquiries (published by Longman) with points on what information should be formally sought and given and what details of the transaction the buyer and seller should discuss personally with each other.

Insurance is available to cover the risk of going ahead without waiting for the results of local searches: if these later reveal lower value for property, the insurance will pay the difference between that value and the price paid. The premium is in the region of $\frac{1}{4}$% of the purchase price.

Q

Putting up with slow solicitors who try and over-complicate matters and clarify every anomaly down to fine detail – my solicitor excepted who moved as fast as I wanted him to.

Agreeing amendments to a draft contract can take time if the contract goes back and forth between the two conveyancers. Rather than sit at home fretting, do not be afraid to ask your conveyancer what is going on if there seem inexplicable delays or silences. But do not pester him daily – that would not be of much use, and you may find yourself paying for any of his time you take up.

Delays not the making of your conveyancer can be the time it takes to obtain a mortgage offer from your building society and to get the result of local searches: some local authorities take many weeks to deal with local searches. You may find that the seller's conveyancer has already initiated the enquiries of the local authority, to cut down on delay (but as yet this procedure is not common).

A good solicitor or conveyancer should advise his client about how long he thinks the procedure will take, judging from his experience of local conditions, and warn that there may be periods when nothing seems to be happening. In practice, however, it is difficult to estimate the time a transaction will take: a chain of buyers and sellers can proceed only at the pace of the slowest party in the chain.

BUYING EXTRA ITEMS

Your conveyancer needs to know the details of any items in the house which you have agreed to buy as an extra, as well as what fixtures and fittings you have agreed with the seller are to be included in the sale.

The standard form of enquiries contains a request for confirmation that all the following items now on the property are included in the sale: trees, shrubs, plants, flowers and garden produce, greenhouses, garden sheds and garden ornaments, aerials, fitted furniture and shelves, electric switches, points and wall and ceiling fittings.

The answer sometimes given by the seller's conveyancer is: "see agent's particulars", but an agent may not have been fully informed by the seller, or the seller may have changed his mind after the particulars had been circulated. So, in order to avoid any misunderstanding or unpleasantness, a buyer should take it upon himself to reach a clear understanding with the seller about what is and what is not included, and make a list in writing. Include this list with the other details you send to your conveyancer, indicating clearly which are included in the sale price and which of the furnishings or other items you are buying separately, together with the agreed prices. Ask him to ensure that all these are referred to in the contract, quoting details such as brand names where appropriate.

BOUNDARY WALLS AND FENCES

A line of trees or a hedge at the side or far end of the garden does not necessarily indicate the limit of the property: it could be within or beyond that line. So, it is important to check exactly where the boundaries lie – if necessary, measuring on the ground and comparing the results with any dimensions given in the title documents.

The deeds of a property may describe the position of the boundaries clearly, and with proper measurements – by words or by a plan. (Traditionally, T marks on a boundary line drawn on an original building plan indicate that that particular wall or fence belongs to the owner of the property inside which the T mark appears.) But some deeds and records are imprecise about where the boundary actually is or, in reality, it is not where they say it should be. In this case, you may have to look for some evidence, such as photographs or letters between previous owners and neighbours, for settling where it should be.

The deeds may say, or you may have other evidence, that a fence or wall on the boundary is on your land – in which case, you own it. Walls dividing semi-detached or terraced properties with supports on both sides are generally regarded as belonging to both, with repairs being a joint expense.

Some deeds specify clearly what your obligations are as regards fencing: the type, or minimum or maximum height. If nothing is stated, you may not need to have a fence at all (unless one would be necessary to prevent damage or injury to others); where there is a fence which you are not obliged to have, you generally cannot be made to repair it, but if it is likely to fall on to your neighbour's land, it is up to you to make it safe or remove it. If you have to go on to a neighbour's land to repair a fence or wall, you need permission unless the right is granted to you in your or his deeds.

Sometimes you are not allowed to fence. Some new estates, for example, impose restrictions against front gardens being divided, and the original planning permission may have been granted on this basis. Corner properties may have special provisions about 'line(s) of sight' for traffic. Under general planning law, you may not erect a fence more than 1 metre high in front of a house, nor over 2 metres high at the rear.

Exchange of contracts

Once contracts are exchanged, you (and, more importantly, the people selling to or buying from you) are locked into a legal agreement from which neither side can withdraw.

It is therefore a serious point in the proceedings. If he is good, your solicitor or conveyancer will take time before you reach the stage of exchange of contracts to see you at the office and go through all the paperwork with you. Do not be afraid to ask him questions on any points that are still unclear. It is important to make sure that everything is right now. It will be too late to change things after exchange of contracts.

Contracts should not be signed until

- preliminary enquiries and local searches are completed
- any surveyor's report has been made and the facts accepted or an NHBC 10-year notice issued for a newly-built house
- the source of payment is settled: a mortgage loan is confirmed in writing
- the deposit of 10% of the purchase price (or less, by agreement) is available
- the date for completion has been agreed. (Completion day is often about 4 weeks from exchange of contracts, but there is no magic in this period and it can be longer or shorter, depending on the wishes of the people concerned.)

Contracts are then exchanged, by your signing one copy which is sent to the seller's conveyancer, and the seller's conveyancer sending to you or (more usually) your conveyancer the contract signed by the seller. It is only when these documents have been exchanged that the two parties become legally bound to the transaction.

After exchange of contracts, a buyer no longer needs to worry about gazumping or a seller whether the buyer really will go through with the deal. But it also means that you cannot change your mind. You have to buy (or sell) even if you lose your job or you discover some dreadful defect in the house you are buying.

CONTRACT
On the sale of a house, this is the legally binding agreement, a document in two identical parts, one signed by the buyer and the other by the seller; when the two parts are exchanged, both buyer and seller are committed to complete the transaction by transferring ownership in exchange for paying the price.

Q

There is a marvellous reassurance associated with an exchange of contracts on your own house, that helps bolster flagging spirits when searching for a new one.

THE DEPOSIT

On exchange of contracts, a deposit has to be paid by the buyer to the seller. Traditionally, the deposit is 10% of the purchase price but a lower figure (say, 5%) can sometimes be negotiated. This deposit (unlike any preliminary deposit paid to an estate agent) is non-refundable and is used as security for the performance of the contract. The amount will be deducted from what has to be paid at completion.

Advice on claiming interest on the deposit paid to a solicitor between exchange of contracts and completion was given in **Which?** February 1988.

Normally, the deposit is sent to the seller's conveyancer as stakeholder, which means he must sit on it and not use it for his client's purposes.

Q

When do-it-yourself conveyancing is involved, a joint bank account should be opened in the names of both buyer and seller to take the deposit: cheques requiring the signature of both parties.

A special condition of the contract may require that the deposit should be paid to the conveyancer as 'agent for the vendor', which means that he does not have to retain it until completion and could pass it on to the seller. If the seller needs your deposit to pay the deposit on his new house, it is difficult for you to object to a request of this nature if you are part of a buying and selling chain and want to ask the same of the buyer of your house. But it does mean that you cannot be assured of regaining your deposit should your purchase fall through, through no fault on your part.

If you do not have the ready money for a deposit, you may have to arrange a bridging loan, to be paid off when you receive the mortgage loan or the money from the sale of your home.

DEPOSIT GUARANTEE SCHEME

As an alternative to paying a deposit, it is possible to take out a deposit guarantee if your solicitor or licensed conveyancer takes part in the scheme (run by Legal & Professional Indemnity).

Instead of paying a deposit, you pay an insurance premium related to the purchase price of the house, which covers a deposit of 10%, up to a set maximum. For example, for a deposit of £5000, the premium for a deposit guarantee is £70 (£42 if you are also selling). This includes a commission for the solicitor or conveyancer (who may decide to pass this back to you). The insurance guarantees to pay the 10% deposit if you default under the contract (but will seek to recover the money from you).

You can arrange and pay for the guarantee scheme at an early stage, if you want to be prepared; it will come into effect the moment you exchange contracts.

This may be cheaper than raising the deposit by way of a bridging loan. But make sure that your solicitor will not make a charge for the deposit guarantee, which would cancel the difference. Your seller may not be willing to accept the guarantee instead of a deposit: he may still insist on cash.

A deposit guarantee does not work in the same way as a normal deposit. It cannot be passed down the line as can happen with an ordinary deposit if all parties agree. And when it comes to completion, you will have to be able to provide the money for the full price.

The chain situation

Unless you are a first-time buyer, you are likely to be selling your existing house as well as buying a new one, and will be trying to time the two operations to run as closely together as possible. While you are occupied with getting a loan and survey on your new house and with the legalities of the two changes of ownership, the buyer of your present home is in a similar situation. And so a chain of buyer and seller, buyer and seller links up. Where there is a chain of transactions, each inter-dependent upon the other, the pace of the slowest can affect all of them.

When a problem occurs along the chain, it affects all those in it. When, for example, the buyer of the house your buyer is selling has a long wait before his application for a loan is granted, this wait slows up all the other transactions. Should his application be refused, one link in the chain breaks; that buyer has to back out of his deal, forcing your buyer to do the same or to delay while he looks for a new purchaser. Obviously, the longer the chain, the greater the risk that one of the transactions will collapse.

There are agencies who are willing in certain circumstances to act as chain-breakers where a buyer is suddenly stuck and unable to go forward with his purchase because his own buyer has dropped out. The chain-breaker buys the property at a discounted price (probably at around 90% of its valuation), so it is a solution of last resort.

bridging loan

If you have to complete your purchase before your sale, your bank will almost certainly let you have a bridging loan provided you have exchanged contracts on the sale of your own property and have a firm offer of a mortgage in respect of the purchase. (Some building societies are willing to provide a bridging loan for their borrowers.)

But beware of bridging finance – unless you are not having to bear the cost (for instance, your employer is footing the bill). It is expensive to set up. Most banks charge a setting-up fee of 1% (or a flat fee of £100+) of the loan just for agreeing to lend you the money. On top of that, you will be paying a higher rate of interest.

There is tax relief on the interest on a bridging loan taken out in order to be able to buy a house or flat. If you are still making the mortgage payments on your previous home because you have not yet managed to complete a sale, there is tax relief for a period on both sets of interest payments. The MIRAS scheme does not apply, so you have to claim this relief specifically.

Some 'open-ended' bridging loans are offered specifically for the chain situation – for example, by Black Horse Agencies and by Home Bridging.

If you have exchanged contracts on your sale, you will at least know that the end is in sight and you can calculate accordingly. But if contracts have not been exchanged, you will need an 'open' bridging loan, because you have no guarantee that the house will sell quickly (some houses take many months to sell). People who take on open-ended bridging loans pay out hundreds, even thousands, of pounds in interest.

Insurance

From the date when contracts are exchanged to buy a property, the house or flat is no longer at the seller's risk for insurance purposes. So, the buyer must be prepared to take out insurance for any damage to the building itself.

Q

Make sure building society gives more than one quote on insurance: we found that at certain times different companies give discounts or offers – we saved £34 per year by refusing first 2 quotes.

For someone getting a mortgage, the lender will make it a condition that the property is insured, and may offer to arrange the cover. If you are getting a building society mortgage, you should be offered at least three companies to choose from although not all building societies keep to this. Most societies will allow you to arrange your own insurance, but they will want to approve the policy as providing adequate cover for their security, and will charge a fee for the 'administrative costs' of doing so.

Q

After completion, lender informed us that they had taken out insurance cover. We had taken out cover already, lender did not inform us that they were dissatisfied with our choice (which was recommended by associate company of theirs!).

A report on house insurance was published in **Which?** September 1986, updated in July 1987; a 'questions answered' feature appeared in June 1988 and a report on house buildings insurance in **Which?** October 1988 gives advice on finding a good policy.

The building society often pays the first premium, to make sure that the insurance is effective, and the amount is then deducted from the money you get when your mortgage loan comes through. Some building societies also pay the subsequent insurance premiums and add the amount once a year to the monthly mortgage payments, or allow the borrower to pay part of the premium each month.

A large building society may arrange insurance by means of what is called a block policy under which a number of buildings are insured. No individual policies are issued, but the building society should give its borrowers full details of the cover provided by the policy.

Check whether the sum insured is adequate.

SUM INSURED

The sum for which you insure should not be the market value – that is, the amount you are about to pay for the house – but the cost of rebuilding it if it should be destroyed, including the cost of clearing away debris and rubble, architect's and surveyor's fees. This is what is meant by the reinstatement cost. Also, there should be an allowance for permanent fittings such as central heating and double glazing.

The amount for which a house is insured governs how much you will get if a fire or other accident destroys it. If under-insured, you may only be paid pro rata: for example, if you insure for £60,000 but at the time of the accident it costs £90,000 to rebuild the house, you will receive only two-thirds of the cost.

The **Association of British Insurers** issues a free leaflet *Buildings insurance for home owners*, available from the ABI, Aldermary House, Queen Street, London EC4N 1TT and at some building society and insurance company offices and citizens' advice bureaux. This tells how to calculate the amount to insure for specific sizes and types of house in various regions of the country, based on rebuilding costs. The figures given in the leaflet are, of necessity, averages. Your house may be more, or less, expensive than the examples shown. If in doubt, ask a surveyor for an 'estimate of reinstatement costs'. He should not charge a lot for this, if you request it when arranging the survey.

Bear in mind that in the case of an older house in a terrace, or in a street of houses of similar type, if yours is destroyed by fire, the planning authority would almost certainly insist that the replacement should be as much like the original as possible, at least the facade. So, even a small victorian terrace house, with a stone bow window, could be very expensive to replace.

Nowadays, nearly all insurance companies issue index-linked policies, with the sum insured linked to the house rebuilding costs index and changing automatically as the average cost of rebuilding changes, although the premium you pay does not change until renewal.

You should hold on to the buildings policy for the house you are leaving because you remain liable under the Defective Premises Act: most policies will cover this liability for 7 years after the sale.

Buying a house at auction

An estate agent may advertise or give you details of a house which is going to be sold by auction. The method of sale in this case differs fundamentally from a sale by private treaty in that when the house is 'knocked down' to a bidder, he exchanges contracts there and then with the auctioneer and cannot back out of the purchase later. He is legally bound to it, even if he were to flee from the sale room without signing anything. Before the day of the auction, the would-be buyer should therefore have taken all the steps which are normally taken before exchange of contracts: made the preliminary enquiries and local searches, had a survey carried out, and completed the organisation of his finances.

Because an auction is likely to attract a number of interested house buyers all needing the answers to a number of questions about the property, a more than usually detailed set of particulars is prepared by the agent. This normally takes the form of a brochure, sometimes with photographs, containing full details of the house itself, with additional facts about the tenure, possession, fixtures and fittings, rateable value, and Special Conditions of Sale. These, along with the Memorandum of Agreement (contained in the brochure) are the equivalent of a contract for sale by private treaty. The problem is that there is no scope for negotiating its terms.

the price

Check if one of the conditions of sale is that the seller is selling 'subject to reserve price' – how much this is is usually not disclosed, although the agent may be able to give you a guideline figure. The auctioneer may, during the bidding, use a phrase like "I'm going to sell this property . . .", as an indication that the reserve price has been reached. If the bidding does not reach the reserve, the auctioneer withdraws the property. If you were among the last bidders for a property that is withdrawn, tell the agent afterwards at what figure you are prepared to buy – the seller may accept your offer.

The publicity for the auction may contain the proviso 'unless previously sold'. In this case, the seller's agent is open to offers and is prepared to negotiate a sale by private treaty before, and instead of, the auction. The seller will still, however, expect to sell on the auction contract so you may have only a few days (or hours) in which to make enquiries and raise funds.

Check straightaway whether the intention really is to go to auction; it may be more of an incentive for offers than an intention and you may lose your chance by waiting for auction day.

Some properties have got to go to auction for legal reasons connected with proving that a proper price has been obtained when it is sold by executors or creditors. If the property is one of these, you will see a phrase such as 'sold by order of executors or trustees'. Do not make a prior offer as this may colour the reserve price.

steps to take if buying at auction

- Study the agent's brochure extremely carefully, reading all the small print. There may be conditions or disclaimers which would make the property unsuitable. Look for mention of any planning restrictions or refusals, in case you would want to make any alterations or improvements.
- View the house in the normal way and be sure that it is what you want. Remember that you cannot back out after the auction.
- As early as possible, send to your solicitor or conveyancer the brochure with all details, and arrange for him to carry out the usual enquiries and searches before the day of the auction. Sometimes the seller's solicitor will carry out the searches and supply a copy to yours. Arrange to have a survey and a valuation done and to get the results before the day of the auction.
- Fix your price limit, and complete arrangements for the necessary finance for the purchase before the day of the auction. A building society or other lender will have to inspect and value the property in the usual way before making an offer of a mortgage.

Resolve not to get carried away during the bidding and so exceed your price limit. If you have doubts about this, appoint someone else to bid for you – such as your solicitor (who will charge for his time).

If you are outbid, you lose not only the house but the expenses of a survey and solicitor, just as you do if you fail to buy by private treaty.

If you are successful, you will have to pay 10% of your bid to the auctioneer straightaway. The Memorandum of Agreement is countersigned by the seller's agent as confirmation of the sale and acknowledgement of receipt of the 10% deposit. The rest of the transaction then follows in the same way as with a sale by private treaty. Completion usually takes place 28 days after the auction, and the balance of the purchase money has to be paid then.

If you cannot complete, the seller can sue you for the difference between your agreed bid and what he realises on a subsequent sale if this is less, and for any expenses he had to incur.

sale by tender

An alternative to an auction is a tender, which invites buyers to put their offer, together with a 10% deposit, in a sealed envelope and return it to the agent by a specified date. A 'Form of Tender' is included in the sale particulars. Check whether the terms of the tender include a contract, in which case you may be bound to the purchase. In other cases, you may still be able to back out after your tender has been accepted.

This method is not normally used for sales of private houses, although a simplified version of it may be in cases where two or three offers have been made near to or at the asking price.

Practical matters before completion

While the legal matters are being taken care of between exchange of contracts and completion day, there are practical things you can get on with and administrative matters you must not overlook.

insurance

From the moment of exchanging contracts, insurance for the house you are buying becomes your responsibility. One of the standard conditions of sale that form part of the contract specifies that the seller is under no duty to maintain insurance on the property (if it is leasehold, however, he may be obliged to do so under the terms of his lease). If the building society who is giving you a mortgage is arranging the buildings insurance, check when it starts and what the policy covers.

Notify the insurers of your present home that the cover for 'contents' should be transferred to the new address from the day you move in. If you are moving in over several days, get the insurers to hold the contents covered for both addresses.

If your buildings insurance is now with a different insurance company because of the building society's requirement, it may be practical to transfer the contents insurance to the same company. (This would simplify matters if you should have a claim involving both the building and the contents policy, such as a burglary claim.) You should claim a refund of the unexpired part of the premium – if the unused part of the insured term makes this worth while.

A report on contents insurance in **Which?** September 1988 gives advice on the right type of cover for your possessions.

The sum for which you insure the contents may have to be adjusted if you are buying a lot of new things for the new house or selling a lot on moving out of the old one. The premium you have to pay may also be different because of the different area and type of house to which you are moving.

You have to tell your insurers if you are not moving into the new home straightaway. The cover on a home which is not lived in is generally less extensive.

Your motor insurers will have to be informed of the new address and whether or not the car will be garaged – which may affect the premium.

The Local Government Finance Act 1988 proposes the abolition of the present rating system in England and Wales and the introduction of a community charge (referred to generally as 'poll tax') to be levied on adults aged 18 and over instead of just property owners. The new system is not expected to come into operation until April 1990.

By the Abolition of Domestic Rates Etc (Scotland) Act 1987, domestic rates in Scotland will be abolished completely by 1992. They will be phased out gradually during the previous three years, starting in 1989. Domestic rates will be replaced by a 'community charge', a tax levied on each adult member of each household. Special provisions will apply to second homes and properties occupied by short-term residents.

Q

Do everything in good time e.g. rates/water rates informed in writing well ahead or you'll be zapped for money you don't owe.

rates and water charges

The rateable value (r.v.) of a property in England or Wales depends broadly on the position of the property and its convenience to facilities, the type of building (detached, semi-detached, bungalow) and its amenities (garage, central heating and so on) and the amount of land involved. The rateable value, which is assessed periodically by Inland Revenue valuation officers, is based on what is known as the gross value (g.v.) – that is, what the annual rent might be if the property were to be let. Certain fixed deductions for costs of maintenance and repairs are made from gross value to arrive at rateable value.

Each local authority decides annually how much per £ of the rateable value to charge its ratepayers. The rating year starts on 1 April. Rates can be paid once a year or twice a year, in advance, or by instalments.

Rates are payable from the time that furniture is put into the house or flat, and cease to be payable when all furniture is removed. So, if there is a gap of a short period – known as a void period – when a house or flat changes hands, provided there is no furniture in it, no rates need be paid (unless this concession has been used up in the current rating year by the previous owner). If the rates have been paid already, a refund can be claimed.

After three months, some local authorities charge up to half rates (empty rate) on property which is still empty; some charge 100 per cent rates (which can cost more than if the building were occupied, because it is 100 per cent of the full rate, without the normal domestic rate relief).

WATER

Water charges are levied by the relevant water authority not by the local authority in England and Wales (in Scotland, water rates are paid along with ordinary rates). For domestic consumers, the charges are generally based on a percentage of the property's rateable value; if metered, on exact consumption plus a standing charge.

A move to a new house may be the moment to change to metered water consumption if you calculate that this would be financially advantageous. The water authority for your new area will be able to give you information about their charges. The *Which?* report on Water in November 1986 included advice on assessing the pros and cons of paying for water by meter.

Even if your water consumption is metered, you have to pay a charge for sewerage and environmental services, based on rateable value of the property. A sewerage charge is not payable if there is no connection to the public sewer.

APPORTIONMENT

The seller is responsible for rates and water charges for the part of the rating year before the completion date, and the buyer for the part after the completion date. For example, if completion takes place on 1 July, the seller must bear the liability for the 92 days which make up the months of April, May and June, while the buyer must accept liability for the remaining 273 days of the rating year. It used to be a convention for rates and water charges to be apportioned on a day-to-day basis, not weekly or monthly. Nowadays, the local authority prefers to make the necessary adjustments as this helps it to keep its records up to date. If apportionments are made, a buyer should satisfy himself that the seller has paid all the rates and charges due for his period of ownership and, if any are outstanding, he would be wise to get an undertaking (preferably through the seller's solicitor) that the seller will pay whatever may be due.

A seller, on the other hand, may have paid out more in advance than the amount for which he is responsible, so that either the buyer or the rating authority has to be asked for a refund of any amounts which the seller has already paid.

accounts

A bank account or accounts may need to be transferred to a branch in your new area. If you have not already noted the address of the one nearest to your new home, your present branch will be able to find out for you. Your bank manager may require a formal letter asking for the transfer to be made on a certain date. Or you can arrange this by visiting the branch you wish your account to be transferred to. You will be given a standard 'transfer' letter to sign. Ask for the new branch's bank code number and your new account number(s) so that you can notify anybody who pays directly into your account or debits it directly. You can go on using your existing cheque book and card until you get the new ones.

With a bank deposit account, it is important that there is continuity so that no

Q

The first rates that we paid were demanded in previous owner's name, despite filling in all the relevant forms.

interest is lost. Check in due course that the closing date at your old branch and the opening date at the new are the same.

Even if you do not need to move your account, you will have to notify the bank of your new address.

For a national savings account at the post office, there is no need to give formal notification; just alter the address in the account book.

CHARGE ACCOUNTS

If you have accounts which are paid weekly or monthly by post or personally with retailers in the area, write or telephone a request for these to be closed and any outstanding account to be sent to you, either to your old or your new address.

If you intend to continue to use a monthly or budget account at a large retail store, you will have to notify your new address, so that the accounts will be sent to you at that address. An inadvertent lapse about paying an outstanding bill (sent to the wrong address) may get you on to a computer record as a bad risk without your realising that this has happened.

You should also notify any credit card company of your change of address.

TV SET ON HIRE

If you hire your television set and/or video recorder, check with the rental firm whether you can take it with you to your new home: if necessary, have your account transferred to another branch. This would be worth doing if you have been paying a reduced rent for an older set. Otherwise, turn in the set and take out a new contract locally for another one.

It is more usual to include a roof TV aerial in the sale of a house – also more sensible. But if you have decided to take it with you, you will have to arrange to have the aerial taken down off the roof (the removal men will not do this) and then to have it put up on your new roof – and will have to pay someone to do this.

forwarding mail

You can collect from any post office a form requesting redirection of mail, to fill in and return to your local sorting office with the appropriate fee. The post office will re-direct your letters and parcels as follows:

letters: for an initial charge (£2.75) for a period of up to 1 month, followed by a further charge (£6.25) for any period up to 3 months, or up to one year (£15).

parcels: a charge equal to the original postage is generally payable on each parcel on delivery to the new address (only inland parcels will be redirected).

Seven days' notice must be given before the date you want the redirection to start. The request form must be signed by all those in the household wanting their mail redirected, and a separate fee is payable per surname if there is more than one. (As an added precaution, make sure that the new owner knows your new address, and ask him to redirect any mail that comes for you.)

The same form contains a section for you to complete for notifying the National TV Licence Records Office in Bristol of your change of address.

change of address cards

If you intend to have your own change of address cards printed, arrange this far enough in advance to allow time for the printing to be done. It is advisable to include both your new and old addresses on it because if you are notifying organisations which keep geographical lists, they will only be able to trace you by your old address. Some removal firms supply cards free.

To help you estimate how many change of address cards you will need, make a check list of organisations you may need to advise and then tick off each one as you send the notification. After your move, you can check against your list any incoming mail which has had to be redirected by the post office and, if necessary, notify any sender you may have forgotten or remind those who on their side have forgotten or not noticed.

One thing that may hold up your preparation for change of address cards is having to wait for your new telephone number.

Q

Telephone: total mess up with change of numbers as previous owner took number with him to his new address. Took over 2 weeks to resolve matter.

BASIC CHECK LIST FOR CHANGE OF ADDRESS NOTIFICATION

finance	
bank	if moving to another area, authorise transfer of accounts to new branch, cancel any standing orders no longer needed
girobank	notify Bootle (use prepaid addressed envelope); if moving to another area, nominate two new post offices; you will be sent a new plastic card
building societies	take account book to any branch
pension/benefit book	notify local social security office; nominate new post office or give new number of account for paying-in; if pension sent quarterly, tell DHSS Central Pensions Branch, Newcastle upon Tyne NE98 1YX
national insurance	notify social security office of old and new address, giving national insurance number (as on your pay slip)
Inland Revenue	tell your inspector of taxes
premium savings bonds	complete notification card attached to your holder's card or form P2767 at a post office and send to Bonds and Stock Office, Lytham St Annes, Lancs FY0 1YN
national savings certificates and save-as-you-earn	send old and new addresses and holder's number to Savings Certificate and SAYE Office, Durham DH99 1NS

stocks and shares	write to registrar (details on share certificate and dividend vouchers); give new bank details if dividend paid directly
credit card companies	
hire purchase company	
local rating authority water authority	amend standing orders for payment by instalments
insurance broker/agent life insurance company any other insurers	
car vehicle registration	complete section on vehicle registration document and send to DVLC, Swansea SA99 1AR
driving licence	complete section on present licence and send to DVLC, Swansea SA99 1AB
motor insurers AA, RAC or other motoring organisation	(premium may change)
medical NHS doctor or private doctor/dentist private health insurers national blood transfusion service	if you are not moving out of the area notify present centre

work and leisure employer firm's (and previous firms') pension fund trades union, professional association	
TV licence records office	Barton House, Bristol BS98 1TL (can be done via post office or on mail redirection form)
children's school(s)	if you are not moving out of the area
clubs, societies or any organisation you belong to, magazine or book club, football pool company	if you want to remain on their mailing list
public library	(and return all borrowed books)
mail order firm(s) any shop or firm you have an account with theatre, concert or other mailing lists	
Which? Holiday Which? Gardening from Which?	complete and send address slip from latest *Which?* to Castlemead, Gascoyne Way, Hertford SG14 1LH

Do not forget to add relatives or friends whom you want to inform – and any individual or organisation from whom you are expecting a communication. For instance, if your children have been offered provisional places at university or polytechnic (pending A-level results or similar), make sure UCCA/PCAS or the college knows (ask for an acknowledgement) lest the places get filled for lack of prompt reply.

Also, leave a change of address card or two for the incoming occupant with a request to forward mail and redirect telephone calls (and leave behind for him any headed stationery you may have left over).

arrangements for new schools

If you are moving into a new area and want to find a new school for your child, send details of him or her to the local education authority of the area you are moving to and ask for help in finding a place. The authority should send a list of all available schools in the area, and may send prospectuses of individual schools. You can write direct to the schools for information and to arrange a visit; do not commit your children to a school until you have visited it.

The Education Authorities Directory and Annual and *The Primary Education Directory* published by the School Government Publishing Company, give information about state schools. The **Advisory Centre for Education** has a publication on *Choosing a school* (£2), available from 18 Victoria Park Square, London E2 9PB.

If you want information about private schools, contact the **Independent Schools Information Service**, 56 Buckingham Gate, London SW1E 6AG or the Regional Director, ISIS **(Scotland)**, 22 Hanover Street, Edinburgh EH2 2EP; ISIS has published a book *Choosing Your Independent School* (£2). The **Scottish Education Department** (New St Andrew's House, Edinburgh EH1 3SY) can provide a list of independent schools.

A number of education yearbooks and guides give information about independent schools (for example, *The Independent Schools Yearbook* two volumes, one for boys' and one for girls' schools, published by A & C Black; *Which School?* published by Gabbitas, Truman & Thring; *The Parents' Guide to Independent Schools* published by SFIA Educational Trust), and should be available in a public reference library.

Information about approved pre-school playgroups and private nursery schools is obtainable from the local authority's social services department, and information about maintained nursery schools and nursery classes at primary schools from the local education authority. Information about nursery, primary and secondary schools in Scotland is available from education departments at relevant regional council offices.

The **Pre-school Playgroups Association**, 61-63 King's Cross Road, London WC1X 9LL, can tell you about any playgroups in an area.

Telephone

It is worth liaising with your seller (and a kindness to do so with your buyer) to save unnecessary disconnection and reconnection charges or having to be without a telephone for a length of time. The telephones at the new address may be owned by the previous occupant, the seller, who may unplug them and take them away. You would then have to make arrangements to buy or rent the telephones you would like to have.

GIVING UP YOUR EXISTING TELEPHONE

You should notify the sales office of your local telephone area at least 7 working days in advance that you will be moving out. The number to ring is in the front of the telephone directory. Give the date when you want to stop renting and being charged for the telephone, and give the address to which your final account up to that date should be sent. At the same time, say if the buyer of your present house or flat wishes to take over the telephone from you, so that the line will be left for him (he will have to apply to take it over). The rental charge will be apportioned between you on your next telephone accounts.

GETTING A TELEPHONE AT YOUR NEW ADDRESS

Contact the sales office in your new area as soon as possible, by letter or telephone (if you are moving out of the area, dial 100 and ask for the appropriate number to ring in the new area). Explain what you want: either to have a telephone installed at the new address or to take over the existing line there. Whether this can happen and when, depends on the availability of telephone lines in that area.

If you do not want any of the extras that the previous occupant had – such as extensions or coloured or special instruments – ask for them to be taken away. This will save the higher quarterly rental for them.

If you own your telephone, you can take the instrument with you if the new house has modern plug-in sockets. If it does not, new sockets, or at least one, will have to be installed. If you do not own a telephone, this may be the time to buy one; but there is no reason why not to continue renting.

When you are taking over an existing telephone and number, there is a

takeover charge of £16. If the number is not remaining the same because the previous occupant is taking it with him or it is required for someone else who has been waiting for some time, the charge is also £16.

If you are moving within the same telephone exchange area to a new address, it is usually possible to take your existing number with you if you want to – but the charge for this is £21.

If you are to have a new telephone line, ask what the likely delay is. An engineer may have to come and see how the wiring is to be brought into the house. There is an installation charge – present maximum £105 for a new telephone customer; for someone who has previously been a subscriber, up to £90. The number is not usually allocated or confirmed in advance of the actual installation – this may hold up your change of address notifications.

A British Telecom booklet *Phones for your home*, with details of the features of phones and systems available for renting or buying from British Telecom, can be obtained from BT shops or by dialling 100 for 'freefone Telecom sales'.

arranging about gas and electricity

In a newly-built house, the builder almost always is responsible for paying to have mains supplies laid on, but you must still make an application direct to the relevant authority for the supply (gas/electricity/telephone) to be connected up and for you to become responsible for payment.

Q

We arranged all the necessary transfers well in advance before we moved in and the transfers all went through smoothly.

Make the arrangements about household services well in advance of your moving out and moving in date so that you can give sufficient notice to book the work to be done on the day and at the time you want. Arrangements can be made to read meters at fairly short notice, but if you want a fitter to connect or disconnect appliances or turn on or off supplies at an appointed time, give at least a week's notice, preferably more. And confirm on the day before that someone is coming at the right time.

If the house you are going to has been previously occupied, the owner should, on his part, tell the local gas and electricity board that he is going and that you are moving in. But some people leave without informing the gas region or electricity board and arranging for meters to be read, so it would be in your interest to have them read on your arrival, too.

British Gas has leaflets on fuel running costs for different regions of the country, comparing the cost of using gas, electricity or solid fuel for heating, hot water and cooking. These – not surprisingly – conclude that gas is cheapest, but do show interesting differences in the estimated consumption in different types of housing.

GAS

If you are going to the area of a different gas region, ask at your present service centre for the address and telephone number of your new one. Then get in touch, either personally or in writing, well in advance, so that you can sign an application form for taking over the supply and make arrangements for the meter to be read and, if necessary, the supply turned on, on the day you move in. At the same time, you can arrange for a service engineer to call to connect any appliance and to alter the gas supply pipe to fit the incoming appliance, if necessary. The charge for connection is normally slightly more than the disconnection charge.

Gas cookers can be fitted with a plug-in flexible hose instead of rigidly, so that the cooker can be easily moved for cleaning. You may want to have this fitted to your cooker when you take it to a new house.

A deposit is not usually asked for when taking over a gas supply unless a customer is known to have been a bad payer or has previously not had a gas account and cannot give an acceptable credit reference or guarantor.

ELECTRICITY

To arrange for your meter to be read on leaving, you should notify the local electricity board, giving as much notice as you can. You may be asked to fill in a form of notification of removal, giving your old and new address and details of your date of departure, and the name and address of the incoming consumer (if you know it at this stage).

You should ask for a meter reader to come on the day of your move before you leave. (There is no charge for this.) Telephone on the day before, to confirm that he is coming and at what time.

You have to make formal application to the electricity board where you are going, for a supply to be made available. There is an application form to be completed. If you are not able to visit the local showroom in advance, write or telephone and ask for the form to be sent to you beforehand, together with details of their tariffs. You can get the address or telephone number from your local (where you are now) showroom.

The application form usually asks for the approximate total wattage you expect

Q

The previous tenant had failed to notify electricity board of his leaving and the board 'split the difference' despite my having a reading done when I moved in. The bill was eventually reduced after letters etc. It took them about 8 months.

to use, so that the electricity board can check that the installation will be large enough to cope with your maximum demand. The figure to put down on the form is the total number of watts the appliances would use if they were all switched on full. (The wattage is usually marked on a plate somewhere on each appliance.)

The form also asks which sort of tariff you want to be on. If you are going to install storage heaters and off-peak water heating, you will want to have the Economy 7 tariff instead of the standard tariff.

You could be asked for evidence of your past record of paying, or asked for a deposit. If you have to pay a deposit, this earns interest, credited to you once a year, and will normally be refunded when you leave the board's area or have established creditworthiness by paying bills promptly. You will not be asked for a deposit if you agree to pay a regular amount each week or month, or if you have a slot meter put in, or if you give an acceptable credit reference or guarantor.

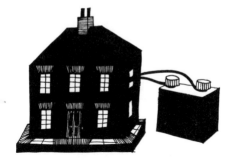

If the house is to be empty for an interim period, the board may ask you if the supply is to be left connected or not (there is no charge for disconnection and reconnection in these circumstances). This may depend on whether you are having any work done before you move in, when the workmen would need an electricity supply for lights, heating, electric drills or other tools. Also, if during the winter you want to keep the central heating on low, it needs electricity to run it, even if it is gas or oil-fired heating.

Going to look at the house again

Find out from the present owner as much as you can about the operation and maintenance of any central heating system and water heating, and ask him to leave you any instruction booklets there may be.

If the system uses oil or solid fuel, check how much fuel is being left and confirm how much you will have to pay for it, and what the arrangements have been for delivery.

Ask for the name of a local plumber and electrical contractor and get details of any maintenance contract there has been, and when a service was last done. Discuss the possibility of taking over the contract.

LIGHTING AND SOCKETS

Get the present owner to show you where the electricity mains switch and the consumer unit and fuses are.

You may need additional or replacement light fittings if the seller is removing any that he is entitled to. He must not remove lamp holders or sockets or leave bare wires. There is no basis for the belief that one electric bulb must be left for the incoming owner: you should be prepared to find none and should be armed with a supply.

Which? May 1985 reported on a survey of how many power points people wanted in their homes: minimum requirement for a 3-bedroom house, 34 sockets.

Compare the number of socket outlets in the house with the number of appliances you have. If you have many more appliances than there are sockets, you will need adaptors to begin with but must be careful not to overload the electrical circuit and should consider installing more socket outlets. Where sockets are in places that would make it difficult to use your appliances, you may have to fit longer flexes on yours or buy an extension lead.

Check that the plugs on your equipment fit sockets in the new house. Where a different type of plug is required, change as many as possible on your appliances in advance. It would be worth trying to arrange with your seller for him to leave you his plugs, provided he does not need them at his next home.

MEASURING FOR CURTAINS AND FLOORING

Look what kind of curtain rails there are (if they are being left) in case you need to change the hooks and attachments on your curtains. Have any curtains cleaned before rehanging them.

To measure windows for curtains for the material you need to make them, a metal rule is easier to use than a tape measure.

In width, you will need at least one-and-a-half times the length of the rail (or the combined lengths of both rails where two overlap). If the material is patterned, you will have to allow extra for matching at the seams and where the curtains meet.

When you measure for new fitted carpets so that you can give the carpet shop 'approximate' details, take the measurements from skirting board to skirting board and explain to the retailer when ordering the carpet that you have not allowed for the turnings required for the edging strips now normally used for fixing fitted carpets. Do not assume that opposite walls in a room are parallel: not all corners are an accurate 90 degrees, nor is every chimney breast the same thickness. The carpet supplier will be responsible for accurate measuring and fitting.

The kitchen, too, needs careful measuring if you intend to put down new tiles or other floor coverings. An accurate floor plan will also help you to work out where your present equipment will fit in and, if you are getting a new cooker or refrigerator or washing machine, what size and shape to order.

When you have measured, chosen and ordered any new curtains, carpeting, floor covering, bathroom or kitchen fitments, get them delivered, where appropriate, to the new address, on or after completion day.

On completion day

On completion day, all the weeks and months of worry and preparation will reach their climax.

The date for completion is agreed between the buyer and seller at the time contracts are exchanged and is specified in the contract. You may well be involved in two completions – one when your new house becomes yours and, if you are selling as well, one when your old one ceases to belong to you. Before fixing the date for completion, both buyer and seller should be as certain as possible that they have somewhere to move to on the day of completion.

Ideally, everyone would have two or three days to move from one home to another but the complex financial arrangements involved in house transfer do not permit this. Unless you are prepared to go to the expense of a bridging loan, you will be stuck with everything happening on the same day. Do not agree to a completion date unless you are sure you can meet it.

If anything should go wrong for the seller's move into his new home, he cannot expect to remain in the old one: on the date of completion, the seller has to give you vacant possession, and to move out on or before that day with all furniture and belongings (except any being sold with the house).

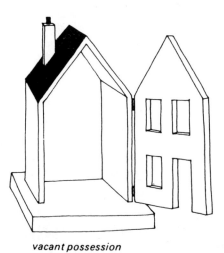

vacant possession

THE MONEY

On the day of completion, the buyer must be able to pay the remainder of the purchase price. The money for this may be coming from various sources made up from

○ anything left over after discharging your own mortgage from what your buyer (or his building society) pays for the house you are selling
○ your new mortgage loan (the building society or other lender's percentage of the purchase price of the house you are buying)
○ any top-up loan
○ a bridging loan if you have not completed your sale or there is a temporary shortfall
○ your own cash from savings.

From the total mortgage loan, the lender may deduct

○ the amount of the first premium for the buildings insurance policy
○ the premium for a mortgage indemnity policy if you had to take one out
○ the lender's solicitor's charges.

If the same solicitor is acting for you and the lender, he may further deduct from the amount of the advance his own fee and any disbursements – the charges he pays on your behalf, such as stamp duty and Land Registry fees, where applicable.

In case the remaining amount will be less than is needed to complete the purchase, ask the solicitor or conveyancer in good time what the deductions and final amount will come to, so that you can make the necessary arrangements to finance the shortfall.

The money you provide on completion day has to be allocated in the way it is needed: for example, a banker's draft payable to the person you are buying the house from and one payable to his mortgagee; where applicable, one to whoever has been providing your bridging loan.

You are charged interest from the date on which the loan leaves the lender (or, with some, the following day), even if you do not make use of it for a few days – so watch timing: do not get your advance too much in advance.

Q

My bank actually ensure that completion monies are paid to solicitor on day before completion to ensure no problems.

If you are getting an endowment mortgage, you will have to pay the first premium on the endowment policy and assign the policy to the lender – until that is done, the mortgagee will not advance the money.

For the money not coming from a mortgage, your solicitor or conveyancer will ask you either for a cheque made out to his firm in sufficient time to have it cleared so that he can draw a cheque on his firm's account for the money, or to make arrangements with your bank for a banker's draft to be prepared and sent to him. A banker's draft is a cheque signed by a bank manager, or one of his staff, on behalf of the bank instead of the customer; it cannot be revoked as a cheque can be and so is treated in practice as being equivalent to cash. A banker's draft supplied by the buyer of your house or his building society may then, if it is endorsed by the person to whom it is made payable – you or your solicitor – be passed on as payment for the house you are buying.

Some solicitors cope with the legal and administrative side by using modern technology to flash copies of documents and money from one side of the country to another.

When the final payments are made, the deeds will be handed over, including the conveyance or transfer to the buyer. You do not, however, get the title deeds of the property or a land certificate if you have a mortgage: the relevant documents are kept by the building society, or whoever is the lender, as security for the money being lent.

It is not usual for either the seller or the buyer to attend personally at the completion (unless they are doing their own conveyancing without a solicitor or conveyancer).

In the days leading up to completion, stay in touch with your solicitor or conveyancer, but get on with the move and let him take care of the rest.

Q

Move as slowly and deliberately as you can: do nothing in a hurry.

Buying a house in Scotland

There are major differences between Scottish and English law. This is particularly so in the law relating to the purchase and sale of houses and flats, and if you are moving from England to Scotland, while the practical aspects of the move are the same as they would be in England, you will find that the legal aspects are very different.

Prices of houses outwith the main cities and suburbs in Scotland are generally rather below the United Kingdom average. Properties in the hills of Scotland are relatively inexpensive, even when they are within easy commuting distance of a major city. But properties in the more sought-after residential areas in and around Edinburgh, Glasgow and Aberdeen command high prices.

The categories of houses available in Scotland are similar to those in England. Most older houses are built of stone with slate roofs and in the inner areas of the Scottish cities there is a good stock of flats, usually in purpose-built 'tenement' blocks.

A noticeable feature of the house market in Scotland is that the majority of property is sold by solicitors, not by estate agents; solicitors are allowed to call themselves "Solicitors and Estate Agents" and often do so.

finding out what is available

There are three main sources of information on properties for sale in Scotland:

○ newspapers
○ solicitors' property centres and solicitors' offices
○ estate agents.

A quarterly list of buildings of historic or architectural interest for sale in Scotland is available from the Scottish Development Department's **Historic Buildings Bureau for Scotland**, New St Andrew's House, St James Centre, Edinburgh EH1 3SZ (telephone 031-244 4405).

NEWSPAPERS

Advertisements in the English national daily and sunday newspapers for Scottish properties tend to cover a limited selection and do not give a realistic impression of the range of properties on the market. However, a wide range of properties for sale is advertised in the principal Scottish 'quality' daily news-papers and each has its main property day – *The Scotsman* (Edinburgh and the Lothians) on thursdays; the *Glasgow Herald* (Glasgow and Strathclyde) on tuesdays, the *Press and Journal* (Aberdeen and Grampian) on tuesdays and thursdays, *The Courier* (Dundee, Perth and Tayside) on thursdays. A good range of properties for sale is also advertised in the smaller local newspapers circulating in various districts.

SOLICITORS' PROPERTY CENTRES AND SOLICITORS' OFFICES

More properties in Scotland are sold by solicitors than by estate agents. This is particularly so in the Edinburgh, Aberdeen and Dundee areas and in many provincial centres, where the vast majority of houses are sold by solicitors and where solicitors' property centres have become established. These are run by solicitors on a co-operative basis and are situated in shopping areas. They provide details of all properties being sold by solicitors in the area. There is a solicitors' property centre in Berwick-upon-Tweed, unique in that it deals with properties for sale on both sides of the border – England and Scotland.

Most solicitors' property centres operate only as information centres and not as selling agents – the solicitors themselves retaining the selling role. The staff at a centre are not qualified solicitors, although generally conversant with house purchase and sale procedures. A customer who is interested in a property is directed to the solicitor actually selling it. All properties are displayed (most with photographs) and full estate agency-type particulars are available for each property, including the name of the solicitor handling the sale. The biggest centres, in Aberdeen and Edinburgh, each have several thousand properties on display at any one time.

Some solicitors' property centres publish regular property lists, most of them weekly, with full listings of all properties registered at the centre in question. Copies can be mailed to prospective purchasers if requested and are available from the particular centre and from all the solicitors practising in the area.

Solicitors' property centres are financed by subscriptions from their member solicitors and by charges made to sellers of property; the service is free to people looking there for property to buy.

A list of solicitors' property centres, with addresses and telephone numbers, is available from **The Law Society of Scotland**, 26 Drumsheugh Gardens, Edinburgh EH3 7YR (telephone 031-226 7411).

Some firms of solicitors have their own property department where details of available property are displayed and from whom you can obtain particulars of properties for sale. Many firms of solicitors employ specialist sales staff who deal with the non-legal aspects of buying and selling property.

ESTATE AGENTS

Until the mid-1960s, estate agents were rare in Scotland. Now an increasing number of estate agents have become established, particularly in the Glasgow area. One of the leading estate agents there is SEAL, owned by a group of solicitors.

The larger estate agencies issue regular property lists and most estate agents maintain mailing lists. Estate agents in Edinburgh have grouped together to publish a fortnightly property list *Real Homes* which is available through offices of its member firms.

Generally, estate agents in Scotland operate in the same way as those in England and the points to bear in mind when dealing with an estate agent in Scotland are the same.

Tenure

The term freehold is not used in Scotland. Most houses and flats, and indeed most other kinds of property, are owned on 'feudal tenure'. For practical purposes, this means that they are owned absolutely and can be disposed of freely in the same way as freehold land and property in England. The property offered for sale is often referred to in Scotland as 'the feu'.

The main distinguishing feature of a feu is that the original developer of the land or estate owner, who is known as the superior, can impose conditions on its future use – for instance, by prohibiting commercial use, extensions or alterations without his consent. It is also usual for the superior to require the maintenance of the property in good condition and reinstatement following damage or destruction.

Once feuing conditions have been imposed, they remain in force in perpetuity unless the superior agrees to waive or modify them. Any purchaser will be bound by the feuing conditions, but it may be possible, once he has bought the property, to negotiate with the superior for a waiver. Normally, the superior charges a capital payment for agreeing to waive feuing conditions. If a superior refuses to vary unreasonable conditions, or if the existence of a condition impedes some reasonable use of land, the owner (or 'feuar') can apply to the Lands Tribunal for Scotland for an order to vary them. A leaflet on land obligations and how they may be varied or discharged, and the fees payable, is obtainable from the **Lands Tribunal for Scotland**, 1 Grosvenor Crescent, Edinburgh EH12 5ER (telephone 031-225 7996). If you think that you may be justified in seeking such an order, it would be wise to consult your solicitor in the first instance.

In the past, the feuar paid an annual cash sum or 'feuduty' to the superior. Since 1974, the creation of new feuduties has been prohibited, and the feuar is obliged to redeem the feuduty when he sells his property. This means that the majority of feuduties have ceased to exist. The feuing conditions, however, still apply even if the feuduty has been redeemed.

FLATS

Flats are owned absolutely on feudal tenure, in the same way as houses, rather than on long leases as is the practice in England; long leases of residential property in Scotland are rare. In the case of flats, the *solum* (the ground on which the block of flats is built), the roof, stairs and common services are normally owned by the proprietors in the block equally or on some other equitable basis. The external walls bounding each flat are owned by the proprietor of it but all the proprietors have an interest to see that they are properly maintained. The title deeds normally set out the basis on which the costs of repairs and maintenance are shared between the various owners.

Buying procedure

The Building Societies Association issues a booklet *Building societies and house purchase in Scotland* which describes and explains the process of house purchase in a step-by-step way; available free from the BSA, 3 Savile Row, London W1X 1AF (send 39p s.a.e. 10in × 7in).

You will need a solicitor. Although in theory you could do-it-yourself, it is not considered practicable to do your own conveyancing in Scotland.

If you do not know a solicitor, the best recommendation may be that of a friend or colleague who has used one for this type of work and who can give you a personal introduction. English solicitors are not permitted to practise in Scotland, but if you are moving from England, your English solicitor may have a Scottish solicitor with whom he deals regularly. A *Directory of General Services* issued by the Law Society of Scotland, giving the names, addresses and telephone numbers of solicitors, is available at citizens advice bureaux and libraries. Also, you will find a full list of solicitors in Yellow Page directories.

The Law Society of Scotland publishes brochures explaining the role of solicitors in buying a house and selling a house.

You should ask your solicitor, at the outset, to give you an estimate of his fees and the outlays (disbursements) he will have to make. There is no scale of fees so you can shop around for competitive estimates.

THE PRICE

The general practice in Scotland is to present a property for sale at 'offers over' a stated figure (often referred to as the 'upset price'). Depending on the demand for the particular property, the price eventually achieved may be considerably higher; it is rare for a purchaser to acquire a property at the asking price, let alone below it.

Sometimes houses are offered for sale at a fixed price. This may be because a quick sale is sought or because earlier attempts to sell at an 'offers over' price have been unsuccessful. Where you want to buy a house which is offered for sale at a fixed price, you should be ready to proceed very quickly, since the first acceptable offer at the stated price will secure the house.

THE HOUSE YOU WANT

When you see a house which you think suitable, tell your solicitor immediately. You can discuss with the seller the price, the date of entry and what contents such as carpets, curtains, kitchen equipment, etcetera, may be included in the sale. An oral agreement for the sale of land and houses cannot create a binding contract and can be repudiated by either party without any consequences. But you should never write letters or sign any document relating to a sale or purchase without consulting your solicitor.

When you tell your solicitor that you are interested in buying a particular property, the first thing he will do is to telephone the seller's solicitor or estate agent to notify him of your interest. The seller's solicitor or estate agent will give you a chance to offer, once your interest has been notified, although he is not legally obliged to do so.

MORTGAGE LOAN

If you have not already made your loan arrangements, the next thing to do is to arrange with a building society, bank or other source of finance, to lend you the money you need to borrow. If you have difficulty in finding a loan, your solicitor will probably be able to help you.

It is wise to make sure at an early stage that the necessary loan finance will be available when it is needed. Most of the leading English building societies and banks, and all the Scottish banks, will lend on the security of Scottish properties, and there are a number of home-based Scottish building societies.

Even before you have a specific house in mind, you should establish that the amount you require will be available on the type of property which you are seeking and that it will be available when you want it – subject always to a satisfactory survey report on the chosen house.

SURVEY

In Scotland, it is customary to have a survey carried out before you make an offer for a property. (This means that if your offer is unsuccessful, you will have wasted the survey fee.) Offers made 'subject to survey' are uncommon, especially if there are competing offers for a property, but occasionally such an offer is acceptable depending on market conditions and the condition of the property itself.

The survey is usually instructed by your solicitor once he is informed that you are interested and wish to go ahead.

Q

Things move so quickly that you really have to have your loan agreed in principle beforehand.

Q

Nobody in their right mind buys without a survey and you won't get a loan without one. If your offer is accepted, you are bound to purchase and it is too late to discover defects or that you can't get a loan on it.

The range of types of survey is similar to that in England. The briefest and cheapest is the building society survey which is little more than a mortgage valuation; the home (or flat) buyer's report gives a wider range of fairly standard information; a full structural survey normally costs much more and is rarely instructed in Scotland.

A building society valuation is undertaken merely for the purpose of satisfying the building society that the house or flat will provide suitable security for their loan to you. The survey is commissioned by the building society which is making the loan and although it is you who pays the surveyor's fee, he will generally not accept professional liability to you. The surveyor or building society will tell your solicitor whether the property in question is suitable for the loan which you require. They normally will also tell you the valuation placed on it, and the main points about the condition of the property. Many building societies now make a practice of giving the borrower a brief written survey report or a copy of the surveyor's report.

A recent decision of the Court of Session indicates that surveyors owe a duty of care not only to the lender but also to the borrower (see Martin v Bell-Ingram 1986 SLT 575).

Making an offer

If the survey report is favourable, the next thing to do is to make an offer to buy the property. It is the usual practice to ask your solicitor to make the offer for you. This is done by a formal letter from your solicitor to the seller's solicitor or estate agent.

An offer is a formal document, usually a letter running to several pages, or sometimes a shorter letter with a schedule of conditions attached. It specifies all the conditions on which you are willing to buy the property.

In making the offer, you will have to decide, with guidance from your solicitor, how much to pay. You should also be clear when you want to move in and what extras you want to buy. If you are the only person interested in the property, your solicitor may be able to find this out from the seller's solicitor or estate agent and may be able to negotiate an acceptable price.

If more than one person is interested in buying the same property, the seller's solicitor or estate agent will normally fix a closing date, intimating to each person interested that offers must be submitted by a stated time on a stated date. You will have to offer 'blind' without knowing how much other people

Q

Guessing what the most acceptable price will be – prices quoted as 'offers over' usually means another 10% to 15% on the price noted.

I feel that it is worth while having a solicitor who knows the market in the area and the seller's solicitor.

Q

Dislike the 'offers over' system some people adopt and would rather know the real asking price – however, Scotland's system of "once the offer is accepted, it's yours" is streets ahead of England and Wales.

will offer. (This is one of the disadvantages of the Scottish system since there may be quite a large gap between the highest and the next highest offers.) It is not possible to get round this by making a bid of "£100 more than the highest offer you receive".

Your solicitor will normally help you decide how much over the asking price you should offer (he probably has access to information about prices achieved for similar properties to guide you in making your decision; the solicitor's knowledge of the market locally is important and usually helpful to you). But the final decision will be yours.

DATE OF ENTRY

Stating the date on which you want to move in is part of your formal offer. Whether this is acceptable is largely governed by when the seller wants to move out. The date of entry is a matter for negotiation between you and the seller: it also depends on how long it will take to arrange the conveyancing formalities and complete your loan. If there are no compelling reasons on either side for a very early or very far-off date of entry, the period between making the offer and moving in is typically between one and two months.

EXTRAS

What extras, such as carpets, curtains, kitchen equipment, etcetera, you wish to purchase may be a relevant factor if there is some competition for the house and one prospective purchaser is offering a better price than another for the contents. Sale particulars normally specify what is, and what is not, included in the price and your offer will normally be drawn up accordingly.

If the extra items included in your price are valuable, you may want to allocate part of the price on them – for example, house £45,000, moveable property £3,000 – as this will give you a small saving in stamp duty. For stamp duty to be saved, the items must be moveable. Heritable fittings and fixtures (fitted kitchens, built-in bedroom furniture etcetera) are transferred by the disposition which will therefore contain a statement of the value of the building + heritable fittings and fixtures.

The remaining conditions of the offer are taken up with technical legal matters such as ensuring that you will receive a good marketable title, that the property is not adversely affected by planning proposals, that structural alterations/extensions have received local authority approval and that you can withdraw from the contract if the house and contents included in the sale are not in substantially the same condition when you move in as when you offered for them.

If there is some special use to which you want to put the property, such as using part of it as an office or as a guest house, or if you plan to make major alterations, you must tell your solicitor so that he can include conditions in the offer to make sure that there are no relevant prohibitions in the title. If you are planning alterations or a change of use, you may have to make the offer conditional upon obtaining planning and/or building control permission. Sellers are not very keen on such offers but sometimes they are unavoidable.

Concluding the contract

If a closing date has been fixed and there is more than one offer, the seller and his solicitor or estate agent will consider all the offers made and decide which one, if any, to accept. Although the highest offer is normally accepted, the seller can, and sometimes does, take other factors into consideration, such as the date of entry proposed and the extras to be included in the sale.

Your solicitor will usually be informed by the seller's solicitor or estate agent, by telephone, within an hour or so after the closing time, whether your offer has been successful.

Before concluding the contract, your solicitor will check with the local authority whether there are any proposals, orders or notices which might adversely affect the property. If this information cannot be readily obtained, the contract will be made conditional on no adverse matters being disclosed. If there are planning restrictions – for example, if the building is listed as being of architectural or historic interest – make sure that your solicitor explains to you exactly what this means in law and in practice.

An oral acceptance is not legally binding; usually the selling solicitor will deliver an acceptance modifying or adjusting some of the terms of your offer, such as the date of entry, or making provision for payment of interest on the price of the house if settlement of the price on the date of entry is delayed through no fault of the seller, and to what extent (if any) the contract to be

Q

I bought my second home in less than 24 hours: saw it in the evening, next morning arranged immediate survey, offer in by deadline of 3pm, accepted by 3.15.

concluded will form a continuing contract after the date of entry. This is called a qualified acceptance and is often delivered within a day of receipt of the offer. If the modifications are acceptable to you (your solicitor will advise you on this) your solicitor sends a letter to the selling solicitor confirming that a binding contract is concluded. This is usually done within a day or so of receipt of the qualified acceptance. Thus, the contract can be concluded within a few days of making the offer.

When matters of detail have been adjusted between the two solicitors, final letters are exchanged between them which create a legally binding contract. These are known in Scotland as the 'missives'. This is the equivalent to the stage of exchange of contracts in England or Wales. But the solicitor makes the offer and concludes missives on the buyer's behalf: there is nothing for you to sign.

Except in the case of new properties purchased from a builder, deposits are not paid in Scotland on the conclusion of missives, the full price being payable on the date of entry in exchange for the keys and the titles.

Whether your offer is successful or not, you know where you stand in the matter very quickly. This is an advantage to the purchaser in the Scottish house-buying system.

INSURANCE

At common law in Scotland the purchaser becomes responsible for insurance of the property from the date when missives are concluded. It is, however, now usual for the missives to provide that the seller will remain liable for any damage to the property until the date of entry, and for its insurance until that date, and that the purchaser can withdraw from the purchase without penalty if the house and any extras included in the sale are seriously damaged or destroyed before the date of entry.

Completing the purchase

Once missives have been concluded, your solicitor will put in hand examination of the title and the conveyancing procedures to ensure that the conveyance (or 'disposition') in your favour is ready for delivery by the date of entry in exchange for payment of the price.

Q

Move to Scotland – much better system, except that the survey valuation has to be accurate so that the offer can be pitched correctly.

MORTGAGE

As soon as the missives have been concluded, you should complete your loan application papers if you have not already done so.

If you are borrowing from a building society, bank or other lender, your solicitor normally acts for the lender as well as for you. He will report to the lender on the title and prepare the necessary mortgage documents, called a 'standard security'. He will also arrange for the loan money to be available in time for the date of entry, and will ask you to sign the mortgage documents by that date.

If you are in any doubt about the terms of the mortgage documents, ask your solicitor to explain them to you before you sign them. Almost all such documents prohibit letting of the property without the lender's consent. They also set out detailed conditions about maintenance, insurance, and so on, and give the lender a wide range of remedies, including the right to sell the house, if you fail to maintain your payments or otherwise fail to observe the loan conditions.

The building society's or other lender's cheque will be sent to your solicitor before the date of entry and he will ask you to pay him the difference between the price and your mortgage loan. If you are selling another house, whether in Scotland or England, and you are relying on the money from the sale, you should make bridging loan arrangements at an early stage and tell your solicitor.

DOCUMENTS

On the date of settlement, your solicitor will meet the seller's solicitor and hand over a cheque for the full price in return for the title deeds, including the disposition in your favour.

Your solicitor will register the disposition and the mortgage document in the General Register of Sasines or, if your property is in an area where registration of title has been introduced, in the Land Register of Scotland. If there is a mortgage on the property, the title documents will be held by the building society, bank or other lender.

If there is no mortgage, your solicitor will hand the title deeds over to you once the registration process has been completed. He may offer to hold them in safe custody for you, for which there should be no charge.

SOLICITORS' CHARGES

After completing the purchase (or sometimes before doing so) your solicitor will send you his account for his fees and outlays (disbursements). Solicitors in Scotland do not charge according to fixed scales.

In addition to the solicitor's fees for the preliminary work leading up to and concluding missives, the conveyancing and the mortgage (on all of which you will have to pay VAT), there will be stamp duty of 1% of the price if it is over £30,000, and registration dues at the rate of £11 per £5,000 or part of £5,000 of price in the Register of Sasines (the same plus £10 in the Land Register) and £7 on the mortgage deed if it is registered at the same time as your disposition.

Outlays must be paid on the date of entry; the solicitor may agree to accept payment of fees a month later or to have payment by instalments.

Ownership

The title to a property can be taken in the names of more than one person – for instance, husband and wife. The rights of common owners, the size of their respective shares and what happens to each share on the death of one of the owners depends on the manner in which the title is taken. Where the title specifies several people as owners, whether they are spouses or not, each owns a separate and distinct share. During life, unless the right to do so has been waived, each can dispose of his share or can demand that the whole property be sold and his share of the proceeds paid to him. After death, the share of each passes in accordance with his will or the laws of intestate succession.

The Matrimonial Homes (Family Protection) (Scotland) Act 1981 severely restricts these rights where co-owners are a married couple.

In addition to specifying several people as owners, it is quite common for two owners, particularly spouses, to take the title in the name of each of them and the survivor. This, however, raises a number of questions upon which legal advice should be sought before the title is completed.

When considering the title, it is advisable to consult your solicitor about making a will (or reviewing your will if you already have one). A will made in England is normally recognised as valid in Scotland and vice versa.

SUCCESSION

If you buy a house in Scotland intending it as your residence or principal residence, you will acquire Scottish domicile. This may affect, amongst other things, the way your property is inherited on your death.

If you die without a will, Scottish law will regulate the distribution of your heritable property (that is, land and buildings) in Scotland and moveable property (all property other than 'heritable') in Scotland and elsewhere.

If you die leaving a will, it regulates the distribution of your estate, but the provisions of your will are subject to Scottish rules of succession which differ in a number of important respects from English law. The most important difference is that a spouse and children cannot be cut out of the succession to the moveable estate no matter what the will may say. They are always entitled to their 'legal rights' which, depending on the circumstances, may be either one-third or one-half of the net moveable estate.

With heritable property (land and buildings), regardless of the domicile of the owner, succession is governed by the law of the country in which the property is. So even if only a holiday home is bought in Scotland, so that there is no question of the buyer thereby acquiring Scottish domicile, the succession to heritable property in Scotland is governed by Scottish law.

In Scotland, a will is not automatically revoked if the person making it subsequently marries, nor are provisions in favour of a spouse automatically revoked on divorce.

Selling your house

You can decide either to handle the sale yourself or to commission one or more estate agents to make the arrangements on your behalf.

Q

D-i-y sale is more difficult than it appears unless you are prepared to spend the time and money any successful marketing job requires.

An agent will do some of the work for you but you must be prepared for this to cost considerably more than if you do it all yourself. Without an agent, you will be spending your time rather than money – and at a time when you are probably occupied with buying as well as selling a house. It may not take longer to find a buyer privately than if you engage an estate agent, but it could do.

If there is new industrial or office development imminent and a firm is likely to be importing new staff, these will probably do their house searching through an agent. Locals contemplating a change, on the other hand, have more opportunity for studying local newspapers and any 'For Sale' boards.

If you advertise your house extensively and do not manage to sell it, you may have difficulty persuading an agent to take over from you. This is not a matter of agents' pique or jealousy but of their practical experience that a house known to have been on the market for a long time acquires a reputation of being unsaleable, with the suspicion that there must be something wrong about it somewhere – even if this is unwarranted.

Selling without an agent

If you want to sell your house privately, these are the steps you will have to take:

○ decide on an asking price
○ decide what items are to be included in the sale, and prices for them
○ draft an advertisement
○ choose the right newspapers or magazine, and place the advertisement
○ decide whether to put up a 'For Sale' board; if so, make (or buy) one and put it up
○ draw up the particulars to give to potential buyers
○ answer all enquiries
○ arrange the appointments to view the house
○ show round all viewers
○ evaluate merits of rival bids
○ negotiate a final price with the buyer you choose.

Q

Check house prices prior to placing on market – the first estate agent suggested a price of £6,500 less than the second agent; the higher price was the price asked and offered by the first prospective buyer.

Q

I used two local estate agents initially for a valuation for selling my house. They were both very seriously wrong: one was £20,000, the other £24,000 out on my sale price (undervalued). I consider their performance very bad, and very glad I did not employ them.

fixing a price

It is not always easy for a do-it-yourself seller to be as knowledgeable as a local estate agent on what would be the right price to ask. An agent's expertise lies in knowing current market trends, what similar local property is selling for, and in judging what would be an attractive but proper price for a particular house and any of its contents.

If your house is one of several similar ones – in a post-war estate, for example – it is easier to judge a price than if it is an older one which may be in a better or worse state of repair and redecoration than neighbouring ones, or a house for which there is no comparable one in the immediate area.

To find out current asking prices in the neighbourhood, study notices in local estate agents' windows and advertisements in local papers for similar houses. Remember that the price being asked is not necessarily the figure at which the property gets sold.

It is not always reliable to believe what neighbours or friends report were the sale prices of neighbouring properties.

The condition of the house itself ought to be considered before deciding on a price. If there are any repairs or redecorations needed, should these be carried out before putting the house on the market or should the price be pitched a little lower to allow for these shortcomings? On the whole, it probably repays doing obvious repairs and having the house in a reasonable state of decoration, so that you do not have to reduce your price. But you have to assess the type of house you are selling and who you think would be interested in buying it. Would they be more likely to want to pay less and do their own repairs and redecorations? Younger buyers who want to rely on a large mortgage may prefer this. Older or perhaps retired purchasers might want to buy a house which they could move into straightaway with a minimum of disturbance.

VALUATION

You can ask a local estate agent to give you a valuation for your house. If you are not selling through him, he may charge: ask first what his charge would be. If you do decide to have a valuation, make it clear that you are asking for a valuation – not instructing him to sell. It is advisable to get the arrangement and fee confirmed in writing.

If you are uncertain about the saleability of your house – whether there are structural problems that could deflate the price or make it difficult to sell – ask a surveyor to look over the house. His survey may reveal one or more faults which would justify a buyer in asking for some reduction on account of them. If so, build into your asking price some allowance for this and keep in mind what figure would finally be acceptable. If, however, you make clear to potential buyers any defects you are aware of, you should not have to reduce the price because of them later.

BARGAINING

Make the asking price as attractive a figure as possible: £64,500 is better than £65,000. It is sensible to set the asking price higher than the one you expect to settle for, so that there is some room for manoeuvre. If you want a quick sale and think a little bargaining will attract a buyer, you can quote a figure and add o.n.o. (or near offer) – and wait for one. Any buyer hopes to start negotiating at a somewhat lower figure than he is prepared to settle for and each party may finally decide to reach a compromise.

The buyer may ask for a reduction because you are not having to pay an agent's commission on the sale, or may try to get as many extras as possible included in the price.

FOR INCLUSION IN THE SALE

You may have included in the asking price any items in the house which you wish to sell with it. Or a separate price can be asked and negotiated for these. In either case, as the seller, you should be quite clear about what will be regarded as fixtures and what you are entitled to take away with you.

You should also consider which items belong to you rather than the house but which it would be more sensible or convenient to sell with it, such as a washing machine or dishwasher already plumbed in, the refrigerator or cooker.

If the kitchen contains units constructed to house a particular size or brand of equipment, it may be more sensible to leave these where they are. As a selling item, a well-fitted kitchen comes high on most people's list and to remove specially designed equipment could be shortsighted. A decision on this may also depend on whether you know yet what you need in your new kitchen.

Made-to-measure curtains, perhaps with matching pelmets, are often best sold with a house since they are unlikely to fit satisfactorily into a different one, and adapting them may be uneconomic. Similarly, all fitted carpets are better left in position, for the next owner. What condition they are in should be taken into account when fixing a secondhand price for them. Bear in mind also what the buyer is saving by not having to buy new carpeting.

FIXTURES

By law, you must sell as part of the house anything that is a fixture (unless it is specifically agreed between buyer and seller that particular fixtures are excluded). There are two legal tests for determining whether or not something is a fixture:

● *the degree of annexation of the object*
In other words, is the article so firmly fixed that to remove it would cause substantial damage either to the fabric of the house or to the article itself? By this test, wallpaper, fireplaces, central heating system and suchlike are fixtures.

This first test, however, may not be helpful in the case of much modern built-in furniture which can be dismantled and removed without damage to itself or to the fabric of the house. To cope with such cases, there is an alternative test·

● *the purpose of annexation*
In other words, was the article added to the property for the permanent improvement of the property or merely the better enjoyment of the article itself? The distinction is frequently a very fine one. One type of gas fire, for example, with mantelpiece and bookshelves, would be a fixture, while another, attached only by the gas pipe supplying it, would be removable.

There may be items in the 'grey' area – special curtain rails, for example, wall light fittings, wardrobes or bookshelves built specifically to fit a wall or corner. Decide whether removing them would cause damage which would have to be made good and whether they are more likely to add to the value of the house if sold with it.

LIST OF ITEMS FOR SALE

When you have reviewed house and garden, and decided what to sell, you should make a list, pricing items according to their quality, original cost, age and current condition. When it comes to showing the house to viewers, point out these items specifically.

To avoid misunderstandings or subsequent queries, it may be worth your while to duplicate a list of any items which you are selling separately, together with other information about the house, on the lines of the 'particulars' which estate agents draw up.

When it comes to final negotiations with your buyer, you may find that he does not want some of the items you want to sell. He is quite entitled to reject these but, if you want to stand firm, you are in a stronger position than he is – if he wants the house badly enough, he may feel obliged to buy the contents you offer.

Drafting an advertisement

An advertisement should include the following basic information:

> type of house (e.g. detached, semi, terraced, bungalow) or flat (e.g. purpose-built, maisonette, block, converted house)
> location
> number of bedrooms
> number of living rooms
> number of bathrooms/separate wc
> heating system
> garage
> garden
> freehold or leasehold
> price
> telephone number for appointments to view
> possibly also the number of floors, rateable value and any desirable amenities such as, for instance, nearness to station.

If there are some special features which are out of the ordinary or which would make good selling points, include these so as to give as attractive picture of the house as possible.

Find out how much the newspaper or magazine in which you are proposing to advertise charges per line or entry, so that you can work out how much you can

Q

Advertise where you would look for a similar property (usually local papers).

afford to say in the advertisement. It would be unwise to skimp on it. You need to draft as comprehensive and attractive an entry as possible.

There are certain space-saving abbreviations which are customary in property advertisements, and costs can be cut by using these. Some of the more common ones are:

CH	= central heating		p.b.	= purpose built
CHW	= constant hot water		conv	= converted
FH	= freehold		rec	= reception
GR	= ground rent		kit/brkrm	= kitchen/breakfast room
WC	= loo		clk	= cloakroom
gge	= garage		exc. con.	= excellent condition
rm	= room		c & c	= carpets and curtains
lge	= large		f & f	= fixtures and fittings
det	= detached		o.n.o.	= or near offer

Using too many of these abbreviations will condense the entry to such a degree that it becomes virtually unreadable, and certainly not eye-catching. Compare the following two advertisements (2 ads) both for the same house:

Arch. des. det. hse. 1975. 4 lge bdrms, 2 bath, 2 WC, 30 ft sit rm, sep d/rm, study, mod. kit/brkrm. gas CH. Dble gge. patio. $\frac{1}{4}$ acre walled gdn. £00,000 FH. Tel . . . .

Architect-designed house, detached. Built 1975 in wooded area 10 mins from town centre, standing in $\frac{1}{4}$ acre of own ground. 4 large bedrooms one with bathroom ensuite; 1 other bathroom, 2 WCs, sitting room 30′ × 14′ with picture window on to patio, separate dining room, study; kitchen recently modernised, pine wall units and breakfast area. Gas CH. Double glazing throughout. Double garage. Well-stocked walled garden. Freehold £00,000. Tel . . . .

If the house, in your opinion, is particularly photogenic and a photo with the advertisement would greatly help to sell it, find out how much this would cost before you start taking one or commissioning a photographer to do so. Small black and white reproductions in newspapers do not always turn out very clear and so may not justify the expense.

Where you place the advertisement will depend on what kind of house (or flat) you have for sale and where you live. You will know what local papers there are. These are usually the best place to start, unless you are selling the kind of property that would be best advertised in one of the national dailies or glossy magazines or the sunday papers. It is unlikely that one entry will be sufficient. Check if there are reduced rates for a series of entries and whether you can cancel within a specified time if you book more than you find you need.

DISPLAYING A NOTICE

Do not forget the corner shop or newsagent's where you can put up a card in the window. People in the locality may be looking out on behalf of friends or relatives who want to be near them. If there is a university or technical college in your town, or a hospital nearby, send a note to the accommodation or personnel officer or bursar, with details of your house for sale.

You may be able to use a 'property shop' in your area. You have to fill in a fairly detailed form giving information about the property and allow it to be photographed. You pay a fee for the details and photograph of your house to be displayed in the 'shop'; some shops charge per week for displaying property, most include indefinite display in their initial charge. The seller and any interested purchasers get in touch with each other direct and negotiate individually. There is no commission to pay on a sale.

In a few places, solicitors' property centres have been set up by local solicitors. At such a centre, details of properties are shown and one of the centre's solicitors undertakes the selling transaction for you. The fee you are charged is based on the selling price of your house and includes display of the property and the conveyancing. The **National Association of Solicitors' Property Centres** (30 Station Road, Cuffley, Herts EN6 4HE) can tell you where solicitors' property centres are.

'For Sale' board

Most people when looking for a new home, drive or walk around an area to get an impression of it. So, a board outside your house is quite likely to attract some viewers. If you make your own board, it need not be elaborate:

> **FOR SALE**
> **APPLY WITHIN**

may be enough, but it should be eye-catching.

There are disadvantages in advertising in this way. You may not wish a neighbour or employer (should he live nearby) to know that you are moving away. Some people feel that a 'For Sale' sign is an invitation to would-be burglars to view a house before planning a break-in.

Since callers may arrive without warning or appointment, you have to be prepared to show them around the house at any time, whether it is convenient or not, and to keep the house looking at its best at all times.

You can buy a 'Self-Sell' kit (£24.99 from Partyline, 216-218 Homesdale Road, Bromley, Kent BR1 2QZ) which includes a plastic weatherproof 'For Sale' board (21in × 18in), a sheet of self-adhesive figures to stick on for your telephone number, 'apply within' as an alternative, cards to put in newsagents' windows, change of address cards, checklist, leaflet guide.

drafting your own particulars

It will help to sell your house if you prepare a set of particulars along similar lines to those of an estate agent. Get hold of a few sets of estate agents' particulars so that you can see how they do it. There is no set form but most particulars include:

- the address of the house, and your telephone number
- a general description of the house and its setting
- a detailed description of each room, including details of such things as power points, telephone sockets, radiators, decorative features, built-in cupboards; put in the dimensions (make sure your measurements are accurate)

Q

If you are a lady living alone, or elderly, then it is unwise to erect a board, for reasons of security and peace of mind.

○ a description of the outside including garden, garage, fuel store; any special features such as patio, toolshed or greenhouse
○ essential information: the rateable value (and actual rates payable); details of which mains services are connected
○ the price
○ directions to find the house (nearest public transport).

Your particulars should be typed. Keep the original and send out photocopies. To give them a professional look, you can stick on a colour photograph of the house.

Do not include in your particulars any items which are excluded from the sale. If you want to keep your options open, you might say at the end of the particulars "The greenhouse (for instance) is not included in the sale but may be purchased by separate negotiation".

If planning permission has recently been granted for an improvement – a conversion or extension, perhaps, or a garage – which has not yet been carried out, do not forget to mention this.

ANSWERING ENQUIRIES

Once you have advertised the house and quoted a telephone number, you ought to arrange for someone to be on hand to answer any enquiries. (If you are available only during evenings and weekends, say so in the advertisement.) Keep a pad by the telephone to record names and times of appointments – you will probably find it easier to deal with one viewer at a time. You must be prepared to abandon whatever other plans you may have and spend perhaps half-an-hour or more showing the callers round.

You may find it difficult at first to assess would-be buyers – who is genuine and who is just curious. It is not easy for you to quiz people on their financial status. But you can ask whether they are – or likely to be – in a chain.

Selling through an estate agent

The advantages of using estate agents to sell your home are:

○ they take some of the work and worry off the shoulders of the seller
○ they have more experience in judging the market value of a house and how best it should be sold (and whether by private treaty or auction)
○ they have better facilities for publicising the sale, and ready access to more would-be buyers
○ they offer better security – for example, an elderly person or someone living alone can ask for the agent's representative to accompany all viewers
○ they can ask if an interested buyer has adequate means or mortgage facilities already arranged and will – if required, negotiate a mortgage on behalf of a buyer.

The agent's prime concern is to achieve a speedy and, as far as possible, a trouble-free sale, for all parties concerned. If an applicant's 'buying power' is established at the outset, it is to the benefit of all concerned. Agents have access to mortgage funds from a variety of sources.

The use of computers by groups of estate agents is increasing. Your property is fed into the multi-list computer system and is then available to all agents participating in the scheme, who can offer the property immediately to prospective buyers over a wide area.

finding an agent

If you have already found a house to buy through an agent, do you then go on to ask the same agent to sell yours? There is something to be said for doing this: the agent will have more to lose if he cannot sell your house. But be careful that the agent does not down-value your house in order to achieve (effectively) two quick sales.

What you need to know about local estate agents is

○ what type of property they sell
○ whether they belong to one of the professional associations
○ the extent of the services offered
○ on what basis they charge and what is included.

Q

The estate agent I chose worked on a fixed price for his services, £500 including advertising, and it was therefore in his interest to have the sale concluded as quickly as possible. I made the mistake of telling him what my minimum price would be and he got it for me within three days. I suspect that I could have had more but everyone probably thinks that. He arranged and conducted all the viewing so I have no complaints about how he performed.

Q

Having made an offer for a house before putting existing property up for sale, we then found it difficult to sell. There was continual pressure from vendors who wanted to put their house back on the market.

Q

Beware: it is not unknown for estate agents (especially those just starting out) to pay for the right to have 'Sold' signs put into people's gardens at strategic places (like the main road into town).

Studying the shop windows, the newspaper advertising and the display boards of different estate agents will give an idea of what business they handle, how extensive it is, and whether it covers a special market or deals with all types of housing. The style and flavour of the text may reflect the style of the firm.

The number of 'For Sale' boards in the area reflects agents' activities and the number of 'Sold' stickers their effectiveness. But some local associations of estate agents agree that none of their members shall erect 'For Sale' boards, and the local authority may impose restrictions.

The Town & Country Planning (Control of Advertisements) Regulations control the display of 'For Sale' boards. Estate agents are obliged to conform to the rule permitting for each property one board, not exceeding $0.5m^2$ in area, or a joined board not exceeding $0.6m^2$ in area. Advertisement consent is required for more than one or for a larger board.

Most estate agents belong to one or other of the professional associations: the Royal Institution of Chartered Surveyors (RICS), the Incorporated Society of Valuers and Auctioneers (ISVA), the National Association of Estate Agents (NAEA), the Faculty of Architects and Surveyors (FAS), the Incorporated Association of Architects and Surveyors (IAAS). They have codes of conduct for their members who have to participate in indemnity schemes protecting the public from fraud. The qualifying letters which would be shown on the letter heading or name plate of a reputable firm of estate agents are FRICS or ARICS, FSVA or ASVA, FNAEA or ANAEA, FFS or AFS, FIAAS or AIAAS.

Be wary of unqualified estate agents; some of these people are not particularly scrupulous. Estate agents do not have to be registered to carry on business, but if convicted or found in breach of certain obligations under the Estate Agents Act 1979, they can, in the last resort, be prohibited from doing estate agency work by order of the Director General of Fair Trading. Any complaints should initially be made to the local authority trading standards department.

Q

How can my estate agent justify a bill of over £1,000 for taking one picture, writing brief details and 6 letters and introducing a couple of clients – it's an absolute rip-off!

THE AGENT'S INSPECTION

Ask someone from the estate agents to call to look at the house. It is a good thing to ask specifically who will be dealing with your house and to meet him or

Q

Get several valuations from local experts when offering your house for sale. My house was undervalued by both myself and the estate agent and as a result we had over 90 visits for viewing and the house was finally sold for considerably more than the asking price (17%).

Q

If buying from a couple who are going through a divorce, try and find out as many facts about them wanting to move and when, before buying their house. We got caught up in a lot of ill feeling between the couple.

her personally at the outset. (Do not necessarily expect the senior partner to deal with you.)

The agent should make a thorough inspection in order to be able to assess the value of the house, taking into account its position and condition. You can then discuss with him, and get his advice on, what would be a suitable and attractive asking price – not necessarily the same figure as the valuation. (If you seek advice from more than one agent, do not necessarily give instructions to the one who suggests the highest asking price. It could just be a not very ethical ploy to get your instructions.)

He should take measurements of rooms, and note other details such as heating, special features and so on, for the description he is going to circulate. You should have ready for him details of rates, any ground rent payable and any service or maintenance charges.

If you want him to, he will offer advice on which items to leave in the house, what price to ask for them, and whether to carry out renovations.

Get the agent to tell you what arrangements he proposes to make for advertising the property. These could be

○ insertion in the agent's list of houses for sale, fed into a computer, mailed to buyers on his register or handed out at his office
○ a special circular dealing only with your property
○ an advertisement in a local, regional or national paper or magazines.

The agent may arrange for photographs to be taken for publicity purposes. The cost of a specially printed brochure, with photographs, may not be included in his fee, and you should check what this cost will be.

If there are any special circumstances (such as that you are selling because of financial problems or a marriage breakdown), tell the agent; point out that there could be circumstances where, through no fault of your own, you may have to abandon the sale.

An energetic agent will return to his office, draft the particulars, print them out and mail them – often on the same day. Also, he may telephone any buyer he thinks would be interested who might visit even before seeing the particulars.

Agents do not necessarily confirm with the seller (or even show him) the house description or an advertisement. You should say if you want to vet the text before it is printed or duplicated. It is worth doing so, even if it causes a day's delay, to make sure that the particulars are accurate.

The estate agent's fee

Under the Estate Agents Act 1979, you must be told in advance in what circumstances an estate agent will charge you and what his fee will be (or at least how it will be worked out) and you must be told if the estate agent or any of his associates has a personal interest in the transaction.

Estate agents generally base their fees on the selling price of the house. The most common commissions are $1\frac{1}{2}$ or 2 per cent, or even $2\frac{1}{2}$ per cent, of the final selling price. An agent may operate a sliding scale, charging, say, $2\frac{1}{2}$ per cent on the first £20,000 of the selling price, $1\frac{1}{2}$ per cent on the rest. An agent sometimes charges a flat fee, irrespective of the selling price.

It is worth shopping around; it is possible to negotiate a fee.

Even where an estate agent has approached you direct asking if you are willing to sell because he has a client anxious to buy your house, he will charge you his commission if you do so.

SOLE AGENCY?

You may instruct more than one agent to sell your house, but an agent may reduce his fee if you grant him sole agency – this means that you put your property exclusively into his hands. It is quite common to give one agent sole agency for a limited period – say, six weeks. If, after the agreed time, no buyer has been found, you can appoint another agent instead of or in addition to the first. In any period of sole agency, it is important not to instruct another agent or you may find yourself having to pay commission to both.

There should be a clear agreement on what basis the agent will receive his commission: namely, that he introduced the buyer who actually completes the purchase. Do not undertake to pay commission to an agent for introducing a buyer 'ready, able and willing to buy': this would mean that if anything went wrong and the sale did not go through, you would still have to pay the agent's

Q

Pay close attention to the percentage charges. The difference between 1% and $1\frac{1}{2}$% doesn't sound much but it's 50%! and is a lot at house price levels. Pay very close attention to what actual percentage flat rate charge represents. But it all doesn't matter too much if the agent delivers the goods. . . .

Q

Do not buy and sell through same agent: this enables the agent to apply subtle pressure.

fee. Nor should you agree to any agent having 'sole selling rights' – this would entitle him to a commission even if the eventual buyer was not introduced by him.

There have been unpleasant court cases where two agents have claimed commission for the same sale, or where an agent has tried to claim commission where no sale has happened. The wording of the agent's letter confirming instructions is very important. If you disagree with what is said, get the matter cleared up then. Do not hope for the best later. In some circumstances, it may be sensible to ask your solicitor to advise you on the wording of the agent's terms.

EXTRAS

There is value added tax to pay on agents' fees and on any advertising costs.

Ask the agent what services are included and what will be extra. If advertising costs are not included, do you have to pay all, or only those above a certain figure? Ask the agent whether advertising is in local or national papers or magazines – costs differ a lot.

If details of the advertising costs which will be incurred, either broken down to the column centimetre rate or per advertisement, are given to you at the outset, you can be aware of the precise charges for which you will be liable. You can set your maximum for extra publicity costs and instruct the agent accordingly.

Some estate agents make a charge for the 'For Sale' board. Do not necessarily accept this, and certainly do not agree to pay for a 'Sold' sign.

Whatever agreement you make with the agent, you should get it confirmed in writing. The agent may well ask you to confirm acceptance of his charges, in writing.

Q

Refund of £50 so they could put up 'Sold' board.

Q

Had to pay extra for not having a 'For sale' board displayed i.e. 1.1% instead of 1%.

Showing the house

Estate agents usually leave the job of showing viewers round a house to the owner, saying that he is best fitted to do it. So, even when selling through an agent, you have to be prepared to give up time to this. You may be able to make appointments ahead, or you may find the agent sending round viewers from his office who want to be shown round immediately. If you are out at work all day, appointments will have to be made for evenings or weekends. (If you can never be home at the times potential buyers might want to view, you should leave a key with the estate agent and make it a condition that someone from the estate agent's office will go round with the viewer.)

If the house is tidy and attractive with windows cleaned, it will make an initial good impression and suggest careful owners who would not have neglected it.

A factor which people living in a house tend not to notice, because of familiarity, is smell. You may have to desist from boiling up fish heads for the cat or cooking curries – the smell hangs about and can be very off-putting. On the other hand, the house need not smell like a hospital clinic; fresh air, a background aroma of furniture polish, and one or two vases of fresh flowers can do wonders.

WHEN VIEWERS COME

A technique for showing people round should evolve after the first attempts. It is sensible to start from the ground floor and work upwards, pointing out one or two good features – without overselling. Always indicate which of the contents are included in the sale.

If you think viewers would like to look round afterwards on their own, you will have to use your own instincts about their trustworthiness. You should not, obviously, leave valuables lying about if you are having lots of strangers going round the place. If a husband and wife (or any two people intending to live there together) seem interested, it can be advantageous to let them make a second tour unaccompanied, to give them a bit of privacy of conversation while they are on the premises. Given a moment together will enable them to order their thoughts and questions better. It may swing them to a decision, whereas if they go away, the moment cannot be revived.

State viewing by appointment only – there is nothing worse than someone calling when you are in a muddle or eating a meal.

Have ready the details of current running costs and other expenses so that any queries can be answered straightaway. If you are asked a question – of fact, that is – to which you do not know the answer, do not guess but say that you do not know. Otherwise, you could find yourself being sued: in law, if a misrepresentation can be shown to have a direct effect on a purchase, there could be an application for damages. For example, suppose you are asked whether there is a damp proof course. You make a guess that there is one although you are not sure. If the house is then bought by that viewer in the belief that it has a damp proof course and it transpires that there is not one, you would have misled him and so could be sued for damages.

Sellers should perhaps beware of extolling virtues of their house and leave it to buyers to see for themselves.

If a viewer says that he is interested but would like to think it over, this is probably true, but it could be because he is too polite to say to your face that he does not like your house. Some experienced sellers say that the most enthusiastic viewers turn out to be the least serious. So, you should be prepared for a certain percentage of enthusing viewers to disappear. Others, however, may adopt a defensive brusqueness so as not to appear too keen.

Warn potential buyers about any others you may have: if they are really keen, you will hear from them again. Be prepared for someone seriously interested to want to come back for at least one further look round and to want to bring other members of family or household, too.

Be prepared for a lot of aggravation – people do not always act logically when moving house; however, do not be despondent if you lose a house – we lost two, and the next one was better each time.

Even if a viewer makes a definite offer and seems genuine in his intention to buy, you would be ill-advised to stop showing others round. Although a deposit from a buyer is an earnest of his firm intent to buy, neither of you is legally bound to a sale until contracts have been exchanged.

WHEN THE BUYER'S SURVEYOR COMES

Expect to have to put yourself to some trouble when the time comes for the valuer or surveyor to inspect. He is unlikely to come on a saturday or sunday, and will not come in the evening, because he will want to inspect in good daylight. A valuation for a lending institution may take only fifteen minutes or so, but a full structural survey on a big house will take some hours. When the appointment is made, enquire how long the surveyor is likely to take, so that you can organise your day accordingly.

It will do no harm to prepare for the surveyor. Have steps or a ladder available if possible; make sure all doors and windows are unlocked, including the garage; check that the roof hatch can be moved; check that inspection covers can be opened; have the hot water system running, and the central heating, too, in the winter. Finally, get someone to take the dog for a walk and restrain the children, or vice versa.

WHEN VACANT

A house which is furnished and, better still, occupied, is a more attractive proposition to viewers than an empty one. Even if the furniture and decorations are not to others' tastes, the house itself will make a better impression. But the situation can arise when you have to move, taking your furniture with you, before finding a buyer. All that will remain in the house you are selling will be the fixtures and fittings and any items which you are hoping to include in the sale.

When the house is empty, it would be advisable to appoint an estate agent to help with the sale. You should agree with him in writing:

- that all viewers be accompanied by the agent or a member of his staff
- arrangements for the custody of the keys (squatters in the guise of potential purchasers have been known to have keys copied)
- a list of the items to be included in the sale, and the price of any others which are being offered separately.

EMPTY HOUSE

If a house is left vacant during the colder months of the year, consider leaving on some kind of heating to prevent the place getting too damp or pipes bursting (not to mention a cold reception for any viewers). A house which has been left empty and shut for any length of time tends to smell either fusty or damp, particularly at a time of year when it would normally be heated.

If a little ventilation can be arranged without risking making it easy for trespassers to enter, this is helpful. In winter, if heating is not possible, the water system must be drained.

Remove the telephone or safeguard it against unauthorised use – so that you will not get a bill because of some yobbo phoning his girl friend in Australia. See that someone visits regularly to clear the stuff that comes through the letter box – it is a bad sign to have to shove the door open against a mountain of circulars.

Choosing your buyer

When you have had one or more offers, you should take into account for each interested buyer not just how keen he is to buy the house or how much you would like him or her to live in it, but how suitable he is as a buyer from the financial point of view.

Many house sales fall through because when it comes to the question of being granted a mortgage, the buyer finds that he cannot get a big enough one, or not in time, or indeed any mortgage at all. Or a prospective buyer may find himself unable to sell his own house for some reason, and so unable to move.

If you have a choice, take a buyer who has already sold his house or had none to sell, or who has exchanged contracts with his buyer or at least has had a firm offer. Choose one who does not need too large a mortgage or who has a mortgage certificate guaranteeing that he will be offered a mortgage, or who has cash in hand. You yourself may know whether your house is unlikely to qualify for a mortgage – because of its age, for example. This is the kind of situation for which an estate agent may be in a better position: he may offer or be asked by a buyer to help in obtaining a mortgage loan.

In talking to your prospective buyers, you should be trying to elicit and evaluate the answers to some questions. For example: has the buyer a house to sell? The answer "no" (a first-time buyer) reduces the risk of chain hold-up. If the answer is "yes", ask further:

- is it on the market yet? (*if not, likely delay*)
- is there a buyer interested? has there been a valuation?
- has it been sold? (*check that 'sold' means contracts have been exchanged and not just that someone has said he would like to buy it*)
- is his prospective buyer part of a chain situation? (*further potential delay*).

Q

Ensure prospective purchasers have a straightforward arrangement i.e. no joint purchases with second cousin's brother's friend etc.

It is not necessarily best to accept the offer of the person who promises to pay the most. It may be better to choose the one who seems the most likely to be able to pay when the time comes, or the one who is not dependent on selling his

Q

I got caught by someone saying they could exchange contracts immediately and then kept hanging about – their chain wasn't complete. In the meantime my nice queue of prospective buyers had gone elsewhere.

Q

Seemed to have purchasers' interests at heart. When they agreed to pay my asking price, my agent asked why they did not make an offer.

own home so will not back out at the last moment because he cannot sell it. It is often not until terms have been agreed that it comes to light that there is a long chain of transactions.

It is important to find out when a prospective buyer needs to move in, in case this is too soon or too late for you. If you yourself are in the process of buying a house, you will probably wish to exchange contracts on your sale and purchase simultaneously. It would, therefore, be unwise to wait until you are ready to exchange contracts on your purchase before accepting a 'subject to contract' offer on your sale: it will take your buyer several weeks to get to a situation where he, too, can exchange contracts.

To speed things up, you can ask your solicitor to send off the necessary forms to initiate the local authority search. When the replies come, they can be sent directly to the buyer or his solicitor. Local authorities take a long time to deal with these enquiries, so this procedure can save time.

NEGOTIATING THE PRICE

There is no need to enter into negotiations about price with a buyer if you have appointed an estate agent – this is what you pay him for. He will act as pig-in-the-middle, passing offer to seller and reconsidered price to buyer. If there are several interested buyers, the agent will try to encourage offers and counter-offers between them. It is in his interest to get as high a price as possible because his commission is based on the selling price. But he may prefer to get a quick sale and forgo an extra £100 of commission.

If you are not selling through an estate agent, you yourself must act as negotiator. You should have in mind what price you may be prepared to accept if no offers are made at the asking figure. When an offer is made to you, you do not need to accept or refuse it straightaway but can say that you are considering it. If you let would-be buyers know what good offers you have received to date, that may encourage them to make a higher one.

You may be asked by a viewer who likes your house or flat to let him have 'first refusal'. If you were to agree to this, you would find yourself hampered from dealing with other offers and could even lose a sale. Instead, counter this approach by suggesting that the viewer makes a firm offer.

Q

A large tree in the front garden eventually had to be cut down – the buyer's building society wouldn't lend them the money until the tree was removed. This delayed the sale by about six weeks.

A buyer's offer is usually 'subject to contract' or 'subject to contract and survey', which allows you or him to withdraw from the transaction if need be. (In fact, even if it is not subject to conditions, he can still withdraw at any time before contracts are exchanged.) At this stage, he will not have a firm offer of a mortgage nor will a survey have been carried out. If his building society valuation or a structural survey reports some drawback, the buyer is quite likely to ask you to reduce the agreed price on that account. He may quote a sum equivalent to the estimated cost of the necessary repair. If you are in any doubt about this figure, it may be worth checking it with a builder or surveyor before re-negotiating.

You may find yourself a victim of reverse gazumping: the buyer may produce some reason (other than a genuine one based on his survey) to reduce his offer, even at the last moment. He may have made several simultaneous offers on various houses, and be trying his hand at obtaining lower acceptances before deciding to go ahead with one of them. There is nothing much you can do about this. In a buyers' market, you may be tempted to accept the lower offer if you are anxious because of your own purchase. Discuss the matter with your estate agent who will have experienced a similar situation many times previously – but the decision will have to be your own.

accepting an offer

Your estate agent may suggest that, as a token of intent, the buyer whose offer you have accepted should put down an initial deposit of perhaps £150. This is of no advantage to you (or your buyer).

Q

Insist that buyers have survey done as quickly as possible to prove genuine interest in property.

You (or the estate agent) must get the buyer's full name and address, and that of his solicitor/conveyancer, and give him yours.

Ask your solicitor/conveyancer what his charge will be for dealing with the legal side of the transfer. (It is less fraught but just as time-consuming to do your own conveyancing when selling as when buying a property.)

If you are using a solicitor/conveyancer, your next step is to inform him that you have a buyer and to give him the relevant details – the buyer's name and address, his solicitor's/conveyancer's name and the address of the firm, the conditions and price you have agreed, particularly the details of any items included in the sale or being sold additionally, so that these can be incorporated

Q

Even when you think you have sold, keep all addresses of disappointed customers (the advantage you have over dealing through an agent is that you know the names and addresses of all prospects). When our last sale fell through after a month, 3 telephone calls and a notice in the window produced 4 prospects and one bought straightaway.

Q

Agent tried to force us into having a sign: we refused but one went up saying 'under offer' – we took it down ourselves.

If you are selling through one of Abbey National's Cornerstone agencies as sole agent, and the buyer whose offer you have agreed withdraws for a reason unconnected with you or the property, you are covered by insurance for legal fees you have incurred up to £200.

in the contract. Also, the completion date will have to be agreed with the buyer so that it can be included in the contract.

The estate agent does not withdraw the house from the market until contracts have been exchanged unless you, the seller, request this. It is your decision whether the property should be left on the market until contracts are exchanged. The estate agent will be in a position to advise you whether or not to leave it on the market in case the initial interested purchaser should drop out for any reason. If any further offer is received, that person must be advised that there is already an offer on the property, and the initial interested purchaser must be informed of a subsequent offer received.

Many sellers are exercised about choosing who will succeed them in the house, and, having found a buyer they like the look of, they do not want to be bothered with any other offers. The agent may not want to disturb your peace of mind, but he does have a clear duty to report all offers to a client, whether or not the property has already been provisionally sold.

If you tell the agent to withdraw the house, he will announce that the property is 'under offer' – often adding this notice to his advertising board outside the house and his shop window if the house is displayed there.

Do not forget to get back the keys from the estate agent if you had left them with him (to show people round while you are at work, perhaps, or to let in the surveyor). If your house was on the books of more than one agent, inform them all when you no longer need them.

You can stipulate that exchange of contracts be within a specified period – for example, one month from the date the draft contract is issued to the buyer is a reasonable time for a registered property. You can offer the property to another buyer if the first one will not or cannot exchange contracts after the time expires.

Your solicitor/conveyancer prepares the contract in draft form to send to the one on the other side.

CONTRACT RACE

Where there are several equally acceptable offers, it is not unusual for a seller's solicitor to send out contracts to the solicitors of each of these potential buyers, with a note advising them that the first received back, signed, will get the house. This can be efficacious, but contract races can rebound on the seller: once the buyers know that they risk losing the property, they sometimes all pull out.

BREAKING THE CHAIN

If you are selling through an agent who participates in a chain-linking scheme and there is a threatened break in a chain of buyer/seller/buyer because your potential buyer has dropped out, ask your agent whether the property is suitable for the chain plan. This means that the agent will arrange to buy your house at a discounted price based on a valuation arranged by the agent, so that the rest of the chain can continue. The house is later sold by the agent, who recoups his expenses out of the proceeds of that sale. (With the *Chainmaker* service, if the house is eventually sold for more than the agreed valuation, the difference usually goes to the original seller.)

Most schemes do not involve you in extra expenses (unless you have to pay towards the valuation) but you have to accept a lower-than-market-value price for your house. Some fairly stringent conditions apply to the different procedures.

Information on their schemes is available from:

Black Horse Agencies (*Chainmaker*)	Homequity (*Goldlink Chainsaver*)	Prudential Property Services (*Chainbreaking*)
Black Horse House	PHH Centre	Winchmore House
Salisbury Square	Windmill Hill	Fetter Lane
Hatfield	Whitehill Way	London EC4A 1BR
Herts A19 5DD	Swindon SN5 9YT	

paying off your mortgage

A charge will be made by the building society for their solicitor to deal with the work involved in redeeming (that is, paying off) the existing mortgage on the house you are selling. Some lenders charge a mortgage redemption fee (this may be as much as 3 months' interest) if the mortgage is paid off within the first years. Most lenders waive this charge, particularly if a new mortgage is being taken out on the next property with them.

Q

The chain was enormously stressful, mainly because one is helpless to accelerate the chain. Nor could we find out what was going on several stages down the chain. Solicitors were pedantic about not speaking to movers except their own clients.

Q

Attracting enough potential buyers was hard but by far the most frustrating and heartbreaking element was the disappointment of finding a buyer, accepting the offer, finding our 'dream home' and having our offer on that accepted, only to find the whole deal came crashing down when, without warning or stated reason, our buyers backed out.

The mortgage deed stipulates the length of notice you need to give (or what interest you will have to pay in lieu of notice) when you want to pay off what you still owe. If your completion date is sooner, you may still have to pay the stipulated interest but building societies do not always enforce this. You should nevertheless give notice to the building society or other lender as soon as you have fixed the completion date. At the same time, ask to be told the exact amount you will be owing on that day. Your buyer can then be asked to have a cheque for that amount made out to your building society's solicitor, to be handed over on completion. If you have a solicitor or licensed conveyancer acting for you, these matters will be handled by him.

INSURANCE

You must continue with the insurance of the house until exchange of contracts, when the responsibility passes to the buyer, but it would be wise to keep your own buildings insurance policy going until completion day. If the place burns down between exchange of contracts and completion, and the buyer has not insured, a lot of litigation might be needed to get your money.

Keep the contents insurance policy going up to completion day. If you are not going to continue with the same contents policy in your new house, do not cancel it until after the move.

LETTING THE BUYER IN

After contracts have been exchanged, the buyer may want to borrow the keys to get into the house (for measuring up, for instance). If the estate agent contacts you about this, tell him to ask the buyer to sign that the keys are issued 'for viewing purposes only: I/we will not take possession'. This is some safeguard against the possibility of an unscrupulous buyer moving in and then causing trouble over completing his payment, possibly even claiming protection as a tenant. As a general rule, however, it is unwise for keys to be released to a purchaser after exchange of contracts without a written undertaking prepared by the seller's solicitors and signed by the prospective purchaser.

Selling by auction

Having assessed your property in the light of prevailing market conditions, the estate agent may recommend that you should not sell by private treaty (the most usual method) but by auction. Holding an auction creates a situation where the price may be forced upwards by a number of keen bidders.

An agent may find a house difficult to put a price on because of its unusual nature – a converted mill, chapel or barn, for instance – and if it is the only one of its kind in the district, he may have no precedent for an accurate valuation. He may, therefore, suggest that an auction would be the best way of ensuring that the seller gets a good price for it. Most firms of estate agents are also property auctioneers.

The seller has to pay the auctioneer a percentage of the price reached ($2\frac{1}{2}\%$ is usual). You should agree beforehand what this will be and whether it will be the same if the property is sold before the auction.

before the auction

A brochure, sometimes with a photograph, describing the house in detail and containing the particulars, is prepared and printed.

The estate agent arranges for extensive advertising (for which the seller pays) in order to get the widest possible coverage for the auction. Posters and advertisements in specialist magazines add to the cost.

Discuss what each expense may amount to (not forgetting photographs for the brochure: his professional photographer may be expensive) and try to agree on limits. You can either agree to pay all the publicity expenses incurred, or fix a set sum for them. Some agents require a lump sum in advance for advertising purposes.

The brochure will include the Special Conditions of Sale (which should be drawn up by your solicitor). It may also include the auction contract with blank spaces for the buyer's name and the purchase price to be inserted.

Some auctions are advertised for 3 or 4 weeks, others for 2 or 3 months, depending on the kind of property involved. Top-of-the-market houses or investment properties usually attract cash buyers rather than buyers needing a mortgage (which takes time to arrange) so the period leading up to the auction can be shorter.

A good auctioneer/estate agent will consult his client halfway to auction date on whether further expense on advertising is justified in the light of response to date.

If, during the period before the auction, a number of would-be buyers emerge, they will want to have surveys and valuations carried out, and you must be prepared to accommodate these. You will probably also have a larger proportion of 'just curious' viewers as well as genuine potential buyers.

The auctioneer's terms may be that you give his firm sole selling rights up to the date of auction and for some specified period afterwards. This means that you would have to pay the commission even if you found a private buyer yourself.

Ask the agent to include in the brochure and advertisements that the auction will take place 'unless previously sold'. This gives you the option of accepting an offer from a private buyer. There are many people who would make satisfactory buyers who will not come to buy at an auction. The idea of bidding at an auction is a daunting prospect for many would-be buyers, and a keen purchaser may be induced to make an attractive offer beforehand. Whether or not you decide to let the property 'go to the room' a buyer will, in any case, have to sign the auction contract. A great advantage of this is that it avoids the pre-contract stress of a sale by private treaty.

But consider carefully before agreeing to accept an offer: the auction may still be the best conclusion.

The agent should help you decide what the reserve price should be. This is usually not revealed to bidders: the sale particulars just state 'subject to reserve price'. If the figure is not reached, the auctioneer withdraws the house. A fee may be payable to the auctioneer in place of commission: this should be part of the agreement made between seller and auctioneer.

at the auction

Public auctions are held on a specified day in a particular auction room or rented hall. A number of properties may be being sold at the same time.

Bidding takes place along similar lines to the auctioning of goods such as antiques or secondhand furniture. The prospective buyers will be people prepared to have gone through the preliminaries (including the expenses) without any guarantee of getting the house, or people who have enough cash and confidence to risk bidding without prior investigations.

The reserve price not being revealed, it cannot be leaked beforehand. Also, if you think signs are propitious (lots of enquiries and a rising market), you can lift it a bit. If, on the contrary, signs are bad, you can pare it down a shade.

Some auctioneers, to encourage bidding, will take dummy bids 'off the wall' up to the reserve price. Some sellers try to encourage bidding by arranging for friends and relatives, unknown to the auctioneer, to make dummy bids in the auction rooms. If you intend to do this, make sure that you instruct your bidder firmly to stop bidding well before the reserve price. And the fewer people who are aware of the reserve price, the better.

When the bidding has reached the reserve, it is usual for the auctioneer to let his audience know, particularly if it seems that competition is flagging. This tends to sharpen things up a bit. On the other hand, if it is rolling along in a lively style, he will not let on that he has gone past the reserve, so that it does not take the steam out of things.

At the fall of the hammer, the successful bidder is committed to buy. He has to sign the auction contract and pay 10% of his price there and then to the auctioneer. This should be held by the auctioneer as stakeholder.

The advantage of selling by auction is that there is an immediate binding contract without the uncertainty of the 'subject to contract, subject to survey' stage. The buyer cannot be gazumped and the seller cannot be let down. Completion is usually within 4 weeks of the auction.

Q

If possible, sell by auction. There is no dubiety about whether the sale has taken place on that date. If the purchaser changes his mind, he has lost his 10% which will more than cover the selling costs at that point. All queries have been settled by that date, including surveys and mortgages etc. If it has not reached the reserve, then you know where you are and can act accordingly.

Drawbacks when selling by auction are

- the cost to the seller is more, sometimes considerably more, than a sale by private treaty – although this may be offset by a better sale price
- the house may be sold before auction so that some of the extra cost will have been unnecessary
- the seller has no choice over who is to be the next owner
- the house could fail to sell if the reserve price is not reached
- you must be prepared to get out of the house and give vacant possession 28 days after the auction.

During the period between exchange of contracts by private treaty or after an auction and the date of completion, you may find that your buyer wants to revisit the house – to check or measure something or to discuss a point with you. He may ask if he can bring his surveyor, architect or builder to inspect or estimate. Provided his requests are not unreasonable, this is quite legitimate. He should not, however, instruct his builder to carry out any work during this time or start to do any himself, and you must not let this happen.

Show him where stopcocks and meters are, and how to operate any central heating system, gas fire or boiler. Arrange to leave behind any instruction booklets there may be for appliances he is taking over, and any details about servicing them. Some owners are even thoughtful enough to leave lists of local shops and services, bus and train times, nearest doctor and so on. This is obviously especially valuable if the new owner does not know the area.

Other information about the house, if available, can be useful, too: plans (particularly of drains) and architect's or builder's specifications, details of maintenance or alteration work done and correspondence about it. This can, for instance, help a new owner to know that he must not cover up or 'bridge' a damp proof course, or that an electrical installation should be checked in 1994 (for example), or that a particular door fitting is part of an important means of escape in case of fire, or that a particular ventilation opening is there in order to prevent condensation.

It is helpful if you cooperate with your buyer over the arrangements about the telephone and for the supply of gas and electricity – whether these are to be disconnected or not – and when the meters are to be read.

As soon as possible after exchange of contracts, and as soon as the completion date is set, both buyer and seller (or their solicitor/conveyancer) should write to the local rating authority and the local water authority, informing them of the sale and completion date. These bodies will then issue appropriate demands or refunds.

Remember that your house must be vacant on completion day; you must move out then, if you have not done so before. Do not make any friendly arrangements to leave behind, for example, some pieces of furniture for collection later: either party could change his mind.

Q

Try to establish rapport with the other party – keep in frequent contact, this may give you an early warning of forthcoming problems – also, the better the parties know each other, the more likely they are to behave normally.

Selling in Scotland

If you are selling in Scotland, you are likely to have already been a purchaser and be familiar with the Scottish system, but in any event many matters dealt with in the chapter *Buying a house in Scotland* will be of interest to you as a seller.

ways of selling

The three most common ways of selling a house or flat are to

> sell it yourself
> employ a solicitor to sell it
> employ an estate agent to sell it.

Whichever you decide on, you should alert your solicitor, before putting it on the market, to the fact that you are about to sell your house. This is because a binding contract for the sale will usually be concluded within a few days of a purchaser making a formal offer and this cannot normally be done quickly unless your solicitor has had an opportunity to

- look over your title deeds to make sure they are in order and check that you have good title to the property. (He will borrow them from your building society or other lender if you have an outstanding loan over the property.)
- order local authority searches to make sure that the property is not affected by any outstanding local authority notices, orders or proposals.

Someone who has been used to the English method of sale, where the solicitor becomes involved at only a relatively late stage, should be aware of the need to bring a solicitor into the picture early in Scotland.

SELLING IT YOURSELF

This entails advertising the property, showing people round it, letting surveyors inspect it, answering all questions about room sizes, the price and what items are and are not included in the sale. You should prepare written particulars similar to those issued by solicitors and estate agents, but stress to people viewing the house that these are provided only as a guide and are not to form part of any contract.

If you decide to sell your house yourself, the only costs which you need incur are those for advertising. Although it is probably not sensible to 'go it alone' the first time you sell, if you have been through the process of buying and selling before, and if you have a readily saleable house in which a large number of people are likely to be interested, you may feel that the saving in sales commission is justified.

If you decide to sell your house yourself, you will still need a solicitor to do the conveyancing and should tell him in advance, and tell prospective buyers that formal written offers are to be submitted to him.

SELLING THROUGH A SOLICITOR

The majority of houses in Scotland are sold by solicitors and not by estate agents. If you ask your solicitor to sell your house, you should expect him to provide a full estate agency service.

He will normally also register your property in the local solicitors' property centre, for which a charge of approximately £55 to £60 (more in some centres) is made. This covers display of the house in the solicitors' property centre until sold, and insertion in the property centre's regular property listing or mailing where there is one.

A solicitor who acts for you in selling your house will charge a selling commission over and above his conveyancing fees. Although solicitors are entitled to charge a sales commission of $1\frac{1}{2}\%$, many charge 1% or slightly less and it is quite common for a solicitor to charge a single percentage fee to cover both the selling and the conveyancing. Ask your solicitor for an estimate of his charges before instructing him to act for you, and if you are not satisfied with the estimate, discuss it with him, or seek an alternative estimate from another solicitor.

If you decide to handle the sale yourself and only need your solicitor to attend to certain specific items, make sure that the basis of his charge is agreed in advance.

SELLING THROUGH AN ESTATE AGENT

Generally speaking, estate agents' terms of business are similar in Scotland to those in England. Commissions are generally $1\frac{1}{2}\%$ of the achieved selling price,

Q

Even if you ask your solicitor to sell your home, you will still be expected to show prospective purchasers round. Quite expensive to get your solicitor to do this as well.

although lower charges may be negotiated, and higher charges normally apply in the case of large country houses or other specialised properties. Ask the estate agent for an estimate and make sure you understand what is included in the charge and whether VAT is in addition and whether advertising costs are extra; you may be charged for the insertion of the property in the estate agent's house magazine.

Even if you instruct an estate agent to sell your house for you, he will normally pass to your solicitor any formal offers which are made. It is important to realise that as well as the estate agent's commission, you will have to pay the solicitor's fee for concluding missives and the conveyancing fees.

THE ADVERTISEMENT

If you are selling through a solicitor or an estate agent, he will prepare the advertisement for you and agree its terms with you.

If you are selling the house yourself, you will have to prepare your own advertisement. Any specially attractive features which make your property stand out from otherwise similar houses should be mentioned as selling points. You might include reference to the view, a good garden, a building listed as being of architectural or historic interest or, in a conservation area, the work of a well-known architect, proximity to public transport, schools and other amenities. It is usual to put the exact address of the property: many people like to drive or walk past a property first before viewing inside.

Arrangements for viewing are normally stated in the advertisement. This may be fixed viewing times or by telephone appointment, or a mixture of both. Remember that the easier you make it for people to view your house, the more people are likely to do so and the quicker you may find a buyer.

The advertisement also normally states the asking price (also referred to as 'upset' price) and it is usual to state the name of the solicitor to whom formal written offers should be sent.

Before inserting the advertisement in the newspaper, because you will be expected to give a quick decision about date of entry and price, you should consider when you want to or are able to move out, what items you want to include in the sale, and which ones you might be prepared to sell if asked to do so. (You are normally bound to leave items which are fitted as part of the structure of the house, unless you specifically exclude them from the sale; if you wish to remove such items, this may reduce the price which you will be offered.)

THE PRICE

It is usual to state an asking price and invite offers over this amount. The asking price should normally be the minimum figure which you would consider accepting. But it is usual in Scotland for prospective purchasers to make a bid above the asking price, and you may decide to take this into account and quote an asking price below your minimum. The amount by which offers may exceed the asking price will vary depending on the type of property, the area in which it is situated and the market conditions prevailing at the time of the sale.

Generally speaking, it is easier to set the value on a house in a modern housing estate where there is a reasonable stock of similar properties; such properties are often sold for prices close to their asking price. However, older properties of character and/or in sought-after residential areas, particularly those in the higher price ranges, often achieve prices considerably in excess of the asking price.

If you are selling your house through a solicitor or an estate agent, he will advise you on both the price you should ask and the price you should expect to achieve. If you are selling your house yourself, you can have a 'pre-sale' valuation carried out by a surveyor. This will normally cost you between £50 and £60 + VAT.

AFTER THE ADVERTISEMENT

With luck, a number of people will come to view your house or flat. When you show them round, point out the main features of the property which you think make it attractive. Do not point out defects or disadvantages and follow the general rule that if in doubt you should stay silent. But if asked a direct question, you must answer truthfully.

You may gain an impression of whether people are seriously interested or not when they come to view, particularly if they return a second time. However, this is not always so and the first sign that you may be going to receive an offer is usually when a solicitor telephones your solicitor or estate agent to tell him that he has a client interested in your property. You should then not sell to anyone without giving everyone who has notified an interest to you or your solicitor or estate agent an opportunity of offering.

Noting interest is usually followed by a visit from a surveyor. If the survey is favourable, it is likely to be followed by an offer.

If you are doing the selling of your house yourself, ask purchasers to lodge formal offers with your solicitor. Never sign a written acceptance of an offer or exchange letters with a prospective purchaser without consulting your solicitor.

Receiving offers

If several people have expressed an interest in your house, it is usual to fix a closing date for offers – that is, a date and time at which you will consider all offers which have been lodged. All those people whose interest has been noted will be asked to submit formal written offers through their solicitor by the date and time fixed. Your solicitor or estate agent will advise you whether to fix a closing date or not, and will suggest when it should be. Often estate agents will advise clients to negotiate with the first person who registers serious interest in the house, whereas solicitors encourage sellers to generate interest from several people before fixing a closing date. Where there is competition, a higher price may well be achieved if you do not rush the sale, although this may be a nerve-racking business for you as the seller.

On the closing date, you and your solicitor or estate agent will have to decide which offer to accept. You are not under an obligation to accept the highest offer or any offer. If offers are close, you may take into account other factors such as the proposed date of entry, what extras are included in the price, or even whether or not you liked the highest offeror. If the price is acceptable but other conditions of the offer are not, your solicitor or estate agent can negotiate these other conditions with the offeror or his solicitor, but it would not be normal in this situation to negotiate further on price.

CONSENT TO SALE
Where the property is owned by two or more people, all of them must consent to any sale.

The Matrimonial Homes (Family Protection) (Scotland) Act 1981 makes it imperative for a married seller whose spouse is not a co-owner to obtain his or her (i.e. the spouse's) consent to a sale at the earliest opportunity and certainly before missives are concluded. Failure to do so may mean that the seller finds that he or she cannot give the purchaser possession of the property as provided for in the missives. This is especially important where the couple are separated or estranged.

CONCLUDING THE MISSIVES

If you are selling through an estate agent, he will normally pass the offers, or at least the offer which is to be accepted, to your solicitor. Once you have received an offer which you want to accept, or identified which of competing offers is to be accepted, your solicitor will adjust points of details with the solicitor acting for the successful offeror. When these adjustments have been made, they are confirmed in writing: this exchange of letters is referred to as the 'missives'. This process normally takes only a day or two. It is important to realise that the conclusion of missives constitutes a binding contract from which neither party can withdraw. The solicitor will accept the offer and conduct the bargain on your behalf. Make sure therefore that you understand what you are agreeing to.

In theory, it would be possible for 'gazumping' to take place between the date when an acceptable offer is received and the date when missives are concluded, but it would be unethical for a solicitor acting for a seller to negotiate with a third party during this period. If in such circumstances you decided to withdraw from negotiations with the successful offerors and to negotiate with someone else, your solicitor would have to stop acting for you and you would have to appoint another solicitor. The absence of gazumping, and the short time between offers being made and becoming binding, are advantages of the Scottish system.

The feuduty has to be redeemed before the sale. This means paying to the superior a capital sum equal to about 10 times the annual feuduty payment.

completing the sale

Once the missives have been concluded, your solicitor will send the title deeds of the property to the purchaser's solicitor so that he can examine them and prepare the disposition (the document transferring title to the purchaser) in favour of the purchaser. He will also inform your building society, bank or other lender that missives have been concluded and obtain a redemption statement to show the amount of loan to be repaid on completion of the sale. He will prepare the discharge document and have it signed by the lender before the date of entry.

Your solicitor will instruct searches in the Registers to demonstrate to the purchaser that there are no adverse entries in respect of the property or against you as seller. He answers any questions raised by the purchaser's solicitor, adjusting the terms of the disposition with him. You have to sign it before the date of entry. Date of entry is the date on which the purchaser obtains physical possession of the property. The purchaser may or may not move in then. The date of settlement is when the disposition is handed over in exchange for the price.

Immediately prior to the date of entry, your solicitor will agree with you what arrangements are to be made about handing over the keys (often it is best to deliver these to your solicitor on the date of entry).

The disposition in favour of the purchaser is handed over in return for the purchaser's solicitor's cheque for the full purchase price. Out of that amount, he repays your outstanding mortgage loan, and any bridging loan, in accordance with instructions received from you or your bank and will then let you have a cheque for the balance of the price payable to you, after deducting his fees and outlays. He should provide you with a detailed statement showing all the financial details; if he does not do so, make sure you ask him for one. You should normally expect your solicitor to send you the balance of the price and his statement on the day on which he completes the sale, or at the latest on the following day.

It is important to realise that once contracts are exchanged and you have agreed on a date for completion, you must move on that day or risk having to face large claims for compensation and court proceedings.

Most people try to arrange for the completion of their sale and purchase to take place on the same day. This means that your old home must be vacated on the day your buyer hands over the purchase money to you, and you must be prepared to move out on that day.

When settling on a date, check the day of the week. Completions are often on fridays at the end of the month. But friday is not necessarily the ideal day on which to move. Even though this would give you a weekend to settle in, if you arrange delivery of goods or the connections of any services – gas, electricity, for example – for friday afternoon, if anything should go wrong with any appointments, you could find yourself without cooker or power for 3 days. Similarly, if you need professional help in an emergency – plumber, say – it is going to be more difficult (and probably more expensive) if it is a weekend. For the same reason, you should avoid bank holiday periods. (Scottish holidays are on different days in different places and are not necessarily on the same days as bank holidays in England and Wales.)

If you are moving some distance away, allow for the fact that the move will have to be spread over two days, with an overnight stop somewhere. Also, if a long distance removal is involved – say, from the south to Scotland – you would have to pay overtime for the remover's staff to travel back on a saturday. Moreover, there are tight restrictions on the hours a driver of a heavy goods vehicle may legally drive in the course of a day or week, so you may have to pay for his weekend accommodation.

Removal firms tend to be heavily booked at the beginning and end of the months, so you may stand a better chance of getting the firm you want on the day you want if you pick a day in the middle of the month. And if you are able to move during a period outside the peak moving periods (school holidays, particularly the summer), the cost may be less.

It is not possible to predict whether the previous owners are the kind of people who leave their home spotlessly clean on vacating it – or at least clear of unwanted rubbish. As well as allowing yourself sufficient time for clearing up your house on leaving it, you should be prepared for the probability that you

Q

Most difficult part was keeping in touch with work done by solicitor and later on keeping an acceptable date for the move itself. It seemed impossible to hurry the solicitor to try to move within school holiday time.

Q

Have all the decisions on what changes you want in the new house sorted out and if possible organise it that you have the house free of furniture for as long as is necessary to get most of the 'dirty work' done. Even if this isn't possible, get the changes started as soon as possible even if it means keeping the furniture stored away.

Q

Buyers wanted everything settled yesterday. So, not to lose the sale, we put everything into storage for three weeks, while we waited for our new house to be sorted out.

will have to clean your new one before putting your possessions into it. If you move in on the day of completion of your purchase, you will have no opportunity for preliminary cleaning. You could find the floors need cleaning before any carpets you have brought with you can be laid.

If you want a little time to clean up, lay the carpets, prepare the house, and generally relieve the pressure, you should assess whether it would be worth completing your purchase a few days before the day of completing your sale – with a bridging loan to tide you over.

When it is your buyer who chose the date because it suits him to move in then and you accepted this, you may not have a new home, or not be able to move into it, on the day you have to vacate your old one. Particularly where a newly-built house is concerned, there is a serious risk that it will not be completed by the promised date(s) due to over-optimistic calculating by the builder.

Whenever you cannot move straight out of the old home into the new one, it may be necessary to put your belongings into store and to find a temporary home, perhaps in rented accommodation, a hotel, or with relatives or friends. These extra expenses can add considerably to the cost of your move.

Putting furniture into store

The expense of putting furniture into store is based on

○ the cost of getting it packed up and taken to the depository
○ the charge per cubic foot for the time it has to be in store
○ insurance
○ the cost of getting the furniture out of storage
○ the cost of delivering it to the new house.

Removal firms with storage facilities can be found in the Yellow Pages or similar local directory or by asking the **British Association of Removers**, 277 Gray's Inn Road, London WC1X 8SY for a list of their members.

Unless there is no choice in the area, you should preferably get more than one estimate.

Storage firms accept the whole contents of a house with the exception of perishable goods such as food and plants, and of flammable goods such as matches, fuel or paint. They recommend that carpets and rugs be cleaned first and some will arrange this for you. Clothes and blankets should be treated with a moth deterrent – the firms do not accept responsibility for moth damage.

Q

We had to get my husband's golf clubs out, as we were 'homeless' longer than we thought, and they charged £15 for opening the crate containing them.

Generally, goods are stored loose, covered but not encased, in a space allocated to you in the depository. You can inspect your goods in the warehouse (sometimes for a small charge) – unless they are housed in containers.

Containerisation is now becoming the accepted method of storage: goods are packed into sealed containers at your home and these are stored untouched in a warehouse until required. The advantage is that the risk of damage by movement or careless handling during transit and warehousing is greatly reduced; also, there is much greater protection from dust and dirt and less possibility of loss.

You should have an inventory (and if in containers, what has been put into which one). Note the value of all items. Insurance premiums are often based on the total declared value; storage charges are more likely to be based on the space required.

INSURANCE

Insurance cover can be arranged through the storage firm, or your household insurers may give you special cover for these circumstances. Make sure it is for a sufficient sum and for 'all risks' including fire, flooding and any other loss or damage. Insurers usually charge an all-in premium covering transit from your house to the warehouse, storage for a given length of time, and transit from the warehouse to your new home. (If you later find that you need a longer period of storage, the cover can be extended by paying an additional premium.)

There may be an individual limit on specific items (of crockery, for instance) but if one item gets broken and that style is no longer made, you would have to replace the set; make sure that the insurance cover is sufficient for such a situation (the premium may be high). Check any policy carefully for exclusions and excess clauses (an excess is the amount of any claim you have to pay yourself).

GETTING GOODS OUT

If you think you will want to take some items away earlier than others – for example, carpets or cooker – you should advise the storage firm at the start so that these can be labelled and stored as 'keep forward' items, accessible for collection when required. If the storage firm delivers these, there will be a charge per delivery. Written authorisation is usually required if you want someone else to collect any of your goods for you.

Find out how much notice is required for getting your goods out of store when you eventually need them. If the delivery is not done by the storage firm, you may have to pay a handing-out charge.

When all your goods are delivered to you, check the inventory as soon as they arrive. Without any attempt to steal or defraud, one packing case might be left behind at the warehouse and it is easier to trace if this is notified at once, rather than some weeks later when the warehouse space may have been filled and the premises re-arranged. Your insurance may stipulate that any claim must be made within a set period.

RENTING STORAGE SPACE

In some places, there are 'self-access' facilities for storage of possessions in specially constructed steel-walled compartments or units, in a secured building or a 'mini-warehouse'. You are the only person who has a key to the compartment you rent or who is told the control code to gain entry, and you are free to go at any time within working hours to get at your possessions. There is an initial refundable deposit, and you then pay monthly, according to the space taken and the period booked. You have to arrange your own insurance cover.

Your new house empty

Some jobs are better done before moving in if your timetable allows this.

There are bound to be one or two, or even twenty-two, jobs to be done in the new house, some of which will be essential ones. They will get done more quickly and easily at this time than they would after family and furniture have been installed.

If you are intending to make any alterations, carry out repairs or redecorate, you should consider carefully as soon as possible whether you can manage to have completion for purchase (of your new home) earlier than completion for sale (of your old home) even at the cost of a bridging loan. This would allow a period for work to be done while your new house is empty.

It is worth notifying your local authority if a property is to be vacant for any length of time, because a rate refund may be payable. If you are carrying out building work which makes the property uninhabitable for a considerable time, you can apply (to the Inland Revenue who do rating valuations in England and Wales) for the building to be temporarily revalued as uninhabitable – which means that no rates are payable.

You should inform the insurance company with which the building is insured: cover for some risks, such as vandalism or theft, is restricted when a property is unoccupied. Also arrange for contents insurance for any items (carpets, curtains, kitchen equipment, furniture) that you bought from the previous owner, which are in the empty house. Contents insurance may exclude theft cover if premises are left unoccupied for an extended period.

Curtains give a house a lived-in look and may be a form of safeguard against intruders. Leave some up at your old home if not sold, and get them up at your new one as soon as possible.

To prevent anyone who is working in the house from running up telephone bills, you can ask the telephone sales manager for an o.c.b. arrangement – that is, outgoing calls barred (£11 charge for barring) until you write to say that you want to revert to normal calling out.

Q

Place pencil and paper by bedside for 'night notes'.

Q

Get organised – make sure you know the facts and can lay your hands on any relevant piece of paperwork at a moment's notice (I carried the 'moving house' file everywhere with me – even to work).

Organising the repairs and alterations

It helps to keep a special notebook (small enough to fit into your pocket or handbag) for notes and decisions, and for recording names and addresses of suppliers, brands and price of articles, and similar other relevant information. Discipline yourself to use only this notebook and not have recourse to backs of envelopes and other scraps of paper.

It is important to plan the correct sequence in which to do the various jobs, or arrange for them to be done. List all the jobs, then draft a programme, day by day and week by week over the period before you move in, in the sequence in which everything would probably be best carried out.

Keep the programme/timetable by the telephone, so that appointments with servicemen, workmen, delivery men or officials can be put down at the time they are arranged. Note the name of the person you have spoken to when booking appointments by telephone, also the date of the call (written confirmation of instructions is an added safeguard).

Some items have a long delivery time and you may need to place your order as soon as contracts are exchanged – for example, for replacement windows, central heating, fitted carpets, kitchen units – and make delivery date a part of the sale agreement: get a commitment from the suppliers in writing.

While the house is empty, you will have to make arrangements about getting keys to the workmen and making sure that someone is there when the delivery men are due to come.

Do not make your timetable too utopian but allow for non-delivery, late delivery, workmen's errors, your errors, unexpected snags, sickness, strikes and other malignant acts of man or fate.

PLANNING PERMISSION

For some structural alterations or improvements, you have to obtain planning permission. Apply in good time: it can take some weeks or even months to come through. Planning permission is usually only concerned with significant changes in external appearance but you should ask at the local planning department whether what you propose needs planning permission. The fee for

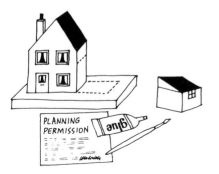

an application for permission to alter or extend a private dwelling is £33.

The Department of the Environment and the Welsh Office publish a free booklet *Planning permission: a guide for householders*, available at council offices, citizens advice bureaux, housing advice centres. There is also a booklet *Planning appeals*, a guide to the procedure you can follow after a refusal.

Advice on how to deal with difficulties, refusals or objections can be obtained from chartered town planners, architects and surveyors. Members of the **Royal Town Planning Institute** (26 Portland Place, London W1N 4BE; telephone 01-636 9107) include not only local authority planning officers but also consultants. The RTPI will be able to suggest where to get specialist advice and publishes leaflets *Your planning application, Should I appeal?* and *What is listed building consent?* which explain how the planning system works.

If you want to use part of your house for a business or build on part of the plot, you will need to find out about the planning history of the house and the local authority's policies. The Royal Town Planning Institute's regional leaflets on *Where to find planning advice* can help you select a suitable consultant.

Do not let any work start until you have the necessary planning permission, listed building consent and building regulations approval, where these are needed.

BUILDING REGULATIONS

The Building Regulations 1985, which have the force of law, operate throughout England and Wales.

The various building regulations are mainly concerned with material work, health and safety, services and fire precautions. They apply to new buildings and extensions, structural alterations to existing buildings, installation of controlled services or fittings.

A copy of the Building Regulations can be consulted in local authority offices or in most public reference libraries. The 1985 regulations are shorter and simpler than previous regulations, and more flexible and easier to use, but a layman would almost certainly need guidance to interpret them. There is a DOE explanatory memorandum *The manual to the Building Regulations 1985* (available from HMSO, price £6.20).

Parts I to IV of the regulations set out the extent of control, what the regulations cover, and how to apply for approval or to use the building notice procedure under which approval is not required. Schedule I sets out the various requirements as to structure – stability, resistance to fire and damp, insulation, ventilation and so on. It also deals with requirements for services or fittings – all heat producing appliances (except electric ones), drains and sanitary appliances.

For some kinds of building work, you do not need to apply for Building Regulations approval or to give notice. For instance, you do not need to if you are merely repairing a building or replacing drains, sanitary fittings or solid fuel or oil-heating appliances where no structural work is involved. Also, the regulations exempt from control certain small detached buildings and extensions. Contact the building control officer of your local authority and find out whether the work you are proposing to have done requires approval or a building notice. If so, he can let you have the necessary formal notification form and tell you what details and drawings are required.

You have to pay prescribed fees to the local authority, in two parts if you deposit plans for approval (on application and on inspection), or once on inspection if you give a building notice. There are flat rate fees for small extensions (up to $40 \, \text{m}^2$) and for loft conversions; fees for other work are based on estimated cost.

Scotland has its own Building Standards (Scotland) Regulations. You apply for a building warrant – for which you have to pay a lodging fee – and the work is inspected before a certificate of completion is issued.

TIMBER FRAME?

If the house you have bought is of timber-&-brick construction, it would be advisable to check what can and what should not be done to the walls, and particularly the cavity, before initiating any alterations that would affect the structure. If you were not given a copy of the booklet *Living in a Timber & Brick Home* by the builder or previous owner when you bought the house, you can get a copy (£3.50) from the **Timber & Brick Homes Information Council**, Kingsgate House, 536 King's Road, London SW10 0TE. The booklet gives explicit instructions about how to carry out work on a timber-&-brick house.

Also, you can ask the local authority building control office to allow you (or your builder) to inspect the drawings and structural calculations submitted by the developer/builder when the house was first built.

RESTRICTIONS

If the house you are buying is a listed building or is in a conservation area, demolition or structural alterations of any kind would need consent from the local planning office. It is a criminal offence to demolish a listed building without consent. Further information can be found in a leaflet *What is listed building consent?* published by the Royal Town Planning Institute.

Some properties are restricted as far as their development or use is concerned by covenants in the title deeds, mostly laid down when the house was first built. A covenant may, for instance, stipulate that certain alterations or additions shall not be made or can be made only with the consent of the person who sold the land on which the property was built. (Some covenants cannot be enforced, but if in doubt, consult your solicitor.) Also, mortgage deeds have a clause stipulating that the building society's (or other lender's) approval must be obtained for any proposed alterations to the house. If a property is leasehold, the landlord's consent will probably be required.

Getting professional advice

For older property, particularly for property constructed before 1850, the **Society for the Protection of Ancient Buildings** (SPAB), 37 Spital Square, London E1 6DY (telephone 01-377 1644) can be asked for general advice. SPAB publishes technical pamphlets and information leaflets on treatment and installations in old buildings, and maintains a card index of architects, surveyors, engineers etc (usually members of the Society) who have experience with work on historic buildings.

It could be useful to have a word with someone at the local authority planning department or engineer's or technical department, or the building control office. He may be able to let you see plans for recent work carried out at the property – layout of drainage, for instance – or of previous structural work or adaptations.

The Consumer Publication *Getting work done on your house* explains the procedure for getting building work done when using a professional and when employing a builder on your own.

If you want a considerable amount of repairs done, or perhaps some alterations or modifications, it is worth getting preliminary advice from a professional – an architect, building surveyor or similar consultant. For new work – such as extensions, creating new rooms, kitchen layouts – use an architect who has special skill in economic layout and design. If the work is largely remedial and repair, a building surveyor may be a suitable consultant.

Architects and building surveyors offer a range of services – preliminary discussions, preparation of designs, provision of documents or drawings, applications for approval from various authorities. They will obtain quotations and arrange the details of contracts with builders, inspect the work periodically and authorise payments. You can make use of all these services, or seek professional advice at selected stages only. The contracts are signed by the employer (that is you, the person for whom the work is being carried out) and the builder; the architect and building surveyor are not parties to the contract. They should, however, be able to give you a rough idea of the costs, including their own fees.

The fees charged by an architect or surveyor are determined by the extent of the services provided. Where the work is extensive, fees are a percentage of the total cost (which cannot be known until the work is completed). Some services may be charged on an hourly basis at an agreed hourly rate, or, if the client prefers it, all fees may be charged on an hourly basis. Before an architect or surveyor starts working for you, you should, in order to avoid misunderstanding, agree the basis of his charge with him in writing.

ARCHITECTS

An architect has to be registered with the Architects Registration Council of the UK and must have specific academic qualifications. He has to adhere to a code of professional conduct.

Most architects are members of the Royal Institute of British Architects (RIBA). Other professional bodies of architects to which an architect may belong are:

> Architectural Association
> Faculty of Architects and Surveyors
> Incorporated Association of Architects and Surveyors
> Royal Incorporation of Architects in Scotland
> Royal Society of Ulster Architects
> Society of Architects in Wales.

No architect has to belong to a professional body and a substantial minority of architects do not belong to any. Architects who do not belong to a professional body, but who are qualified, are known as 'unattached architects'. The fact that an architect elects to belong to a professional body is a matter for him and does not confer on him any additional qualification or status. The registration qualification is exactly the same for all architects, whether they belong to a professional body or not.

Registered architects in private practice can be found in the Yellow Pages directory, and some local planning authorities keep a list of local architects. The RIBA has regional offices with lists of local members, and their office in London (66 Portland Place, London W1N 4AD) has a free clients' advisory service. The RIBA has a free leaflet *On working with your architect* on smaller building projects, and details of architects' fees and services are in the RIBA booklet *Architect's appointment: small works* (£1 plus postage from RIBA Publications, Finsbury Mission, Moreland Street, London EC1V 8BB).

All the professional bodies of architects also provide an advisory service to help people find the right architect for the right job, and provide booklets relating to terms of appointment and scale of fees. These various booklets are advisory only, in that they are the basis for negotiation, and no professional body of architects compels its members to work to a fixed scale of fees.

BUILDING SURVEYORS

If you had a structural survey done of the house, the surveyor who did that should also be qualified to advise on building work. If not, you can contact the **Royal Institution of Chartered Surveyors** (12 Great George Street, London SW1P 3AD; in Scotland, 9 Manor Place, Edinburgh EH3 7DN) or to the **Incorporated Association of Architects and Surveyors** (Jubilee House, Billing Brook Road, Weston Favell, Northampton NN3 4NW) or to the **Faculty of Architects and Surveyors** (15 St Mary Street, Chippenham, Wiltshire SN15 3JN). These bodies provide an advisory service to help people to find the right building surveyor for the job; and all of them suggest a voluntary scale of fees.

BUILDING OR DESIGN CONSULTANTS

Firms and individuals who call themselves consultants of various types – architectural, building, design, architectural surveying – are not formally qualified and not registered as architects, but carry out work similar to that of registered architects. They are not bound to adhere to any professional code (and may not be insured for negligence). You should ask the consultant during an initial discussion what his charges are likely to be based on. Check that the person you want to use has professional indemnity insurance cover. If he does not, it would be difficult to have a claim met should things go wrong.

BUILDERS

Generally, the best way to get a good builder is through a recommendation. If you have just moved into a new area, ask neighbours and local estate agents. If you are consulting an architect or building surveyor, he should be able to advise you on a suitable builder, as part of his services. Some builders advertise, or put their name on boards outside houses where they are working.

The **Federation of Master Builders** (33 John Street, London WC1N 2BB) can be asked for the names of members. Those on their national register of warranted builders are bound by a code of practice and offer a warranty that defects arising

within 2 years due to faulty workmanship or materials will be put right by that builder or another registered builder. The warranty also provides payment (maximum £8000) towards any reasonable additional costs if the builder ceases trading while your work is in progress.

The **Building Employers Confederation** (82 New Cavendish Street, London W1M 8AD) has regional offices throughout England and Wales (the Scottish Building Employers Federation covers all areas north of the border) which can supply the names of suitable member firms or give a full list from which you can make your own choice. Members of the Building Employers Confederation participate in a guarantee scheme which includes a 6-month defects liability period, a further 2-year guarantee period covering structural defects and some cover if the builder goes bankrupt or defaults.

If possible, estimates should be obtained from two or three builders, particularly if extensive work is involved. Write out a list of the work you wish to be done, so that each one can estimate for exactly the same job. If you want the new work to match in with the existing building, you must make this clear.

The work

Knocking down walls, dismantling wooden fitments, getting at pipes or wiring and so on, are all jobs which create an amazing amount of dust, dirt and debris. Any floor coverings should be protected or removed, and any fittings in the house or flat covered or moved away where possible before any workmen start.

If fitted carpets have to be lifted, see that these are rolled, not folded, so that they do not become badly creased. Watch out that builder's rubble is not 'tidied' under floor boards, in the roof space or even on to a neighbour's flat roof.

Any work that involves making holes in the wall, putting things into or behind walls or ceilings (particularly plumbing or electrical work) is likely to necessitate replastering afterwards and probably repainting. Such work should, therefore, be done before redecorating and final cleaning.

Where a large amount of rubbish and builder's rubble results from demolition work, make it the builder's responsibility to remove it.

HEATING AND INSULATION

You may be able to get a grant towards the cost of installing central heating if it is part of a comprehensive improvement plan for your house – but not if you are installing central heating only, or central heating combined with inessential other work. Apply to the local authority about this grant.

Installation may necessitate

○ estimates and preliminary discussion
○ up to two weeks' work, depending on the type and size
○ water supply temporarily turned off
○ plumber/electrician/plasterer.

The **National Association of Plumbing, Heating and Mechanical Services Contractors** (6 Gate Street, London WC2A 3HX, telephone 01-405 2678) and the **Heating and Ventilating Contractors' Association** (34 Palace Court, London W2 4JG) can be asked for the names of members in any area.

Grants are available to private householders from local authorities in some circumstances to pay a percentage of the cost of insulating an inadequately insulated loft and for lagging pipes and water tanks. A Department of the Environment leaflet about the homes insulation scheme is available free from the local authority and citizens advice bureaux.

DAMP, ROT AND WOODWORM

A builder may be able to find and deal with minor localised problems caused by a defective damp proof course; putting in a new or replacement damp proof course is a specialist job. An improvement grant from the local authority may be obtainable to help pay for this, but remember that it takes time to get such a grant and you must not start work before it is approved.

A report on getting rid of damp in houses in *Which?* March 1985 deals with reducing condensation, spotting and curing penetrating damp and rising damp, and the various types of damp proof course and points to check. A *Which?* report in January 1987 *A lot of rot* deals with dry rot, wet rot, woodworm, and compares advice given by treatment firms.

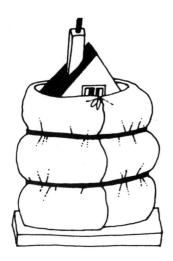

Technical pamphlet no 8 *Treatment of damp in old buildings* (£1) and information sheets (40p) on timber treatment and the treatment of rising damp in old buildings, available from SPAB.

If you are getting a mortgage, the building society or other lenders may require that damp, rot or woodworm problems be dealt with immediately, as a condition of the loan. They may want a guarantee for the work, in which case it will have to be done by a specialist firm (preferably backed up by the Guarantee Protection Trust in case the firm goes bankrupt).

Names of specialist firms who are members of their relevant trade association can be obtained from the **British Wood Preserving Association** (6 The Office Village, 4 Romford Road, London E15 4EA) and the **British Chemical Dampcourse Association** (16a Whitchurch Road, Pangbourne, Berks RG8 7BP).

ROOF REPAIRS

A report on roof repairs was published in **Which?** March 1984, and the report on outdoor maintenance in April 1988 includes information on caring for your roof.

It is worth checking the roof again at this stage for any signs of loose tiles or gutters blocked by leaves and dirt. Overflowing gutters are often the cause of damp soaking through walls or under eaves. Fitting mesh guards will prevent leaves from being washed into the tops of any down pipes.

Chimneys may need to be repointed, or the flashing replaced. Check that any television aerial is securely attached, but is not damaging the chimney itself. If any chimney is used to flue-in a gas appliance, it is worth having a 'cage' put over the chimney pot, to save having to call in the RSPCA or fire brigade to release a trapped bird – birds seem prone to falling down chimneys, perhaps overcome by fumes as they perch.

ELECTRICITY

Plan what lighting you would like in the new home at an early stage, in case any new wiring – for spot lights or wall lights, for instance – will be necessary.

Depending on the age of your new home, it may be a pre-condition for obtaining a mortgage that its electrical installation is examined in detail to confirm its safety (previous owners may have altered it incorrectly).

In any case, if the house is more than 30 years old, the wiring will almost certainly need replacing if this has never been done. Switches, socket outlets and pendent light cords that are more than about 15 years old are also likely to need replacing.

The electricity board or a private electrical contractor will survey the wiring and provide a report or an inspection certificate. You can get the names of approved electrical contractors from the **National Inspection Council for Electrical Installation Contracting** (NICEIC), Vintage House, 36/37 Albert Embankment, London SE1 7UJ (01-582 7746) or from your public library or electricity board shop. The list also indicates those who are members of the **Electrical Contractors' Association** (34 Palace Court, London W2 4HY). The **Electrical Contractors' Association of Scotland** (23 Heriot Row, Edinburgh EH3 6EW, freephone 8490) will supply a list of their members in any area and has free leaflets with advice to householders.

The survey will also tell you how the electrical installation is arranged and enable you to plan what lighting, additional sockct outlets (for portable appliances) and fused connection units (for stationary appliances) you would like, in case any additional wiring is necessary. Sockets to provide power for electrical power tools or portable devices, such as lawn mowers, must be fitted with a special safety device.

Consider the electricity consumption of lights which stay on for a long time, to luminate a dark corridor or staircase, for example. Modern, fluorescent lamps use considerably less electricity than tungsten bulbs of similar light output, and have a longer life and in some situations recoup the initial higher cost quickly.

An advantage of rewiring completely, whether this is absolutely necessary or not, is that it gives you the chance to increase the number of socket outlets or to re-position existing ones, according to how you want to use them and where you plan to put your furniture.

The Electrical Installation Industry Liaison Committee has recommended the following minimum number of socket outlets to be provided in homes:

kitchen	4	single bedroom/teenager's room	3
living room	6	landing/stairs	1
dining room	3	hall	1
double bedroom	4	store/workroom	2
single bed-sitting room	4	central heating boiler room	1

Rewiring or extending electrical circuits, putting in or moving a socket may mean temporary disconnection of the electricity supply and replastering after running cables under the plaster or through ceilings.

A report on light bulbs in **Which?** July 1987 is a guide to the types of bulb available, and shows how you can save money by choosing the right bulbs.

Reports on power points were published in **Which?** in May 1985 and July 1986.

When completed, a new installation (a new circuit for a first-time electric cooker, for instance) or a major alteration should be tested by a qualified electrical engineer (a member of the NICEIC) and a formal test certificate issued. You should notify the electricity board who may inspect before connecting or re-connecting the supply.

PLUMBING

The existing plumbing may need to be modified to install a new sink or basin, an extra wc or shower or to plumb in an automatic washing machine or dishwasher, for example.

New installation or renewal of plumbing may mean replastering and having the water supply temporarily turned off.

Sanitary plumbing and drainage has to comply with the Building Regulations; if you are in any doubt, consult your local authority's building control department.

Any water fitting to be installed (a shower, for instance) has to comply with the water bye-laws, to prevent waste, misuse, undue consumption and contamination of water. The installation of fittings is subject to the approval (and possible inspection) of the local water authority who interpret and enforce their own bye-laws and who should be notified at least seven days before work starts on the installation.

A report on plumbing and problems appeared in *Which?* March 1986 and on plumbers in *Which?* September 1983.

The **Institute of Plumbing** (64 Station Lane, Hornchurch, Essex RM12 6NB; telephone 04024 72791) maintains a register of plumbers and can supply a list of registered plumbers in business in a particular area (send s.a.e.). The register is continually monitored by the British Standards Institution under the PRIMA (Public Register Inspection Maintenance Assessment) scheme. The Institute also publishes an annual *Business directory of registered plumbers* (available in public libraries).

FLOORS

Wooden floors should be checked for loose joists or supports, loose boards or nails, projecting knots and warping, and big holes or cracks which would have to be filled in.

Flooring has to be laid after any piping for central heating or any rewiring has been completed. Ensure that any nailing is not where pipes or wires run underneath. It is a good idea to mark the floorboards with the position of cables and pipes beneath; this will make them easier to find if anything goes wrong later.

Kitchen flooring – other than carpets or carpet tiles – should be laid before floor-standing kitchen units are fitted and before a dishwasher or washing machine gets plumbed in.

A report on choosing and fitting carpets was published in **Which?** February 1988.

Carpets and underlay should not be laid until floors have been finally cleaned and allowed to dry thoroughly. It is easier to lay new carpets before moving in, but make sure that they will be protected during the move.

TELEPHONE

In most older houses, wiring for the telephone is on the surface along skirting boards or picture rails. The telephone wiring can be concealed in conduits or channels built in while a house is being structurally modified.

If the house has an old-style telephone, new plug-in connections can now be installed or extra sockets added to an existing line.

Once you have one plug-in socket and line installed by British Telecom (cost £25 plus VAT), you can yourself add other sockets if you wish by buying a d-i-y kit from BT (£9.95 for one socket, £14.95 for two sockets, including wiring, clips, tool) or in a shop. Or you can get an electrician to do the connection for you.

Telephones were included in a report *Rent or buy* in **Which?** October 1986, and a **Which?** report in November 1987 assessed the telephones then on the market.

There is now a wide range of telephone styles that can be used in a plug-in socket, varying in shape and colour and sophistication – and price. British Telecom has a leaflet showing all the models that you can buy or rent from them, and there are many other models for sale through shops and other outlets.

Any telephone or socket kit you buy should be one approved by the British Approvals Board of Telecommunications as suitable for use with British Telecom lines, and which therefore carries the BABT approval label with a green circle.

The **Telecommunications Industry Association** (364-366 Fulham Road, London SW10 9UH, telephone 01-351 7115) can give information about items of equipment and the names of independent contractors.

BURGLAR ALARM

A report on protecting your home in **Which?** November 1987 includes advice and information on burglar alarms, and one in June 1988 warns about sales methods of burglar alarm firms.

It would be sensible to review the security of your new home as soon as possible.

Each house or flat presents different problems. You can ask at the local police station for a crime prevention officer (CPO) to come and give you free advice on the security measures that would be appropriate to your home.

Burglar alarms, usually installed by specialist firms, can be fitted to doors and windows, and so can special locks. Some burglar alarms are triggered by pressure mats under carpets or flooring and should be placed in position before carpeting is laid and in places where they will not be set off by any pieces of furniture when these are later put in their permanent places.

The **National Supervisory Council for Intruder Alarms** (Queensgate House, 14 Cookham Road, Maidenhead, Berks SL6 8AJ, telephone 0628 37512) maintains a register of companies that it has approved as alarm system installers.

Inadvertent damage may be done to an existing burglar alarm system during building work, so check when all the work is finished.

HOUSE CLEANING AND DECORATING

A **Which?** report on decorating and design advice was published in February 1987.

Redecorating of any rooms is considerably easier, quicker and less messy if the room is empty of furniture, carpets and curtains; a professional decorator should therefore charge somewhat less.

Thorough cleaning of the house or flat includes washing paintwork, walls, insides of cupboards, scrubbing floors, cleaning windows. There are firms specialising in general cleaning work who will supply people to do the cleaning with the necessary equipment. Ask for estimates first.

Carpet cleaning firms will clean fitted carpets in situ. Have this done after all other work is finished but allow a few days for them to dry before furniture is moved in. Loose carpets and rugs can be taken away for cleaning on the firm's premises, to be returned before moving-in day. Various types of carpet shampooers can be hired. Some removal firms undertake carpet cleaning.

The Which? book of do-it-yourself gives information about materials, tools and techniques for doing a wide variety of jobs.

A report in **Which?** August 1987, *Buying d-i-y materials*, includes a survey of shops, showing where you can buy at the lowest prices.

doing your own repairs, alterations, decorations

If you are a do-it-yourself enthusiast, you may look forward to doing a lot of the necessary work in the home. There are some factors you should take into account when deciding whether or not to do any of these jobs yourself.

- *how difficult is the job?*
  This may depend on your age, fitness and temperament, as well as your previous d-i-y experience, and what tools and equipment you have.

  If it is something you have not done before, you will need to spend some time learning about the job – how systems work, how to design your own, what equipment to use, how to go about it, and so on. The bigger the job, the more diverse the range of small tasks it is likely to involve. Plastering and advanced carpentry are two jobs which require skill and practice.

- *does it save you money?*
  Doing it yourself saves money mainly because you do not have to pay for someone else's time, overheads and profit on materials. The most profitable jobs to do for yourself are those for which the professional rates are high.

- *are there any risks?*
  You can hurt yourself while doing the job (advice on some of the hazards and how to avoid them is given in *Which?* June 1985). The results of some d-i-y jobs could be dangerous, particularly electrical work. (Only qualified gas fitters are allowed to work on anything to do with connecting gas supply to an appliance.)

HIRING EQUIPMENT

You may need equipment for repairs or decorations which you would not normally use and so would not want to have to buy and store. There are d-i-y hire shops in most large towns. If you do not know of one, look in the local paper or under 'Hire contractors' in the Yellow Pages directory.

Which? February 1986 contains a full report on where and how you can hire equipment, which items are better hired or bought, and what to look for when hiring.

Arranging the move

Q

It is well worth spending the money – it would have taken us two tiring days to move ourselves – the removal firm arrived at 8am and we were unpacked at 2pm!

Q

Don't be tempted to do your own move. I was very impressed with how hard and fast the men worked. Worth every penny + a fat tip.

A report on moving home, published in **Which?** May 1988, includes advice on choosing a removal firm.

Q

Removal companies needed 3 to 6 weeks notice – impossible from exchange date.

Using a removal firm is a more expensive way of moving than borrowing or hiring a van and being your own removers with the help of friends or relatives.

A lot will depend on how much stuff you have to move. If you have a considerable quantity of furniture or belongings or a number which are large, heavy or awkward to move, or if there are any difficulties of access, flights of stairs or long distances to carry furniture out or in, do not do it yourself unless you are very tough and strong and prepared for really hard work.

The preparatory work of clearing up before leaving a home, plus organising and preparing the new one, can be extremely tiring. If this is then to be followed by one or two days of very hard physical work, lifting and carrying for hours on end, the effect can be cumulatively one of total exhaustion.

If you are working full-time, or if you are elderly or unfit, pregnant or have small children, you may think it worth the cost of paying for all the packing and moving to be done by experts, so that all you have to do is the supervisory work, plus transporting yourself (and your family) from one place to the other. Even with a removal firm, the actual day of the move is a tiring one.

Removal men are usually experienced, and pack and move quickly – much quicker than you could. They may not seem to be as careful with your belongings as you would be but a professional remover is used to handling articles in a way that avoids damage.

If you are moving a distance, particularly if you have a lot of furniture, using a removal firm will be more practical than hiring a self-drive van with which you would have to make several journeys (plus one more in order to return the van to its owner).

With a removal firm

If you decide to pay for a firm to do your removal for you, you should set about choosing one well in advance. Find out the names of local firms as well as of the larger national firms and ask friends and neighbours for recommendations and warnings.

The **British Association of Removers** (277 Gray's Inn Road, London WC1X 8SY) will give the names and addresses of members and send leaflets *Your key to a successful removal* and *Moving home* if you send a stamped self-addressed envelope. Many firms who are members of the BAR provide similar leaflets – or a whole kit of them – for potential customers.

Prices vary considerably, so you should get at least two, preferably three, estimates. These are usually given free. If you are moving to a different area, consider getting a quotation from firms in the area you are moving to.

Q

Get more than one quote from removal firm, as our quotes varied by up to nearly £500 for a move from Yorkshire to Devon.

getting an estimate

As soon as you have some idea of the date of your move, ask the removal firms to send a representative to give you an estimate. It is not wise to accept an estimate given over the telephone: you may find yourself supplied with too few men or too small a van when the day comes (or too large a van – and bill).

When the estimator arrives, he should inspect all your house or flat and garden to see what quantity and type of furniture and belongings are involved. Do not forget to show him the contents of any loft, garage or garden shed. Also point out if any items are to be left behind so that these are not included in an estimate, or if any have to be picked up from some other place or are being bought before the move.

Q

Get a good quote by someone who comes round to actually look. Don't accept a telephone quote of an hourly rate. It could take ages longer than the estimate and probably will.

Charges are calculated either
- *according to the quantity and type of belongings to be packed and moved*
  The firm's estimator can judge how many van loads and how many men will be needed. He will take into account whether the move is a local one which can be completed in one day, or, if it is a long distance one, what length of time it will take and what overnight stays there may have to be.

or
- *according to the time taken over the packing and move*
  Charges can be based on an hourly rate (not suitable for a move of any distance), by half a day or day. Check what the hours concerned are: when does morning/afternoon begin and end? is a day 8 hours, 12 hours or 24 hours? does the rate per hour vary according to the hour of the day? when would overtime start, and at what rate? (If you do not get access to your new home until, say, after lunch, you could be involved in overtime.)

Hourly charges are normally based on a depot to depot principle, but mealtimes are usually excluded from the charge. Charges may be more (or less) expensive for a move on certain days of the week, but this would not help you if you are committed to move on a certain day because of your completion date.

Charges are often quoted excluding VAT, so check if VAT is an extra.

If you are able to reduce the quantity to be packed by doing a lot of it yourself beforehand, you could reduce the cost. If you are moving only a short distance and have access to your new home before the day of the move, you can transport small loads yourself in advance.

Things to discuss with the estimator

WHETHER YOU ASK THE FIRM	PRO	CON
to pack everything	important if you work full time/are elderly/unfit/have small children	more expensive
to pack only your crockery and glass for you	cheaper	needs effort and plenty of time in advance to pack contents of wardrobes, cupboards, bookcases
to provide chests, crates or purpose-made cardboard cartons for you to do packing	even cheaper	needs time in advance, effort and skill in packing breakables properly; if you pack and they carry, you may have difficulty in getting compensation for any breakage
to do the unpacking for you	important if you work full time/are elderly/unfit/have small children	more expensive; need to know at once where in new house items are to be unpacked (tiring exercise at end of moving day)
to do no unpacking and collect cases at later date (may not be possible for a move to an area some distance away)	unpacking can be done at leisure; cuts cost, especially if charge is on hourly basis (unless there is a charge for collecting later)	needs somewhere to store emptied cases to await collection deposit payable for cases left, may be only 50% refund on collection
whether the move needs to be spread over more than one day	possibly less wear and tear/pressure	extra expense (including overnight accommodation)

Q

Let the professionals do the packing and unpacking and open a bottle of champagne when it's all finished.

Removal firms do not generally accept responsibility for damage to any items which have not been packed by them, and nor do their insurers.

You should point out to the estimator any of your belongings that may need special packing, or may present problems in handling or transporting, such as
    pictures
    audio equipment, records
    collection of valuable objects
    antiques, fragile items
    books, if a large quantity or of special quality
    freezer, home safe
    wine
    plants, animals
    any heater or appliance fuelled with LPG.

Point out any built-in cupboards or shelves that will need dismantling to get them out (but they may not be designed to be dismantled and reassembled – some of the cheaper chipboard systems will not fit together again satisfactorily).

For pictures and mirrors, there are corrugated packs which the removal firm might offer to supply; mattress sacks also are available.

Some firms offer special cardboard cartons or 'travel boxes' for use with an inner paper sack or liner (which can be filled separately) that fits into the box. The advantage is that the paper sacks can be sent by post to the client who can fill them ahead of time, and they are then left to be unpacked at leisure after the move. The cartons are less likely to snag the carpet or scratch the floor than the old-fashioned tea chests, and can be carried by one person.

PIANO

Some firms have the special trolleys ('shoes') and webbing for transporting pianos and are accustomed to handling them. Others subcontract to a specialist transport firm, particularly if there is any difficulty about getting an instrument in or out of a house or flat – through a window, for instance. Check with the estimator, and if your piano is a valuable one or there is any problem about moving it, consider engaging a specialist firm. Look in the local classified telephone directory or contact any local concert hall, theatre, or piano retailer for advice.

CARPETS

If any are to be moved, discuss whether the men will lift and re-lay these, or only spread them out on delivery, or just unload them. Lifting and re-laying, particularly of fitted carpets, may be charged extra.

CLOTHES

Ask whether clothes, linen, other contents can be left in drawers, and whether the removers can provide 'wardrobe' packing cartons to hang clothes in (these are large, collapsible cardboard cartons in which there is a clip-on plastic rail on which clothes can be hung straight from a wardrobe). Some firms will leave these for collection later, so that the cartons need not be unpacked immediately.

ACCESS

Q

Wall units were unable to go through front door and had to be lifted over a back fence into garden.

If the approach to your new home (or to the present one) is at all difficult, mention this to the removal firm's estimator. A steep drive might be too much for a large van, or a narrow entrance or approach road could mean having to use two smaller vans. Many houses do not have direct access for a van, so if belongings will have to be carried a long distance from van to house, tell the removal firm's estimator.

If there are parking problems at either end – for instance, restrictions on parking during certain hours – you will be expected to make arrangements with the local police for permission to load or unload, or pay to have a parking meter suspended. The removers may ask you to reserve a parking space if possible the night before.

If the move is into or out of a block of flats, tell the removers about the availability and size of any lifts, and whether there is permission to use them for goods (some landlords insist on removals going up the stairs).

Check with the estimator who is to provide coverings for the floor (at either end of the move). For example, parquet floors or fancy stone tiles in kitchens may need to be boarded over before heavy items are rolled over them. If the firm agrees to provide coverings, it is wise to get this confirmed in writing.

Go over in your mind the layout of your new home and assess whether there could be any problems about getting any of your furniture into it. Narrow staircases or awkward corners, for example, could mean temporarily taking a window out in order to get access to a room, and the removers might need to bring special equipment to deal with this. Do not leave it until the day of the move but warn the estimator when he is with you – otherwise, you could be faced with extra charges for difficulties in unloading.

Do not think that if you say nothing about likely difficulties they will not add to the cost. On the contrary, if there is any serious delay, you are likely to get an extra bill.

If anything is not absolutely straightforward, confirm your requirements in writing so that the firm has no excuse to say that it was not agreed or included in the estimate.

acceptance of the estimate

The firm's estimate is likely to be on a standard form which incorporates the terms and conditions. Study carefully the small print concerning claims, exclusion clauses about liability (even though, in law, they may not be enforceable) and insurance cover. If a removal firm is a member of the British Association of Removers, it will probably use a standard contract, the clauses of which have been drawn to protect the firm. You may be able to add terms of your own or ask for unacceptable ones to be deleted.

Although the terms and conditions are usually the same, prices can vary considerably from firm to firm. Many firms ask for payment to be made in advance; you may be able to arrange to pay on the day of the move. Some firms accept Access or Barclaycard; this can help to spread your outgoings.

When you accept an estimate, you are expected to give a firm date for the job and, having booked a date, you would have to give reasonable notice if you want to change it, otherwise the firm may well charge a cancellation fee.

the removal men

The estimator's principal job is to assess how much the firm should charge you, rather than make arrangements for the practical aspects and convenience of the move. He will not be there on the day. He should pass on any messages or warnings about what is involved and any special requirements of yours direct to the foreman of the team who comes. But do not rely on this: write down all the relevant details and send them to the firm in advance, to be given to the foreman.

Ask how many men will be provided. There should be at least three if the removers do all the packing, so that one man can be packing china, glass, kitchenware, etcetera, into containers while the others carry and load large items. Ring up on the day before the move to confirm the time when the men and van(s) are due to arrive.

insurance for the move

While the contents of your home are being moved from one building to another, they may automatically remain insured by your household contents policy. (If your contents policy includes 'contents temporarily removed', do not assume that this covers a household removal: check with the insurers.) If not, most insurers will extend an existing contents policy to take in the increased risks of a removal, at an additional premium (likely to be at least £25). Insurers are unlikely to be willing to issue a separate household removal policy if you have no existing insurance with them.

Provided you are going to have the removal undertaken by a specialist firm of removers, you should have little difficulty in getting insurance.

The cover offered is usually on the basis of what is called 'all-risks' insurance for loss or damage, and includes accidental breakages, but excludes scratches and dents. Very often, you are expected to pay a part (which may be as much as £50) of any claim. This is called an excess.

Ask whether you would get the replacement value for any article lost, or the value at the time allowing for depreciation and wear and tear. Make certain that you insure for the maximum value of your goods: if you are under-insured, you may receive only a proportion of the amount of your claim.

Watch out for the 'pairs and sets clause' which means that the insurers will not pay for the cost of replacing any undamaged item forming part of a set when replacements cannot be matched – this could leave you with an odd one out.

Tell the insurers if your removal necessitates overnight storage in the van, to make sure that the policy will cover this. A householders policy does not cover storage at the removal firm's depot; other policies can be extended to do so.

Removals insurance generally excludes the loss of or damage to bank notes, shares, bonds, deeds, stamps, securities; also, loss or damage due to atmospheric or climatic conditions, strikes, delay, the nature of the goods insured. There are likely to be other exclusions, depending on the insurers. Melamine furniture, for instance, is likely not to be covered.

Consequential loss is also excluded: removals insurance does not cover any additional expenses you may incur due to the loss of your furniture or belongings. For instance, unlike a householders contents policy, you cannot claim for having to stay in a hotel or for the expense of making arrangements for new furniture to be bought.

Check the time limit within which a claim must be made in writing both to the insurers and the removal firm. Three days of the delivery of the property sounds reasonable enough. But if for some reason you are delayed or arrangements have to be made for delivery in your absence, it could technically invalidate a claim later.

It is also as well to find out whether the policy is restricted to goods that are professionally packed – which most policies are. If so, remember to allow the removers' men to pack everything. Do not help them do it, even if it means you have to stand around and watch all day, because if you help and something gets broken, the insurers will be able to repudiate your claim because you did not comply with the condition. Remember also that, for the same reason, the removers must unpack everything.

insurance through the removal firm
If insurance is part of the removal firm's contract, there may be a specified (low) limit on what will be paid as compensation.

Members of the British Association of Removers have to undertake to provide a specified minimum standard of insurance cover for their customers.

Ask what the premium would be for the amount you want to insure and what the maximum payment would be for any one item. You should insist on seeing in writing exactly what is covered, the time limit for making a claim, how much of each claim you will be expected to bear and all the principal exclusion clauses before paying the premium and accepting the insurance.

As I moved on a do-it-yourself basis, I had to have helpers but this turned out to have bad side effects as well. Family and friends turned up and order was difficult to keep and time was lost instead of gained. Also one has to take into account the cost of feeding a band of helpers for the day.

Allocate everyone a specific job.

A do-it-yourself move

The advantage of a do-it-yourself move is that it is cheaper than a professional move: the basic cost is the hire of a van plus petrol, or only petrol if a van can be borrowed from a friend who owns one, or from your employer.

If you can take the opportunity to help someone else with a d-i-y move, you will learn a lot about the knack of negotiating stairs and doorways with pieces of furniture, also about packing a van to make maximum use of its capacity.

The disadvantages of a d-i-y move are that it

- is physically very tiring
- needs strong and willing helpers who can be available on the day(s) of the move
- needs plenty of time in advance for pre-packing since the day(s) of the move will be spent carrying and loading
- is not easy if you have a lot of things or heavy equipment to move and they have to be carried up or down stairs
  or where there are difficulties of access – for example, where the house is in a pedestrian court
- is only practical for moves of short distances – say, not more than 50 miles; a number of journeys with a small van over a greater distance adds to the time and cost, and the hired van has to be returned to its depot at the finish
- necessitates providing your own packing cases and packing materials, rope or webbing to secure items in the van, blankets or other protection for polished surfaces.

hire of a van

Before you decide on a self-drive van, you should be sure that you could cope with driving an unfamiliar vehicle. One that is larger than a private car can take some getting used to, and parking a van which has restricted rear vision may also be quite difficult. But an experienced car driver, even if unused to handling any type of van, can probably cope with a laden 18 cwt van.

A self-drive van may be hired from nationwide companies specialising in this type of hire or from a local hire firm. Look in the Yellow Pages directory or the

Q

Extra day's hire of van: too exhausted at the end of first day to return in van.

Q

Packing everything ready to put in the van took 3 times as long as I'd expected. Driving the van was slow and noisy. Again the journey took twice as long as I'd reckoned and the noise and vibration were such that I felt I had a hangover the next day!

small ads columns of your local paper, or ask friends or colleagues for a recommendation.

The bigger firms may have several sizes of vehicle from 8 cwt vans up to 7 ton trucks, which can be driven on an ordinary driving licence. For trucks or lorries above $7\frac{1}{2}$ tonnes laden weight, an HGV (heavy goods vehicle) category licence is necessary. You are allowed to drive small goods vehicles (up to $3\frac{1}{2}$ tonnes laden weight) from the age of 17, between $3\frac{1}{2}$ and $7\frac{1}{2}$ tonnes laden weight from the age of 18.

Hire firms may stipulate any other minimum age limit, or that a licence has been held for at least a year, and is a clean one. When you hire a self-drive van, the company will want to see your driving licence so do not send this off to the licensing authority to notify them of your change of address until you have completed the move.

If you prefer to hire a van plus driver – which will probably cost a bit more – find out whether the driver will help you with the loading and carrying or not. Whatever the size of the van, he will be subject to the regulations on goods vehicle drivers' hours – he must not drive more than 9 hours in the course of one day, and must take the stipulated rest breaks.

SIZE

The hire firm will gave you the dimensions and cubic capacity of the various vehicles. It is difficult for the amateur to estimate from the capacity of a van what loads it will take and therefore the number of journeys that will be necessary. Because you will not be experienced in loading economically, work on the basis of needing more capacity and making more journeys than you may at first think.

The size of the door opening of different makes of van varies, so if you have large items of furniture, measure these first and choose a van with sufficient door size. This is especially important if a refrigerator or freezer has to be moved because these should always be kept in an upright position.

A van with a low kerb height or a let-down tailboard can be very useful; a truck with a hydraulic tail lift is invaluable for loading and unloading cooker, wardrobes or other bulky furniture. Alternatively, see whether some form of ramp can be built up into the rear of the van. Find out about hiring or borrowing a trolley or a wheeled platform for moving a cooker, refrigerator, washing machine, and other heavy items.

COST OF HIRING A VAN

Charges may be either

- a fixed sum per day or week for unlimited mileage during the period of the hire or
- a smaller fixed sum per day plus a mileage charge, or an allowance of free miles followed by a mileage charge.

Ask whether VAT is included in the charge, or will be added.

Work out whether it would be cheaper to pay a higher daily rate and nothing for mileage, or a lower rate plus mileage costs. To make this comparison, you need to have some idea of how many miles you will be driving during the period of hire. Subtract the lower rental charge from the higher one and divide the answer by the charge per mile. The result will give you the breakeven point: if you drive more than this number of miles, the firm offering unlimited mileage is probably cheaper; if fewer miles, the firm charging so-much per mile will be cheaper.

Check the exact hours of hire and what happens if the van is returned late – there could be a penalty charge, or you may be charged for another 24 hours' hire. If you know you are going to be late, let the firm know – if only for the sake of the next hirer waiting.

Find out when a day starts and ends (whether it is 24 hours, or perhaps 9am to 6pm). Consider whether it is worth starting the hire on the day before the move, so as to be able to get most things packed in, ready for moving off early the next morning (after a night's sleep). But do not load a van the night before a move unless you can lock it securely and park it safely, or put it in a lock-up garage.

You will have to return the van to the hiring place, so you have to cost in the extra mileage and time. It may be more sensible to hire in the place to which you are moving, so as not to have a return drive at the end of moving day (plus an extra return journey then).

Find out what insurance is included and what is excluded. There may be an excess of £200 or more which you would have to pay towards the cost of any damage to the vehicle. It may be possible to pay a small extra premium to have the excess clause waived. Some van hire firms will arrange goods-in-transit insurance cover, if required.

You will be asked for a deposit when hiring the van, but will get it back when you return the van. Some hirers ask for a deposit to cover the amount of the insurance excess.

In your calculations of the cost of petrol to cover however many journeys you think you will make, remember that an 18 cwt van does no more than about 20 mpg. Ask what the tyre pressures should be for the van when laden, so that you can check them before driving with your load.

loading a hired van

Remember that the order in which the items are put into the van will be the reverse when unloading. You will want to offload any carpets first, so these should go in last. Also, any heavy items that will be upstairs in the new house should be loaded near the end so that at the unloading stage the toughest work can be done at the beginning. But keep in mind the stability of the van – heavy items should be packed low down and distributed overall.

When stacking the van, try to make flat surfaces and use rugs or blankets on top of pieces of furniture to protect them from scratches. Damage can be caused if the furniture moves about while in transit, so make certain everything is wedged firmly to prevent this. The contents of the drawers of a chest of drawers can be left in them, covered with newspaper or towels. Remove the drawers while loading the emptied chest on to the van, replace them for travelling, and reverse the process when unloading. It may be wise to code the drawers as they are not always interchangeable. Cupboards and wardrobes can be filled with small boxes when they have been loaded into the van.

There may not be enough space for your helpers to travel in the van once it is loaded, so remember to arrange separate transport for them if you want the same team to help you unload at the other end.

Q

I moved all my possessions myself and took 4 days to shift all the odds and ends – that was planned, but I hadn't realised just how tired I would be after unpacking and refilling boxes up to 3 times. Next time I'll hire enough crates and keep them for one week before and 2 weeks after the move.

timetable and check list for moving

	TICK WHEN DONE	NOTES/DATE
about 4 weeks to a week before	Get 3 removal firms' estimates and/or quotes for d-i-y van hire charges Choose firm; confirm arrangements D-i-y: alert friends/family for help on the day (packing, driving, providing meals, cleaning up, being available) *old address* Arrange for meters to be read Arrange for disconnection of cooker – washing machine – dishwasher Arrange for carpets to be cleaned if required *new address* Arrange for taking over – gas – electricity Arrange for reconnection of cooker – washing machine – dishwasher Arrange for carpets to be laid	
	Notify telephone sales office of date account to be closed *new address* Apply to take over telephone or request new telephone to be installed extra sockets if required	
	Change of address cards – buy, or order printing (after new telephone number known)	
	Arrange insurance of contents at new house from date of move and during removal	
	Start sorting and throwing out things, getting rid of surplus Arrange extra rubbish disposal	
	Get boxes, packing materials, strong string Buy stick-on labels	
	Arrange any hotel booking that may be needed	
	Children – arrange to leave with relatives/friends Pets – book kennels	

1 week before	Prepare diagram of new house with location of furniture
	Send off change of address cards
	Bank etc. – arrange for transfer of account Post office – apply for redirection of mail *old address* Arrange cancellation of deliveries and settlement of accounts: – milk – newspapers – laundry *new address* Arrange deliveries e.g. milk
	Put valuables and documents in bank/safe place Tell police of imminent move
	Check arrangements for hiring van/borrowing car Get own car serviced
	Confirm arrangements and timings for meter readings and disconnection/connection at old/new address: – electricity – gas Arrange with seller and buyer about leaving off/on: – electricity – water – heating
	old address Arrange for leaving keys *new address* Check arrangements for collecting keys
	Finish packing and labelling
	Prepare survival kit
day before	Pack personal overnight case(s) Organise meals/drinks for moving day Switch freezer to maximum (if moving it with contents) Take children to relatives or friends to stay Deliver pets to kennels Get supply of cash (e.g. for tips, meals, petrol, coins for emergency telephone calls) Defrost refrigerator Go to bed early
moving day	See page 253 *et seq*

Preparing to move out

Allow plenty of time to sort out your possessions and, if you are going to do so yourself, to pack them. How long to allow for preliminary sorting will depend on how much you have accumulated, and this will probably be related to how long you have spent in your present home. Far too many of us keep junk stored in loft, garage or garden shed. Tackle these hoarding places as early as possible – months ahead, if possible – because they take longest to sort and clear out.

If you are moving into a smaller house or flat, you will have to decide what to keep and what to discard.

If you want to delay a decision on some things in case you would regret discarding them, ask friends or relatives if they would like to house any item while you think about it, making clear that you might ask for it back. But you can do this only with very close friends or relatives.

It will help to draw scale plans of each room in the new house or flat, then cut out shapes to scale (as far as possible) for each piece of furniture, and see how they will fit into the room. (Remember to allow for the position of electric sockets.) This will not only enable you to see which items to keep but, when you come to the move itself, you will be able to direct the operation so that no pieces of furniture finish up in the wrong room.

Once you have worked out where everything can go, list it room by room so you can direct the removal men (they come thick and fast when they are unloading). Mark the furniture with a code for each room – perhaps with coloured stickers (red for one room, green for another).

Be ruthless about parting with any surplus furniture or equipment – you will not do it once you have moved. Make each member of the family do this, particularly the squirrel-type hoarders.

Disposing of things

Sort unwanted possessions into groups of what you think are saleable items, those which could go to charities or jumble sales, and those of no value to anyone. Disposing of things takes time and can be difficult – another reason for allowing yourself plenty of time to make any arrangements.

SALEABLE ITEMS

Do not get rid of things without checking whether the incoming buyer might not want to buy them at a reasonable price.

CLASSIFIED ADVERTISEMENTS

The local papers (weekly or daily) will serve as a guide to the types of things which are wanted and to current prices. Some localities have publications dealing only with articles For Sale and Wanted.

Find out the advertising rates for your local paper and whether there are any 'free' ones. *Exchange & Mart*, the weekly paper for advertising secondhand goods, has a wide coverage; it is used particularly by advertisers and readers in London and the south of England.

If the article is a piece of special equipment, it might be worth advertising it in the appropriate magazine on the subject. It can take some weeks to have an advertisement included in some magazines, so check this.

You will have to be in to answer the telephone and show the items to prospective buyers. Make sure you get paid before you let any item go.

AUCTION ROOMS

Some towns have permanent auction rooms where regular sales are held. Look in the Yellow Pages directory and for advertisements in the local press.

Go along to the auctioneers and explain what you want to sell. Some auctioneers divide goods offered for sale into groups according to quality, or handle only those of a certain standard. If they think your goods are not suitable for their auctions, they may refer you to a secondary, or chattel, sale room which deals in miscellaneous selections of lots.

Remember to find out what percentage commission (plus VAT) will be deducted from the sale price by the auctioneer. If any items are of good value, discuss whether you should place a reserve figure on them – that is, a sum below which you do not want an item to be sold. You will have to arrange for the goods to be delivered to the sale room, and collected if not sold.

SECONDHAND SHOPS AND DEALERS

Local knowledge is probably the best way of discovering dealers. (Some removal firms are also secondhand furniture dealers.)

Before approaching a dealer, try to gauge current secondhand prices by keeping an eye on advertisements or secondhand shops.

Ask a dealer (or two) to call to inspect what you wish to sell. It may be helpful to have someone with you when he comes, to give you moral and factual support. You may feel diffident about bargaining when you feel you are not being offered a good enough price. The dealer will probably collect the items from you if he agrees to buy them, and you should take this factor into consideration. If your problem is to clear your bulk, do not let the dealer pick out the bits he wants – insist that he takes the lot. Otherwise, you will be left with the unwanted residue.

Books, particularly non-fiction books, may have a saleable value to collectors or specialist secondhand dealers. You may find one through local knowledge or the Yellow Pages directory; ask him to call and make you an offer.

Q

Our sale on the lawn in a marquee was a huge success – well attended and surprised us by the size of the day's takings.

You can organise your own sale by putting the things into the garage or on the lawn, with prices clearly marked, and advertising the fact that they are for 'Sale on sunday between 2pm and 6pm', or whenever.

There may be a 'boot sale' location near you, where you offer whatever you want to sell from the back of your car. You should decide beforehand what prices you will charge – and be prepared to come down (or not). It will take a day out of your pre-move weekend and timetable.

ITEMS FOR CHARITIES AND JUMBLE SALES

Some articles would not be worth selling but could not be considered rubbish – for instance, old clothing, curtains, bedding, toys, crockery, ornaments. Among general secondhand shops are those run for charities which have permanent shops in some towns and may take temporary rent-free premises in others. Consult your local telephone directory, or ask at the citizens advice bureau or a council for voluntary service.

Local private housing associations or homes are sometimes grateful to be given unwanted furniture, carpets or curtains. You could also try the local branch of the Salvation Army if there is one, or your local church, social services department, Red Cross, voluntary organisations. Some voluntary organisations run a 'charity auction': donated goods are auctioned in the conventional way, half the price going to the donor, half to charity.

ITEMS OF NO VALUE

If you finish with a residue of undisposable items – rubbish – you may have to make a special arrangement with the local authority for this to be taken away. There may be a charge for a special collection of this kind. Ask your dustmen first, and if they are unable to collect it as normal domestic refuse, telephone your local council offices and ask what to do.

Some local authorities have established sites where unwanted household waste, old appliances, mattresses, broken furniture can be taken and dumped by householders free of charge. The authority then disposes of it.

For large quantities of rubbish, and where no local authority facilities are available, it may be necessary to hire a container or skip from a commercial firm. Look in the Yellow Pages directory under 'Waste disposal services' or 'Skip hire'. Containers of varying capacity can be hired for the day or for a number of days – over a weekend, for example. It is wise to book ahead. The firm who delivers also comes to collect and gets rid of it. The cost varies according to how near you are to a disposal site. Payment is usually required on delivery of the container.

If the container or skip cannot be left in a garden or driveway and has to be deposited on a public highway (that is, any road), a licence is required from the local authority. It is free and should be applied for a few days ahead. There are regulations concerning the placing of warning cones and, if the container is parked overnight, red warning lights. These can be hired from a local hire shop.

A parked skip can be an invitation to two-way transactions. You may find it the next morning filled up by neighbours' junk – or that some of your discards have disappeared.

your car

With so many additional problems to cope with at this time, the servicing of the family car may be neglected – you may have mentally added it to the list of things to be done after the move is over. But if you will be transferring goods in your car over the period of the move, or even just ferrying yourself and your family with personal luggage on the day, be sure to take precautions beforehand in order to avoid a breakdown on the way: check oil level, battery, water, fan belt. The car may be carrying a lot more weight than normally, so check the brakes and, if necessary, adjust the tyre pressures. If there is anything about the car that has been worrying you, get it seen to before the move.

If you do not own a car, try to borrow one for the day of the move. It may even be worth hiring one. Check about insurance cover.

Do your own packing: I was told this beforehand by others experienced at moving home, but didn't listen. At least you know where to find the kettle!

Allow removals men to pack everything: this will avoid house being in chaos for a long period of time.

Packing

Both sorting and packing take longer than most people estimate and they find that they have too much still to do on the actual moving day. So, start packing well in advance, particularly if you will be doing the move yourself or the firm of removers will not be packing and unpacking everything. The advantage of pre-packing items which are not in daily use is that they can be stored in their containers somewhere until you move, and in the new home can be left to be unpacked at leisure later.

lifting and carrying

Many a physiotherapist has patients who have come for treatment for muscular strain after a move, as a result of the unaccustomed lifting and carrying of heavy weights done incorrectly.

Consumer Publication: *Understanding back trouble.*

Here is some advice to help you avoid back trouble when lifting, shifting and carrying:

You should always try to anticipate and size up the job. Think before you move: how heavy is the object? can levers be used to reduce the stress? is the floor space clear to move about without kicking or stumbling over an obstruction? is the floor slippery? where are you going to put the object? where can you grasp it? is it a two-person job?

When you lift or shift an object, get as close to it as possible, with your feet around it rather than to one side or behind it. Put your feet so that you are firmly balanced, one foot ahead of the other, ready to move off in the right direction. Keep a straight back: do not tackle lifting jobs with your back rotated, twisted or bent sideways; your shoulders and pelvis should be facing the same direction. Bend the hips and knees until the object can be reached. Grasp it firmly and get a good grip. If there is nothing by which to hold it, use a sling or ropes.

Q

At 66, moving wardrobes etc is difficult and foam-backed carpets are very heavy – use an established removal firm next time.

Lifting, heaving or carrying with arms outstretched throws needless strain on the chest, upper back and shoulders. Keep the load close to your body; the farther from your body you hold it, the greater the stress – hence the risk when lifting a box out of the car boot. Whatever you are lifting and carrying, keep its centre of gravity as near as you can over or under your own centre of gravity.

When dealing with something large and heavy, lift it first at one end only, and get it on to a higher level before you take the full load. This halves the stress. Rather than carrying a heavy load, pull it on a trolley. If that is not possible, divide it into two smaller loads, one for each hand – or make a second journey, if need be.

When putting things down, if you cannot safely drop the object (which is the best way), put the lifting drill into reverse. Keep the object close to your body, and put one end down first.

Packing containers

Q

Keep plenty of large plastic bags for rubbish – the bin soon fills up.

You should start in good time to collect plenty of boxes and other containers and newspaper.

Chests, crates or cartons may be provided ahead of time by the removal firm. (Tea chests are becoming hard to obtain.) Some removal firms may send you a

Q

Obtain sufficient packing cases well in advance of the move and retain them for at least a week afterwards so that you can unpack and place in cupboards etc at leisure.

batch of paper liners for the crates in boxes they use, for you to fill (with non-breakables). The paper bag is shaped to fit into the box, to be lifted into it and carried away for transporting by the removal men on moving day.

Try the local supermarket or food shop or off-licence for cardboard cartons and discarded boxes; the partitioned kind are ideal for packing food jars, bottles or breakable vases, and suchlike. Remember that cartons will get stacked on top of others, and that the bottom carton in the pile will collapse if it is not strong enough to take the weight.

For transporting larger breakables, ask electrical retailers and china shops if you can have cartons with the straw or shavings or packing materials in which goods have been delivered to them. Obviously, use all your own suitcases, trunks, holdalls, and borrow more from friends and relatives (tie on a label straightaway to identify the lender – you will have to return the empties eventually).

Wearing gloves while you do the packing will protect your hands (you will b surprised to see how dirty they get).

When wrapping china and glass, it is not so much the paper that protects them as the resilience of crumpled paper. When packing china in tea chests or boxes, put in first a thick bottom layer of crumpled-up newspaper. Large plates and lids should be individually wrapped and can be packed vertically round the sides of the box or chest, to be held in place by other items. If you are packing fragile items for transporting, it is sensible to label these as 'fragile' or 'this way up'. Do not – obviously – put heavier items on top of breakable smaller ones.

Do not fill chests or boxes too full, particularly with heavy items, such as books; otherwise, they become impossible to lift or carry any distance. Instead, use a greater quantity of smaller cartons, and tie them with string to make them easier to carry.

labelling

It is essential to label boxes and cases as you pack them, to identify their contents. You may think you will remember what each contains – you will not. Also, keep a list of the contents of boxes or cartons which are not going to be unpacked straightaway, identifying the room to which they belong.

People devise their own systems of labelling: per room or per type of contents or for unpacking chronologically. Choose whatever method appeals to you.

Containers which are to be emptied immediately need only be labelled or numbered to identify in which room in the new home they are to be deposited. Provided you put up a correspondingly labelled or numbered plan in a prominent position in the new house or flat, everyone should be able to see where things are to go. Some people use a colour code or a letter code – allocating a colour (or letter) to each room in the house and sticking the appropriate coloured sticker or letter on each door and on the furniture and containers.

Preferably put the labels on the side not the top of boxes, so that they can be seen when stacked one on top of the other. Be careful not to put a self-adhesive label on a polished surface, or on any normally visible surface: after a day or so, the fixative may harden and then you may not be able to get it off without leaving a mark.

Some removal firms will supply labels free of charge. Stationers sell packets of adhesive labels of various sizes, also coloured stickers. Buy about twice as many as you first think you will need.

Put labels also on items not to be removed from the house, so that they are clearly identifiable on moving day.

KEYS

Sort out all the keys to rooms, cupboards, garage, outhouse, as well as sets of front and back door keys, and label them. It will be an act of kindness to the incoming owner, and may avoid any unnecessary queries later, if you make a list of how many keys exist and which, if any, are missing. Make sure that all the keys are duly rounded up eventually – husband and wife have their own set, the children may have keys, near or distant relatives, trusted neighbours, the 'daily' help.

Make sure you tell your buyer where you are leaving all the keys – but do not let him have them until you know that completion has taken place.

Furniture

If you have any furniture that needs renovating or re-upholstering, or you want carpets cleaned, it can be a good idea to get the firms to collect before you move and to deliver to the new home. This is a good time to get all these jobs done, while you are living in chaos anyway, and it means that someone else is doing some of the removing for you. It is, however, only practicable if you are moving locally.

When pieces of furniture, shelving or kitchen appliances have to be dismantled, any screws and fittings should be kept with the items to save time when re-installing. Tape them to the piece of furniture, on an inside surface with adhesive tape, or ask the removers to do so.

Label all keys of cupboards, chests of drawers, wardrobes, etcetera, and keep them together in a clear polythene bag; some removal firms provide key bags.

Ask the removers whether they prefer any drawers to be locked or left unlocked – this could depend on the weight of the piece of furniture. Drawers can be used as packing containers: cover the contents with rugs, old sheets or polythene sheeting.

Q

To save time and confusion at the end of moving day, pack each person's bed linen, blankets, night clothes into strong polythene bags and label each with the owner's name or the code for the room in the new home.

BEDS

Bedsteads are usually dismantled by the removers. Check if they will also put them up again at the other end (make sure the bedstead spanner stays with it). Put identifying labels on mattresses and bedsteads or bases for matching up at the other end. Some removal firms provide special mattress sacks.

CARPETS

Carpets should be rolled, not folded, to prevent creasing. Label the pieces of underlay (with a stick-on label) to identify which carpet they belong to. Some of the foam varieties of underlay may be found to have disintegrated into dust, particularly where there has been much traffic (stairs, for instance) so you may find nothing to take away and will need new underlays at your new home.

VALUABLES

If the move is a local one, valuables could be lodged with your bank for the period of the move. If you have to take them with you, consider packing jewellery and other small valuables discreetly among your clothes. But remember to make a note of where you put them.

CLOCKS

You will have to immobilise any clock that has a detachable pendulum or weights. If you are unsure how to do this, consult a local clock repairer before attempting to remove any weights. Some removal firms specifically exclude responsibility for any internal damage to clocks.

FLAMMABLE ITEMS

Run down or remove any fuel remaining in oil heaters, oil lamps, lawn mower. The removers will not accept them with fuel, nor half-used tins of anything volatile, nor paraffin.

CHILDREN'S TOYS

If you have small children, do not forget to keep out a selection of their favourite toys and games and books to have at hand over the period of the move.

TOOLS

Before packing up workshop, garage or tool cupboard, prepare an emergency tool kit to take with you, readily accessible. Include such tools as screwdriver, pliers, sharp knife, adjustable spanner, nails, hammer, screws, hooks, fuses or fuse wire, adhesive tape, rope, string, light bulbs, plugs, torch.

DUSTBIN

The dustbins at both houses are likely to be overflowing by the day of the move. Invest in a new dustbin, and liners, and take these – kept empty – for use as soon as you arrive at the other end.

MOVING HOUSEHOLD APPLIANCES

Do not forget to check that there are sockets for portable electrical appliances and fused connection units for stationary appliances in convenient positions in your new home. There should be a socket outlet or connection unit within 1.8 metres of all likely locations of electrical appliances.

Q

On the whole, it may be a good idea to consider selling your freezer with the house, and either buy a new one or buy the one left as a fixture by the seller of your new house.

COOKER

Remember to switch off the electricity supply at the mains position before disconnecting the cooker.

FREEZER

Ideally, run down stocks before moving; defrost and dry out the cabinet.

Freezers are not designed with the strength needed to be transport containers. Some removal firms will not take a freezer with its contents, mainly because of the extra weight. The vibration during a move and weight of the contents can damage the pipework.

If you must move it with frozen food

○ reduce stocks to no more than 25 per cent of the freezer's capacity
○ switch to maximum freeze for at least 24 hours before removal
○ do not open the door or lid after refrigeration is switched off.

A risk in moving frozen food is the possibility of thawing: refreezing partially defrosted food can spoil its taste and can be a health hazard if it had been left long enough for the food to go off.

Even when the freezer is empty, it is vulnerable to damage during the move. If it is tipped more than about 30 degrees – to come down some steps, for instance, or when negotiating doorways – this can cause an airlock in the cooling system. A freezer that has been moved must be left to stand in its final position for a minimum of 2 hours before it is switched on.

REFRIGERATOR

Defrost just before the move, and leave the fridge dry and empty. Pack any remaining perishables in an insulated picnic bag or wrap them in plenty of newspaper and put into thick cartons.

Remember that refrigerators must be carried upright.

DISHWASHER AND WASHING MACHINE

A plumbed-in dishwasher or washing machine with a stop valve on the supply pipe does not need a plumber to disconnect it. (Leave a label telling the new owner 'This is a water supply pipe'.) But you may need a plumber at the new house for fitting a stop valve to the supply pipe there.

If the washing machine has a revolving drum, this should be immobilised before moving it. Ideally, find the restraining bars which came with the machine when it was new. If you cannot, consult the manufacturer or a local retailer for advice. Tilting a front-loading machine can cause damage to it. Some machines have bearings or gear boxes with an open reservoir of oil – if the machine is not kept upright, you will have an indelible dribble over everything.

survival kit

Before packing up the contents of the kitchen, you would be wise to prepare a survival kit to be taken with you in your car, or in the van if you are travelling with it.

The kit should contain:

> kettle (do not forget the flex for an electric one)
> teapot
> tea and/or coffee
> milk (longlife, tin or powder)
> sugar
> disposable or plastic cups/beakers
> teaspoons
> towel(s)
> soap
> lavatory paper
> candles, matches
> corkscrew, tin opener
> first aid: sticking plaster, scissors, aspirin
> coins and phone card for telephoning from a public call box
> and have somewhere accessible the telephone numbers of
> ○ the estate agents
> ○ your solicitor
> ○ the seller
> ○ your buyer
> ○ electricity board
> ○ gas services.

And . . . at least a dozen assorted light bulbs (in case your sellers are so mean that they have taken them).

If you are moving over two or more days, you will also need an overnight bag of personal belongings for each member of the family. And do not forget to take with you the tool kit you have prepared.

Children on the move

Most adults find moving house a traumatic business. Children can find it disturbing, too – which, in turn, will be an added worry for the parents. So, it is important to protect the children as much as possible from the upheaval and to settle them down in their new surroundings as smoothly and as quickly as possible.

Q

If you have young children, let them help to pack their toys and see you packing other items. Have a friend take care of them for the afternoon before the day you move.

Older children should be encouraged to look forward to a move and to feel involved in it. If it can be organised, take them to see the new house beforehand. Let them have an opportunity to imagine themselves in their future surroundings, to inspect their new bedroom and perhaps to choose their own decorations for it.

Even if the children are very young, talk to them well in advance about what is to happen; they may not fully understand what it is all about, but they will be getting some warning of what is to come.

A baby in a carry cot can be less trouble than an older child – provided you take with you enough milk, baby food, drink and nappies.

Q

Put pets in kennels
Put children in grandma's
Put beer in fridge

If it is practicable, it may be better to 'farm out' a toddler or small child, with relatives or a neighbouring family with children, over the day or days of the move. This will avoid letting the child get caught up in the upheaval, and relieves the grown-ups of the added burden of coping with the child.

When the time comes to collect the children from relatives or friends for their first night in the new home, arrange this so that there is sufficient time for them to find their way round it, and to explore a little, before it is their bedtime. If there is any spare time or energy left, use this to make their bedroom as familiar as possible by putting out their toys, clothes, and so on. They are at first going to feel insecure in the strange new surroundings, so anything which can be done to reduce this – such as providing them with their favourite toys – will help.

As soon as possible after the arrival in a new area, make it a priority to locate any neighbouring children of the same age for yours to play with. Your children will miss their former friends considerably, and will need new ones quickly if they are to enjoy the change.

Moving any pets

The societies for the prevention of cruelty to animals are ready to give advice on any problem to do with animals. The head offices are

for England and Wales:	for Scotland:	for Aberdeenshire:
RSPCA	SSPCA	AAPCA
Causeway	19 Melville Street	6 Bon-Accord Square
Horsham	Edinburgh EH3 7PL	Aberdeen AB9 1XU
West Sussex RH12 1HG	tel: 031-225 6418	tel: 0224 581236
tel: 0403 64181		

Q

The hamster died – upsetting for children. The dog survived with usual fortitude.

DOGS

Whether you would be wiser to put the animal into kennels or not depends on the kind of move, the distance, the protractedness of the changeover – and on your dog. A good guard dog might find the comings and goings of workmen or removal men a strain, in which case it would be less harassing for dog – and owner – if it were not about the house. And if there is any chance that your dog might escape and run off while doors are left open during loadings of the furniture van, or that it would continually get under everyone's feet, it would be kinder and safer to board it out for this stage of the move or to ask a neighbour to have it for the day.

If you can leave the dog for the day with a relative or friend, so much the better, but it may be necessary to put it into kennels for a day or so, if you are involved in a lengthier operation. If you do not know of a local kennels, consult your local vet or look in the Yellow Pages directory. If you are moving some distance away, it would be more practicable to find kennels near your new home if arrangements can be made for the dog to be delivered there beforehand. Good kennels get booked up in the holiday season so make your booking as soon as you know the date of the move and get any required injections done; a recent certificate of vaccination will almost certainly be required.

Q

Got sedatives from vet but they took many hours to have effect – should have been given about 5am!

Do not forget to check the new garden (if there is one) to make sure that it is dog-proof before releasing your dog into it.

CATS

A cat can be more of a problem, particularly about settling into the new home. It is probably best to take your cat with you in the car. If possible, use a travelling basket, preferably of the wickerwork kind. If you have not got one, buy or borrow one; some removal firms provide cardboard pet carrying cartons. Whatever you choose, it should measure at least 50 × 28 × 28 cm (20 × 11 × 11 in.). It would be wise to let the cat get used to the basket or carton before the journey.

If your journey is to be a long one – say, over 4 hours – or a disturbing one, ask your local vet whether he would consider prescribing a tranquilliser. This would depend on the age, size and fitness of your cat, and how accustomed it is to travelling. Also, if you are taking a country cat into an urban environment, you may be wise to have it jabbed for cat 'flu: in cat-crowded areas, there is more chance of infection. Seek the advice of your local vet.

Immediately on arrival, choose one of the rooms as the cat's temporary quarters and release it in it, keeping the windows and door shut. Warn everyone, or even lock the door, to avoid the cat being released accidentally, and leave it there with food, water and a dirt box (and perhaps its favourite chair or cushion) while the unloading goes on. At the end of the day, close all windows and doors and then allow the cat the run of the rest of the house. Do not let it out until at least 24 or even 48 hours later, and then only do this just before its feeding time. (It may, however, have taken refuge in a safe corner – under a stack of packing cases, perhaps – and may need to be coaxed out.)

For the first week or so, just to be on the safe side, put a collar on the cat, with a tag giving your name, address and telephone number. It is important to make sure that the collar is made wholly or partly of elastic, preferably with a quick-release fastener for safety.

SMALL CAGED BIRDS

Birds should be no problem because they can be transported in their cage covered with a cloth. Make sure that there is adequate ventilation and remove any loose articles that could move around inside the cage. Birds are susceptible to changes in temperature, so be careful not to leave the cage in a draughty spot during transit or in the new house while everyone is occupied with moving in. Empty the water and seed containers and remember to fill them again after you arrive. Alternatively, use non-spill containers.

OTHER SMALL PETS

Mice, guinea pigs, gerbils, hamsters and rabbits should be transported in 'chew-proof' well-ventilated containers. Water should be provided in a securely fixed inverted bottle with a drip tube, making sure that the end of the tube is at a convenient height for the animal to drink. Some food and bedding (not the synthetic variety) should be provided in the container.

FISH

For fish being moved from a pool you need a non-spillable, well oxygenated container: for instance, a large polythene bag quarter-filled with pool water, placed in a bucket for protection and support during transit. Polystyrene chips can be used to 'cushion' the bag and maintain the temperature of the water.

For tropical fish, get the advice of the local aquarium expert or pet shop about maintaining the correct water temperature, and tell the removers.

Q

When moving, have patience, keep calm and pray for a fine day.

Q

Be patient – be fit – expect things to go wrong – keep smiling!

Q

The day of the move was psychologically disturbing due to new owners moving in directly on the heels of us moving out and feeling somehow displaced in the middle of it.

Q

. . . with electricity, gas and BT – reps from the first two came to get final readings on the removal day and we tripped over them – despite being informed in writing well in advance.

Have a good night's rest and start the day with a large breakfast, since the next meals may not materialise when most needed. Some people are able to enlist the help of one very good friend to be responsible for making the innumerable cups of tea or helping with last-minute packing or cleaning and generally giving moral support.

Last-minute jobs will be the stripping and packing of beds, and the final clearing and packing of foodstuffs in the kitchen. Prepare any packs of sandwiches or snacks you have planned, and fill a thermos (or two) with soup or hot drinks or just hot water for making drinks with.

Wear sensible clothes, with large pockets (tuck notebook into one of them), comfortable shoes: you will be doing a lot of running about and standing around. Keep out a stool or folding chair to sit on during the day whenever you can.

Arrange to keep to one side the vacuum cleaner or a broom and dustpan and brush, and any other basic cleaning equipment, to be loaded among the last, so that they can be used at this end for a final clean-up if needed, and will be readily available at the other end.

Collect your survival kit to go with you in the car (do not let it go with the removal van in case it does not reach your destination as quickly as you do). Decide where you will put any documents you may need on the day, and your valuables. Do not place temptation in the removal men's way by leaving cash or jewellery around on moving day. There is no need for absurd security, but take commonsense precautions.

You may need to cash a cheque unexpectedly during the move (to have the money for tips, for instance, or to buy fish and chips or a dozen light bulbs) so keep your cheque book and bank card handy.

If arrangements go according to plan, the servicemen from the electricity board and gas region will call early in the day to read any meters and disconnect any appliances you are taking with you. (This may mean no more hot water, hot food for you there.)

When the removal men arrive, make friends with the foreman and show him round, not forgetting any loft, garage or outhouse. Explain to him the labelling

Q

Don't move in the rain! (we did).

Q

I had to leave a friend in the new address while still removing at the old because that was the only time BT could (would?) attend. If this had not been done, I would have been phone-less until they saw fit to come round.

system you have adopted and indicate which items are not to be removed. Check whether the requests you made to the estimator have been passed on to the foreman. If they have not, telephone the management right away, or get the foreman to, so that it can be sorted out as soon as possible.

Carpets in the entrance hall should be protected with druggets, plastic or dust sheets, especially if it is a wet day. Be prepared to provide these coverings in case the removal men do not bring their own. See that they are brought away in the van.

If the removal men are to do all the packing and loading, leave them to it at this stage as far as possible, keep out of their way, and only give further instructions to the foreman. Cups of tea or coffee will be welcome several times.

When all is loaded on to the van, make a final tour of inspection both inside and out, to check that nothing has been left behind (look into built-in cupboards) but that all items included in the sale have been left.

Check that you have left the heating system on or off according to the arrangement made with the new owner, and turn off the mains water if this has been agreed with him. This could be important if the house is to stand empty and unheated for any time in winter. Close and lock all windows and doors, and leave the keys wherever you have arranged with the new owner.

Before the removal men leave with the van, check that they have the new address, and give clear instructions how to find the house if it is at all difficult. Make sure you have made arrangements about what they should do if they should arrive first – you could be delayed en route for some reason. (An emergency contact telephone number might also be useful, such as your mother-in-law's.) But try as far as possible to be at the new house in time to supervise the unloading, or to have a reliable friend or relative there to do so.

Completion and handover of keys

While you are moving out, your conveyancer should be dealing with the legal (and financial) side of completion. Unless you are doing your own conveyancing, neither the buyer nor the seller is there. The crucial factor of completion is the handing over of all the money.

Q

Try to ascertain whether people moving themselves can keep to the deadlines set.

Normally, the keys of a house are not released until the purchase money has reached the seller's solicitor. Strictly, the seller should get a set of keys to his solicitor, who will hand them over to the buyer's solicitor and the buyer gets them from him. This can be physically difficult, and complicated by the venue where completion takes place.

Q

The previous owners locked the keys in the house!

Although it is more usual for the solicitor to do this, it may be more convenient for the keys to be handed over by the estate agent. The seller would have to arrange for his solicitor to authorise the handing over as soon as completion has taken place.

Q

Possession not until 4pm as solicitors withheld key until money had changed hands.

Delay in money reaching the solicitor or in the estate agent being notified of completion will delay the buyer being able to get hold of the keys and can cause a hiatus in the moving-in operation. Waiting outside your new home for some time before you are able to start unloading could prove expensive if your removal is being charged on a time basis.

At the new home

Before any furniture is unloaded, see that any carpets in the entrance, hall, or stairs are protected with coverings of some kind. These can get very dirty, especially on a wet day or in a house on a new estate where there is still a lot of mud on the site.

Q

Insist that all previous occupant's rubbish is removed prior to possession.

If you have adopted the method of labelling each item with a colour or number corresponding to the room in which it is to be put, label the rooms accordingly and stick the plan in a prominent place by the front door. Or you may prefer to position yourself there and to indicate the correct room as each item is unloaded. Remember with the heavier pieces of furniture to specify exactly where in the room each should be put – you should have worked this out beforehand – to avoid finding yourself having to heave them about later. If you have been living in a flat and are moving into a house, you may not have appreciated the importance of knowing at this stage on which floor your furniture is to go.

When the foreman tells you they are ready to go, have a look inside the van just to make sure that nothing has inadvertently been left there.

The removal men will expect a tip. If you feel they deserve one, you can give a sum to the foreman for distribution or give individually to each man (and the driver). But if you are not satisfied, say so. If you give a tip without comment, it can sometimes lead the removers to suspect that any claim you may subsequently make is exaggerated or even false.

You may be asked to sign a discharge document that the job is completed. (It may incorporate a receipt for payment, if you pay at the end of the moving operation not ahead of time.) This is the document on which to write down if you have any reservations about how the work has been carried out. If you have not yet inspected your belongings, sign as 'unexamined'.

Switch on the water heating. Make up the beds as soon as they are unloaded, so that they are ready to be collapsed into when needed. If it is possible to hang curtains in the bedrooms, do this as well.

Unpack only essentials – not only because you may want to clean any fitted cupboards and shelves before putting your belongings into them, but because you should not tire yourself out on jobs that can wait. Also, the more items that can remain packed in boxes or containers, the less the chaos. But you will have to empty the chests or containers that the removal men want to take away.

Be prepared for

– a lot of discarded packing materials
– emptied containers waiting for collection/disposal
– piles of books unloaded but not put on to shelves
– pots, pans, crockery everywhere on the wrong surfaces
– debris and dirt.

Do not expect to be fully organised at your new house straightaway. If you try to be, you could be heading for a nervous breakdown.

There may be a kind friend or new neighbour who will feed you. But if you are planning to prepare some sort of meal the first evening, you will have to locate

---

Q

They were late arriving at the new house, in a hurry to get back, left boxes full instead of unpacked and broke/damaged various items.

Q

. . . the mental anguish of not believing the whole process had gone smoothly until unpacking the kettle in our new home.

Q

They moved out finished at 5.30pm. We made up the beds, cooked a meal (from the freezer made beforehand) and relaxed. Super!

Q

If you empty tea chests yourself, check every piece of packing paper very carefully before you throw it out.

Q

After moving in, one needs a pot of cash to spend on unforeseen yet important initial purchases i.e. doorbell, curtain rail etc.

crockery and food. If you find you are too exhausted to want to prepare a meal at this stage, find a cafe, a take-away or a fish and chip shop.

CLAIMING FOR DAMAGE OR LOSS

If anything gets broken or damaged, try to make a written note of it at the time, and ask the removers' foreman to sign or initial it. Such an aide-memoire should not be altered or amended after signature. Keep your copy carefully, to support any claim.

You may not spot deficiencies, loss or damage in all the hurly burly straight-away. Make a list of anything that has been broken or damaged as soon as possible, and notify the insurers and the removal firm's head office that there is a likelihood of a claim on the removal insurance policy.

If something prevented you from being present when the goods were unloaded, or everything is not being unpacked straightaway, it would be wise to tell the insurers (and the removers) at once that you are unable to comply with a claims time limit.

If damage is caused to your goods as a result of negligence on the part of the removers, they should, as far as possible, put it right by repairing or replacing it or compensating you financially. Take the advice of your solicitor. Many solicitors will not charge extra for sorting out the odd problem after completion if you have to claim on your insurance policy.

The claim form you receive will not have been designed specifically for this type of insurance: many questions may be irrelevant – or missing. Describe the circumstances as precisely as possible in the blank space provided. If only a few articles have been damaged, you should list each item. Depending on the extent of the loss, the insurers will either ask you for further details before taking up the matter with the removers or send you a cheque rather than waste time and money with enquiries about a small sum. Keep any bills or receipts for repairs or replacements to produce in support of your claim.

If a lot has been destroyed (by fire or a major accident perhaps), the insurers will arrange for a representative to call to formulate some idea of what has been lost and what can be salvaged, and the value. Do not agree to a figure if you think it is too low.

After the move

Q

When just moved in, we had people ask if they can view the house because estate agents still had the house on show.

You may think it wise to have the locks of the outer doors changed. There may be unaccounted-for keys: you never know who else had keys from the previous owners.

Your insurance company may want to inspect your new home if your contents and all-risks policy is for more than a certain figure, and may recommend that you fit certain door and window locks, or an alarm system.

DOCUMENTS

You should keep safely in one place all the documents, certificates, policies, guarantees, and other paperwork connected with your purchase. In spite of probably feeling that you will never move again, some of these papers would be required if you did so at any time in the future. If any are being kept by your solicitor, bank or mortgagee, make a note of this in the file.

TAX RELIEF ON MORTGAGE INTEREST PAYMENTS

You get tax relief on interest you pay on the first £30,000 of your mortgage: you will be making mortgage payments to the lender net of basic rate tax under the system of mortgage interest relief at source (MIRAS). If you are a higher rate taxpayer, in order to get the additional tax relief due to you, you have to give the tax inspector details of the mortgage so that the extra relief can come to you through the PAYE system or, if you are self-employed, by direct assessment. There may be some delay in your getting this relief on the first interest payments.

CAPITAL GAINS TAX

Normally, you do not have to worry about capital gains tax when you are selling your home. So long as you have lived in the house throughout your ownership and have lived in (or owned) no other house as your principal residence, no tax will be payable. But tax might be payable if, for instance, you have spent time abroad and let the home to tenants, or if you have not actually occupied the home (even if you owned no other). You might also have to pay tax if part of the house was used for business purposes or the land sold with it was more than an acre.

Capital gains tax is payable only on the net profit on the sale (after knocking off the costs of buying and selling and improvements – other than things such as redecoration). The first £5,000 is exempt (1988/89 tax year) and tax is payable at your income tax rate on the rest. The profit is based either on the value of the property in 1982 or, if acquired after 31 March 1982, on the price you paid when you bought it.

There are specific exemptions to having to pay CGT. For instance, you can overlap two houses if you buy your new home before selling your old one but for no more than 2 years. The 'dependent relative exemption' which enables a second house to be sold free of capital gains tax if it has been occupied throughout your ownership rent-free by certain relatives applies only to property acquired for this purpose before April 6 1988.

a will

If you have become a property owner for the first time, it is important to make a will or amend an existing one, making clear what you wish to be done with your estate after your death.

It is not too difficult for the average person to draw up a will but it is essential that this is done correctly. The Consumer Publication *Wills and probate* explains how to draw up your own will. If you think your case is at all complicated, it would be worth consulting a solicitor (also if you have moved to or from Scotland). Some solicitors will make a deal with you over fees if you make a will at the same time as you move if he is doing the conveyancing.

You should keep your will in a safe place – and tell your executors where this is.

changing your doctor

A report on GPs was published in **Which?** in June 1983 and on patients' rights in February 1987.

When you move to a new area, register with a new doctor as soon as possible: do not wait until you need treatment.

The local Family Practitioner Committee produces a list of all National Health Service general practitioners in its area, and a list of these doctors is kept at FPC offices, main post offices, local social security offices, public libraries, citizens advice bureaux.

You can choose any NHS general practitioner, provided he or she will accept you. However, you may find it difficult to find out enough about doctors to choose one from the list. Personal recommendation seems to be the most satisfactory method, so start by asking neighbours or other local people about the doctors in the area. Choose informants who have similar circumstances to your own – with children or elderly or diabetic, for instance.

When you have got a short list of GPs, it would probably be worth your while visiting a few surgeries to see where they are and what they are like. Find out whether the doctor has an appointments system, what the surgery hours are, whether it is a group practice or attached to a health centre, and what happens about home visits.

A doctor can refuse to accept you as a patient (without giving any reason) unless you need immediate treatment. Even if a doctor treats you in emergency circumstances, it does not mean that he has accepted you as a patient.

When you have found a doctor willing to take you on to his list, both you and the doctor fill in the appropriate sections on your medical card (or if you have lost or mislaid your medical card, a registration form) and the doctor sends it to the local Family Practitioner Committee. You will get a new medical card, and your new doctor will be sent your medical records. Although you do not have to inform the previous doctor you are leaving, it would be courteous to do so. If you change your address but are staying in the same locality and want to keep the same doctor, you have to tell him your new address and ask him if he will continue to treat you.

If you are unable to find a doctor who can accept you, the local Family Practitioner Committee has powers to allocate you to one, if necessary.

If you do not get on with a new doctor or for any other reason feel dissatisfied, it is open to you to change, although this is not always easy. Information on how to go about this is on the NHS medical card.

THE DENTIST

The report on caring for your teeth in **Which?** January 1985 included advice on finding a good dentist.

You do not register with a dentist in the same way as with a doctor. You can choose to go to any dentist (the local library, post office or citizens advice bureau should have a list) at any time, provided he accepts you. You will need to give your NHS number, which is on your medical card.

Q

. . . the whole process is a very emotionally-charged situation. You must be prepared to take a few risks (e.g. go for a large mortgage), you must be determined to persevere until you get what you want, you must have great patience and accept setbacks philosophically. It's worth it in the end – we're very happy with our new house.

. . . and finally

If moving has turned out particularly complicated or strenuous in spite of trying to foresee all the hazards, try to get away even if only for a couple of days. A break at this point from the physical and mental effort can make all the difference. You should find that you return eagerly to your new home, ready to enjoy in it a new period of your life.

Glossary

Here are some terms you may come across in connection with conveyancing, insurance, mortgage.

advance
the mortgage loan (also capital sum, principal sum)

all risks insurance
insurance that covers all happenings that are not specifically excluded in the policy (as against a policy of specified perils which covers only the happenings that are listed)

APR
annual percentage rate of the total charge for credit: standard way (laid down by the Consumer Credit Act 1974) of working out the true interest rate; by law, the APR has to be shown by banks and building societies alongside their quoted rates for each mortgage term, to enable potential borrowers to compare equally what is being offered

assignment
the transfer of ownership to another person of some kinds of property such as an insurance policy in the case of an endowment mortgage, or a lease

balance outstanding
the amount of loan owed at any one time

bonus
additional amounts paid on with-profits policies – periodically (reversionary) or at end of policy term

bridging loan
a loan, usually from a bank, to tide a person over between the time when he has to pay the purchase price of one house and the time when the proceeds of sale of another and/or mortgage funds become available to him

capital
the mortgage loan (also advance, principal)

capital reducing mortgage
repayment mortgage

cash-in value
see surrender value

charge
any right or interest, subject to which freehold or leasehold property may be held, especially a mortgage; also used to denote a debit, or a claim for payment

conditions of sale
the detailed standard terms which govern the rights and duties of the buyer and the seller of a house, as laid down in the contract which they sign; these may be the National or the Law Society's conditions of sale

conveyancing
the legal and administrative process involved in transferring the ownership of land or any buildings on it, from one owner to another

covenant
a promise in a deed to undertake (if covenant is positive) or to abstain from doing (if restrictive covenant) specified things

creditor
someone owed money; the lender

differentials
when lender operates a 'banding system' under which extra interest is charged on larger loans: the 'bands' are known as differentials

early redemption
paying off loan before the end of the mortgage term

early redemption charge
the sum charged by a lender to cover administration costs in the event of a loan being repaid before the end of the mortgage term

easement
the legal right of a property owner to use the facilities of another's land – for example, a right of way

endowment insurance
life insurance which will pay out a specified sum, or more, on a specified date (or on death, if sooner)

endowment mortgage
a loan on which only interest is paid throughout the term; it is paid off in one lump at the end with the proceeds of an endowment insurance policy

freehold
property held absolutely (that is, until the end of time)

joint tenants
two or three or four people holding property as co-owners; when one dies, his share of the property automatically passes to the survivor(s)

Land Registry
a government department (head office in London and district registries in various other places in England and Wales) responsible for opening, maintaining and amending the registers of all properties in England and Wales which have registered titles

leasehold
ownership of property for a fixed number of years granted by a lease which sets out the obligations of the leaseholder, for example regarding payment of rent to the landlord, repairs and insurance; as opposed to freehold property, where ownership is absolute

local search certificate
an application made to the local authority for a certificate providing certain information about a property and the surrounding area

low-cost endowment mortgage
a mortgage secured by a mixture of endowment with-profits and decreasing convertible term insurance, so that the guaranteed sum insured payable on death is equal to the loan; the reversionary bonuses added to the endowment policy normally ensure that the loan can be repaid at the end of the term

low start mortgage
premiums start low and increase by a certain percentage each year until the full level premium is reached

MIRAS
Mortgage Interest Relief At Source: mortgage payments are paid net of basic rate tax (rather than paying the gross amount with adjustment to tax code)

mortgage
loan (usually for house purchase) for which a house is the security or collateral. It gives to the lender (usually a building society or bank) certain rights in the property, including the power to sell if the mortgage payments are not made. These rights are cancelled when the money advanced is repaid with interest, in accordance with the agreed terms

mortgage deed
the document enshrining the conditions of a loan secured on a property (also called a legal charge)

mortgagee
the lender

mortgage indemnity policy
compulsory insurance required by building society for loan above normal percentage valuation of a property (also called mortgage guarantee policy)

mortgage protection policy
life insurance taken out by borrower which would pay off the outstanding mortgage loan in case of borrower's death

mortgagor
the borrower (whose property is security for the loan)

premium
payment (one-off or periodical) for an insurance policy, the amount depending on the sum insured and the type and degree of risk to the insurer

principal
the amount of money that has been borrowed and on which interest is calculated

redemption
paying off a loan: the final payment of principal, interest and costs of the mortgage; if all or part of the loan is repaid early, an additional charge may be payable

registered land
land (including buildings, houses on it) the title to which is registered at the Land Registry, with the result that ownership is guaranteed fully or to some degree by the state; in many parts of the country, registration of title is compulsory

repayment mortgage
loan on which part of the capital as well as interest is paid back throughout the period of the loan

retention
the withholding of part of a mortgage loan, should structural defects need to be repaired on the property in question; the amount is normally the sum required to carry out the repairs, and it will be withheld until the work has been completed satisfactorily

stakeholder
one who holds a deposit as an intermediary between the buyer and seller, so that the deposit may only be passed on to the seller with the permission of the buyer, or returned to the buyer with the permission of the seller

sum insured
the amount that will be paid out when a term insurance policy matures or the event insured for happens (such as, for life insurance, the death of the policyholder; for household insurance, loss of or damage to property)

surrender value
the amount of money a policyholder receives if life insurance policy is terminated before the expiry date (other than on death) – for instance, when endowment mortgage paid off early

tenants in common
two (or more) people who together hold property in such a way that, when one dies, his share does not pass automatically to the survivor but forms part of his own property and passes under his will or intestacy (this is in contrast with what happens in the case of joint tenants)

term insurance
a life insurance contract which pays out only on death within a specified period (also known as temporary insurance); is used to cover the period of a mortgage

term of mortgage
the number of years at the end of which the loan is to be repaid; the shorter the term, the higher the monthly repayments (and the APR)

title
ownership of a property

top up mortgage
additional mortgage from another lender when first lender does not provide enough finance to purchase a house

vendor
the seller

with-profits policy
a life insurance policy where bonuses (varying according to the company's profits) are added regularly to the original sum assured paid when the policy matures; type of policy often used for endowment mortgage

Index

CA Publications are available from Consumers' Association, Castlemead, Gascoyne Way, Hertford SG14 1LH and from bookshops.